Physiology and Behavior Therapy

Conceptual Guidelines for the Clinician

THE PLENUM SERIES IN BEHAVIORAL PSYCHOPHYSIOLOGY

Series Editor:
William J. Ray, *Pennsylvania State University, University Park, Pennsylvania*

PHYSIOLOGY AND BEHAVIOR THERAPY
Conceptual Guidelines for the Clinician
  James G. Hollandsworth, Jr.

Physiology
and
Behavior Therapy

Conceptual Guidelines
for the
Clinician

James G. Hollandsworth, Jr.
University of Southern Mississippi
Hattiesburg, Mississippi

Plenum Press • New York and London

Library of Congress Cataloging in Publication Data

Hollandsworth, James G.
  Physiology and behavior therapy.

  (The Plenum series in behavioral psychophysiology)
  Bibliography: p.
  Includes index.
  1. Behavior therapy. 2. Psychology, Physiological. I. Title. II. Series. [DNLM: 1. Behavior
—physiology. 2. Behavior Therapy. 3. Psychophysiology. WL 103 H737p]
RC489.B4H6   1986   616.89′142   86-558
ISBN 0-306-42180-1

© 1986 Plenum Press, New York
A Division of Plenum Publishing Corporation
233 Spring Street, New York, N.Y. 10013

Printed in the United States of America

For my mother, who taught me to be critical,
and my father, who taught me to be curious

Foreword

Despite the widespread use of psychophysiological concepts and methods in behavior therapy, there is no text devoted specifically to the subject. The publication of this book is necessary and timely, and should promote a better appreciation of the physiological roots of behavior therapy.

The important connections between physiology and behavior therapy receive insufficient recognition nowadays, despite the fact that historically one of the two main streams of behavior therapy grew out of a physiological basis. Wolpe's early work was closely connected to physiology, and in contemporary behavior therapy, Lang's critical contribution is firmly based in psychophysiology. The physiological component is prominent in Lang's highly productive three-systems analysis of emotion and in its application to psychological disorders. In addition, there are philosophical reasons for maintaining the close connection between behavior therapy and physiology.

The existence of these connections, and their justification, can raise few objections, and it is therefore curious that a book on this significant subject has not appeared earlier.

The importance of physiology for behavior therapy can be illustrated by considering the nature of a behavior therapy deprived of its physiological connections. It would survive, certainly, but as a rather scrawny, uninteresting orphan among many clamorous competitors. The physiological roots are essential for the healthy continuance and growth of behavior therapy. The danger that behavior therapy might degenerate into a mixed bag of disparate, atheoretical techniques has, I believe, passed. In some measure, these physiological connections were responsible for ensuring the integrity of behavior therapy.

The recent growth of behavioral medicine owes a great deal to physiological research, and here even more obviously than in the case of behavior therapy, it is essential to maintain a continuous interplay between physiological and behavioral phenomena. It is worth mentioning that the preexisting connections between behavior therapy and physiology probably played a valuable facilitatory role in the birth of behavioral medicine.

Hollandsworth's systematic and lucid approach to the subject is welcome, and the result is a book that is both instructive and interesting. I hope and expect that it will raise the level of interest in physiology and behavior therapy, and in turn, help to enrich the subject.

S. RACHMAN

University of British Columbia

Preface

Physiology is the unifying science of living organisms, just as chemistry is at the molecular level and physics at the atomic. As such, physiology provides a foundation upon which knowledge from many disciplines can be integrated. This allows for the consideration of multiple factors that contribute to human behavior by emphasizing the interactive effects of many variables, no one of which is sufficient by itself to explain why we do what we do.

The book is designed to be a self-contained instructional aid for advanced undergraduates, beginning graduate students, or more advanced practitioners with a limited background in physiology. As such, everything needed to understand the concepts and applications in the book is contained within the work itself. The academic preparation of the reader will determine which chapters are most useful and which will benefit from the addition of supplemental reading.

To assist the reader in tailoring the book to his or her needs, the chapters have been organized into three parts. The first, Preliminary Concepts, consists of introductory (Chapter 1: Physiological Control) and background information (Chapter 2: Physiological Systems; Chapter 3: Central Nervous System). If the book is used as a text, these can be read with little if any elaboration in class (depending, of course, on the level of the students). For example, in using this material with graduate students, I assign the first three chapters to be read outside of class and then cover the material in class by answering questions about specific points.

Part II, Basic Issues, actually begins the process of integrating physiological principles with behavioral concerns. Consequently, the material in this section deals with a number of important and persistent issues. For example, the first chapter in the section—Chapter 4: Nature and Nurture—deals with the issue of biological versus environmental contributions to learning. This provides the basis for the next chapter—Chapter 5: Triple Modes—which considers ways in which one might conceptualize clinical problems so that physiological as well as psychological factors are taken into account. Chapter 6, Biofeedback, raises questions concerning the degree to which we can be made aware of basic physiological processes and the extent to which we are capable of exerting control over these responses. This discussion provides a lead-in to the next chapter—Chapter 7: Emotion—in which differing views concerning the role of awareness in defining, understanding, and treating emotional problems are presented.

Part III, Clinical Applications, is where supplemental readings are clearly warranted. The book is not intended to be a comprehensive treatment guide. Although several of the more promising and widely used modalities for treating anxiety (Chapter 8) and depression (Chapter 9) are covered, guidelines for implementing specific interventions should be sought elsewhere. A final chapter, Physiology and Behavior Therapy, attempts to integrate things by discussing basic assumptions that facilitate the integration of physiological concepts with behavioral practice.

It should be noted up front that this book is not a text on psychophysiology or an introduction to behavioral medicine, two areas that are intimately involved with the integration of physiological with psychological concepts. Although the present work could not have been written without major contributions from each, both areas are more specialized than what is attempted here—psychophysiology as a specific strategy for studying psychological phenomena (Hassett, 1978) and behavioral medicine as a specialty area requiring advanced (i.e., doctoral and postdoctoral) training (Stone, 1983). It might be more appropriate to think of this volume as a preparatory step in the pursuit of these more advanced interests. As a result, a presentation of psychophysiological methods will not be attempted here in that they normally require expertise and sophisticated instrumentation generally not available to many readers. Likewise, with the exception of a brief summary in the final chapter, the extensive literature on behavioral medicine will not be reviewed either. Readers interested in behavioral medicine specifically will find a number of recent works (e.g., Garfield, 1982a; Pinkerton, Hughes & Wenrich, 1982; Prokop & Bradley, 1981) that cover this topic in depth.

It can be readily seen that this book is not an end point in itself, only a beginning. By presenting the physiological aspects of behavioral problems and applying these ideas to the treatment of clinical disorders, it is expected that the reader will be encouraged to seek more information on his or her own. The area is complex, and there is much we do not know. But there is much we do know, and it is hoped that *Physiology and Behavior Therapy* will serve to further the integration of knowledge from these different yet compatible perspectives.

Of the many people to whom I owe a debt in the writing of this book, none are more important than my students, without whose constant encouragement I would not have written it in the first place. More specifically, I would like to acknowledge the individual contributions of the following who gave me invaluable feedback on the book as it progressed: Mark Barron, Pitt Beam, Joyce Benefield, Suzanne Brooks, Catherine Capelli, Colleen Carr, Kathy Cherney, Brian Delpape, Victor DiLio, Margaret Dillard, Barbara Ellender, Tony Ferretti, Paul Finn, Gary Gintner, Noah Kersey, Schumpert Kline, Jeannie Koestler, Kim LaJoie, Matt Lambert, Jeff Matranga, Eric Morrell, Don Nicholas, Rodger Pinto, Lupo Quitoriano, Terry Shafer, David Sprague, and Earl Rectanus. Special thanks go to David Gunter who worked with me so patiently in drawing the figures that appear in Chapter 3. In addition, the contributions of Milt Becknell, Debbie Hill, Priscilla Marotta, Paige Powell, and Jan Seville deserve special recognition, as does the patience and support of my most valued colleague, Brenda Dawson.

JAMES G. HOLLANDSWORTH, JR.

Hattiesburg, Mississippi

Contents

PART I

Preliminary Concepts

In this part, two basic proposals will be made. First, it will be argued in Chapter 1 (Physiological Control) that human behavior is the complex product of multiple regulatory systems operating on many levels throughout the body, some that we are aware of and some of which we are not. This view of behavior calls for expanding one's scope of interest to include physiological as well as psychological factors. Second, it will be proposed in Chapter 2 (Physiological Systems) that behavior can be thought of most profitably as a system. This perspective based on systems theory emphasizes the interactive and multidetermined nature of one's actions and warns against thinking of behavior in terms of unidimensional explanations involving single cause-and-effect relationships. A third chapter (Central Nervous System) provides an overview of the anatomical and physiological foundations upon which systems of behavior are based.

1

Physiological Control

This book is about assumptions, about our understanding of why we do what we do. It is an attempt to question some of our assumptions by introducing concepts from the discipline of physiology. For example, in this chapter we will question the degree to which human beings are capable of understanding and regulating their own behavior. It will be proposed that our ability to comprehend the reasons for many of our actions is limited by the realities of physiological design and regulation. This does not mean that we are ignorant of what we do, but it does suggest that there is much that goes on that we are unaware of and over which we have only partial control. The death of John Hunter is a case in point.

An Example

John Hunter was born on February 13, 1728, and died on October 16, 1793. During his 65 years, Hunter was an active, outspoken, blunt, often rude and overbearing man. The brother of another famous physician, William Hunter, John became a noted surgeon, anatomist, physiologist, and pathologist. He is credited with several successful surgical innovations, the most notable being the tying off of an artery above an aneurysm. In recognition of his contributions to medicine, he has been termed "the founder of scientific surgery" (Stephen & Lee, 1917/1937–1938).

A picture of Dr. Hunter in an 1832 issue of *The Penny Magazine* (July 7, p. 141) shows a heavyset man with a short neck, prominent eyebrows, and a high forehead. His daily habits revealed him to have been both punctual and impatient. He often arose at 5 or 6 o'clock to perform dissections. His day was spent seeing patients, performing surgical experiments, preparing lectures, and dictating the results of his studies. He stopped his routine only briefly for meals, working often past midnight. No doubt, were he alive today, Hunter would be described as a perfect example of the Type A (coronary-prone) personality.

John Hunter's problem was his temper and his heart. The two, working together, caused him much distress and were to become the reason for his death. Whenever he became angry, he experienced angina of the worst kind. The chest pains would become so severe that he was completely incapacitated. Hunter is said to have exclaimed, no doubt in frustration over this peculiar vulnerability: "I'm at the mercy of any rogue who cares to annoy and tease me."

In addition to being an exceptional surgeon and brilliant pathologist, it must be said that John Hunter was a dedicated and gifted teacher. Some credit this to be his greatest contribution. It was Hunter who, through his lectures, directed attention to the physiological processes of disease and repair upon which the practice of surgery is based. However, his dedication to teaching was such that he created great

[John Hunter.]

Figure 1. John Hunter (from *The Penny Magazine*, July 7, 1832).

animosity among his colleagues at St. George's Hospital in London by accusing them of being more interested in making money from their lucrative private practices than in teaching their students.

Things came to a head in 1792 over the issue of several staff appointments. Under the direction of Dr. John Gunning, the senior surgeon at St. George's, Hunter's colleagues conspired without consulting him to draw up certain rules concerning the admission and regulation of students. One rule prohibited the admission of students who had no previous medical instruction. In the fall of 1793, two young men from Scotland (Hunter was Scottish) traveled to London, ignorant of the new rule, and appealed to Hunter to speak in their behalf at the next board meeting on October 16. Hunter, realizing that the meeting might be heated, expressed his concern on the morning of the 16th that the excitement of a dispute might prove fatal to him. While he was speaking at the meeting in favor of the young students' request, he was flatly contradicted by another surgeon (probably Gunning). Hunter immediately stopped, left the room, and fell dead in the arms of Dr. Robertson, another physician at St. George's.

What killed John Hunter? Was it his anger or his heart? The obvious answer is his heart. At autopsy, it was found that the coronary arteries were occluded, the valves ossified, and the heart generally diseased. In short, John Hunter's heart simply gave out. But what of the circumstances of Hunter's death? Certainly his angry reaction to Gunning's challenge must be seen as contributing to the disastrous outcome. A man (or woman) of more even temperament might have responded with less excitement, thus avoiding the coronary crisis.

Understanding John Hunter's death requires an accounting of both physiological and psychological factors. We know that Hunter functioned quite well when in control of his temper; thus, the pathology of his heart was not sufficient in itself to end this productive life, at least not on October 16, 1793. A fit of anger, on the other hand, is unlikely to kill someone by itself, unless the predisposing pathophysiology is already present. The reason for John Hunter's death, therefore, lies in the interaction of two types of responses, one that we are normally aware of and one that we are not aware of.

Levels of Control

Understanding the manner in which an emotional response can kill someone requires a basic knowledge of how the neuroendocrine system of human beings is organized. This system, which allows us to interact with the environment, determines how information is sensed, integrated, and acted upon.

We might start by acknowledging that there are limits to what we are able to sense. Contemplation of one's kidneys, for example, is a very different (and difficult) process compared to reflecting on the day's events. The reason is simple. The neural wiring to and from the kidneys is sparse in comparison to the millions of neurons assigned to the task of memory and recall. Further, the pathways that do exist to carry information from the kidneys (afferents) terminate in very basic structures of the brain. Therefore, most of the information that is sensed in the kidneys never makes its way into the consciousness of the individual. In short, the "hardwiring" of the neuroendocrine system allows us to be aware of some things and prevents us from being aware of others.

The reason why the conscious parts of our brains are allowed to sense some information but not other is based on how the neuroendocrine system is organized. As it turns out, some information is sensed, integrated, and acted upon at the local level, whereas other inputs must be transmitted to some central processing unit before the appropriate response can be made. In other words, there are systems operating at many different levels throughout the human body, only some of which require central control (Depue, Monroe, & Shackman, 1979). Why this is the case can be seen readily when we consider that humans, like most organisms in whom we are interested, are segmented creatures.

Segmental Control

Segmentation, the defining characteristic of all vertebrates, simply means that the body is divided into sections that are capable of functioning somewhat independently of each other. If one cross-sections the body of a vertebrate, like cutting a swordfish steak, one notices two, distinct parts. First, one observes a rather rigid, muscular body wall (the soma). The body wall provides protection, structure, and allows for movement. As such, the soma is concerned with the organism's interaction with its external environment. The second distinct part of the segment is the internal organs (the viscera). These organs are concerned with a number of bodily functions, such as keeping fluids in balance, extracting nutrients, and eliminating waste products. The viscera, therefore, are concerned with regulating the organism's internal environment.

Each segment is organized around a section of the spinal cord contained in and around a single vertebra. As we shall see, many responses are integrated and initiated entirely by these circuits. Frequently, however, there is the need for a coordination of responses between segments. In cases such as these, the so-called "higher" or "central" centers of the nervous system organize and initiate patterns of responses. Nevertheless, the important and even necessary role of each segment should not be forgotten.

The crossed extensor reflex is a good example. When one touches a hot surface, such as a stove, a coordinated response occurs almost immediately. The injured hand instantly withdraws, whereas the other hand pushes the body away from the stove. This is not, in spite of the speed with which it occurs, a simple response. After the stimulus is sensed, some muscles are inhibited, others excited, and all of this must be carried out in a coordinated fashion. Fortunately, one does not have to "think" about this response. It occurs very quickly (i.e., within 200 to 500 milliseconds) and is accomplished entirely at the segmental level. Obviously, it is advantageous not to have to think about responses such as these that serve to protect the body from physical harm.

Another example of segmental control is the bladder reflex. When the bladder fills to a certain point (approximately 400 to 500 ml of urine), the resultant distention sends signals to the spinal cord. There the information is integrated so that muscles responsible for contraction of the bladder can be activated causing a series of contractions. Yet urination will not normally occur even then because an external sphincter around the urinary tract prevents the flow of urine. This external sphincter is under voluntary control by the higher brain centers. Thus, urination normally results from the coordination of signals arising from segmental distention and the conscious centers of the brain (Guyton, 1981).

This arrangement illustrates an important point. Although central and local control may complement each other, both are still necessary for a complete response to occur. What usually happens, however, is that we are aware of the voluntary responses under our control and consequently recognize their importance. Those responses under segmental regulation are generally beyond our awareness and thus are often unappreciated.

Local Control

As it turns out, there are levels of control even more basic (i.e., more localized) than that of the segments. In fact, in order to understand the interaction of the systems that killed John Hunter, we must deal with two, additional levels of control—one at the level of the individual cell and the other at the level of the individual organ.

Control at the cellular level (also called tissue control) is common among all living organisms. In fact, many organisms function quite well without any nerves at all. Regulatory processes at the tissue level are accomplished via biochemical changes around and within individual cells. It may come as a surprise to learn that even in an organism as highly developed as the human being, many of our cells also respond primarily in this manner. For example, gastric secretions in the stomach are in response to the physical distention of the stomach wall and the resultant release of a local hormone (gastrin). Swelling induced after scratching oneself with a sharp instrument or being stung by a bee is also controlled entirely at the tissue level. A number of local messengers (prostaglandins) are released by the cells in response to local stimuli such as these. In fact, although aspirin (acetylsalicylic acid) is often taken for a "head" ache, its action occurs at the tissue level by preventing the synthesis of prostaglandins. This mode of action is quite different from the centrally acting analgesics, such as morphine, that modify the perception of pain in the brain itself.

Another example of tissue regulation is a phenomenon called *autoregulation*. Autoregulation is the property of tissue to adjust the flow of blood to match the tissue's need for nutrients, primarily oxygen (Cowley, 1980). Active tissue, as during exercise, uses more oxygen. Consequently, the arterioles relax, allowing more oxygen-laden blood to have access to the working muscles. When the flow of oxygen exceeds the tissue's needs, the arterioles automatically constrict, reducing the flow of blood to the level of need. This process is accomplished entirely at the cellular level and involves no additional control, either segmental or central.

A second level of local control involves regulatory systems contained within the organs themselves. Although these systems may be influenced by the higher centers of the brain, they exert a strong regulatory effect independent of other control mechanisms. One example is the ability of the healthy heart to adjust its pumping capacity to eject all the blood that enters it. How this occurs is twofold. First, stretching the atrial walls due to increased blood flow automatically increases heart rate by 10 to 30%. Second, the contractility of the ventricles also increases with increased stretch of the heart muscle (homeometric autoregulation). These changes are the result of increased metabolic activity at the local level and physical properties of the heart muscle. The response is regulated within the heart itself, quite apart from external control (Guyton, 1981).

In summary, much of what goes on with us everyday is regulated at a level that does not involve the higher centers of the brain. Because we

are generally unaware of this activity, it may not strike us as very important. But, as we shall see when we return to the case of John Hunter,
these involuntary, locally controlled responses can be very important
indeed.

Central Control

Segmental and local control of physiological responses has obvious
advantages. As noted earlier, it frees us from the responsibility of having to direct these numerous, life-sustaining activities consciously. This
independence, however, has its disadvantages. Too much autonomy
could mean that diverse responses might work against each other. Fortunately, we have developed other systems that coordinate responses
across systems. This does not mean that local control is relinquished
entirely. What appears to happen is that these "higher" control systems
modulate or complement local systems without abrogating their independent function.

The most obvious way of coordinating the activity of the different
segments is to link them together. This is accomplished by the spinal
cord. Numerous neural pathways from each segment enter the spinal
cord and travel up the cord to a central aggregate of neurons called the
brain. Likewise, pathways originating in the brain run down the spinal
cord, branching off at each segment.

The communication of all of this information presents obvious logistical problems. Perhaps a simple organism could share all of the information from one segment with all other segments. In higher organisms,
such as humans, this is simply not possible. The number of pathways
required to do this would be so great that the spinal column would come
to resemble a tree trunk rather than a slender cable.

The way nature has solved this problem is twofold. First, afferent
signals from different sites often share a common pathway, making it a
"party line," so to speak. Having one pathway perform several functions reduces the number of fibers necessary to transmit information to
the brain. However, this may also lead to some confusion on occasion.
For example, pain originating from visceral organs may be "felt" as pain
from some other area of the body. This "referred pain" explains why the
individual experiencing a heart attack may attribute cardiac sensations
to indigestion.

The logistical problem of transmitting information is also solved by
passing on some data and failing to pass on other. Important news, such
as tissue damage, is relayed relatively intact to the higher centers for
consideration. Other information that is unnecessary or even distract-

ing, such as pressure sensations from organs crowded together in the abdomen, is not.

Even when one moves to the higher levels of control in the brain, there are still various levels of control, some within our awareness and some not. Conscious activity, and thus voluntary control, seems to reside within the highly developed cerebral cortex. Yet, it has been proposed that tucked away beneath the folds of this thin layer of cells is another brain, one concerned with the operations of the more primitive, life-sustaining functions of the body (Kety, 1970). This brain, the paleocortex as MacLean (1973) calls it, is primitive only in the sense that other structures are capable of more elaborate feats, such as abstract reasoning. It is not primitive, however, in the sense that it directs the highly sophisticated activity of numerous visceral responses.

The fight–flight response is a good example of how the more primitive structures of the brain organize complex patterns of visceral responses. The paleocortex organizes our internal organs in preparation for danger. Operating through the hypothalamus, the paleocortex can cause cardiac output and blood pressure to increase as well as direct the flow of blood away from organs that will not need it, such as the intestines, and to the active muscles. In addition, the rate of cellular metabolism is increased throughout the body due to the release of excitatory hormones. The level of glucose (sugar) in the blood in increased, and the liberation of energy within the cells themselves is facilitated. Mental activity is enhanced, and additional red blood cells are released into the circulatory system from the spleen to aid in the transport of oxygen. All of this occurs automatically when the organism prepares for vigorous muscular activity for defensive or aggressive purposes. Once set in motion, the higher centers of the brain are essentially powerless to reverse the process (Guyton, 1981).

The Organization of Behavior

It is misleading to suggest that any one level of physiological control is more important than another, or that human behavior is the product of one or two regulatory systems alone. For example, it would be inaccurate to attribute defensive or aggressive behavior solely to the paleocortex. To the contrary, we have reason to believe that physiological systems on every level are involved in the production of behavior. Further, the environmental context in which the behavior occurs also plays an important role in determining which responses emerge and which do not (Valenstein, 1973).

The idea that behavior is a composite product of many systems is well established. Delgado and his colleagues (Delgado, 1967, 1970; Delgado & Mir, 1969), for example, have proposed what he calls a "theory of fragmental representation of behavior." He proposes that different areas of the brain are responsible for organizing "fragments" of behavior, such as autonomic responses, vocalization, facial expression, and both tonic and phasic motor activities. These fragments, in turn, are organized into more complex behaviors by other neural structures. Some of these fragments contribute to several behaviors (e.g., sexual arousal and aggression), whereas others are tied to a particular response (e.g., certain facial displays). From this perspective, behavior is seen as the complex result of numerous, semiautonomous responses.

To illustrate this point, we might consider the fight–flight response. Certain areas of the neocortex are involved with recognizing the presence of danger and giving direction and purpose to the motor response. Other areas of the neocortex provide the fine-motor control of the motor component, allowing for effective movement in response to the challenge. The paleocortex, in turn, organizes the more visceral aspects of this activity, whereas additional physiological systems at every level respond accordingly.

The Case of John Hunter

John Hunter's case illustrates the process clearly. Hunter encountered a challenging situation. His angry response likely set in motion a fight–flight type of response controlled by the paleocortex. Among other physiological changes, Hunter's blood pressure and heart rate increased. Unfortunately, autoregulation prevented the vascular beds from dilating because his socially appropriate response was one of muscular inactivity. The arterioles remained constricted, increasing the blood pressure even further as the programmed response was carried through to completion. The heart, in turn, automatically pumped more vigorously in the face of the higher pressure. A critical point was reached at which the coronary arteries, in their occluded state, could no longer supply a sufficient supply of oxygen-carrying blood to the cardiac muscle. When this occurred, portions of the myocardium failed. With the pumping ability of the heart impaired, the delivery of blood to the cardiac muscle decreased even further. As a consequence, the heart failed completely, resulting in death. The irony is that all of the systems in Hunter's body were acting as they were supposed to. Only the weakened heart could not cope with the "normal" course of events.

Conscious versus Unconscious Control

Most responses in which psychologists are interested involve coordinated activity on many levels throughout the body. Some of these responses, such as cognitions, reside in higher centers of the cortex. Other responses, such as many visceral reactions, are essentially outside our awareness and are controlled either locally or by more basic regions in the brain. Traditionally, psychologists have tended to focus on the higher levels of control. Because language is our most easily employed tool and because language is a sophisticated result of higher cognitive function, it is not surprising that psychologists who rely heavily on language may overestimate the contribution of higher cortical control to behavior.

Much of what goes on, however, may result from operations that are beyond the control or understanding of higher cortical areas. An interesting example of this can be found in a description of "running amok." The term *amok* refers to an aggressive frenzy observed among Southeast Asian societies, particularly in Malaysia. One observer, van Wulfften Palthe (1936), describes it as follows:

> Suddenly, without warning, without those around him being in any way prepared for it, a native springs up, seizes the first weapon he can lay hands on, usually a sword or knife, and rushes like one possessed through his house and garden into the street. Like a mad dog, he attacks every living thing that gets in his way, and succeeds with marvelous skill in dealing deadly stabs and blows: *his mental eye may, indeed, be clouded* (the natives call the condition "meat gelap," clouded eyes), *but his primary motor and sensory functions have in no way shared the clouding* [italics added], and it is not seldom than an amoker will in a moment or two leave five or six dead or desperately wounded persons on the ground in his wake! (p. 529).

A less esoteric example of limits to our awareness can be found in the area of physical fitness, something that affects us everyday. One might expect that his or her perception of fitness is closely related to one's actual physiological state. However, this may not be the case. We found that a measure of perceived fitness was only weakly related to an index of physiological fitness and that the former was much more closely associated with one's mood at the time of testing (Born & Hollandsworth, 1985). It is possible that something as intimate as one's own physical well-being is only poorly perceived and perhaps influenced more by fluctuations in mood than by an accurate awareness of our capacity for physical activity.

The idea that much of what we do is beyond our immediate awareness or control is, of course, not new. Freud proposed that much of our observable behavior could be attributed to psychic processes of which we are not aware and over which we have little control. The construct of the "unconscious" from the psychoanalytic perspective, however, is not analogous to what has been proposed here. According to Freud, the unconscious is comprised of thoughts and memories that we are not aware of but that can be made conscious by the expenditure of considerable effort (Freud, 1915/1953). Defense mechanisms, such as repression and reaction formation, are said to prevent these thoughts from reaching consciousness. As such, the unconscious is not beyond awareness but only blocked from awareness. From a physiological perspective, however, we are not designed to "know" and thus control everything our body is doing. Instead, those aspects of our behavior that are "unconscious" are not the result of conscious thoughts gone underground but are due to regulatory control on levels below the conscious areas of the brain.

This difference in opinion is important when one considers the implications of each position in working with patients. From the psychodynamic perspective, "an inability to use appropriate words to describe feelings" is called *alexithymia* and indicates that the patient is a poor candidate for therapy (Sifneos, 1979). These *alexithymic* patients are seen as rigid, impulsive, and suffering from a poor fantasy life. In order to counter these characteristics, the therapist may seek to teach the patient how to express his or her feelings. On the other hand, if one believes that many thoughts and feelings are essentially beyond verbal awareness, attempting to provide the patient with words to describe these phenomena may be viewed as providing labels or attributions that may have little relationship to what is actually occurring.

Understanding Our Behavior

The possibility that we often make up explanations for things we do not understand has been advanced by Nisbett and Wilson (1977). Drawing on the experimental literature in the area of information processing, the authors argue that "when people attempt to report on their cognitive processes, . . . their reports are based on a priori, implicit causal theories, or judgments about the extent to which a particular stimulus is a plausible cause of a given response" (p. 231). In other words, people tend to make attributions based on preconceptions, biases, or arbitrary impressions. It is suggested that these explanations arise from many sources, such as cultural or subcultural norms, previous learning, or the linking of novel stimuli with novel responses. Although this does not mean that individuals are incapable of reporting accurately why they do what they do, it does mean that they are likely to be in error unless the causes are obvious and the circumstances of the situation are clearly understood.

Applying this thinking to psychological problems for which cause–effect relationships are usually vague and often obscure, it can be argued that the patient's verbal reports may more accurately reflect the perceptions and subtle guidance of the therapist rather than increased awareness on the part of the patient. This possibility is supported by the finding that "insights" following traditional psychotherapy can be predicted most successfully from knowledge of the therapist's theoretical orientation rather than from the client's actual history (Bandura, 1967; Mischel, 1968). (The realistic limits to our ability for interoception will be discussed at length in the chapter on biofeedback [Chapter 6]).

Nisbett and Wilson (1977) suggest that we rush to provide answers because it is desirable in terms of prediction and feelings of self-control. Whatever the case, the evidence clearly suggests that making causal attributions is common to the human condition (Weiner, 1985) and that it is most evident in those areas about which little is known. In commenting on the tendency to "psychlogicalize" cancer, the national columnist, Ellen Goodman, notes that "mystery lends itself to mythology. Myth rushes in to fill a scientific vacuum. . . . But it is amazing how quickly myths disappear when there are cures" (1985, p. 9A).

Susan Sontag provides an excellent example of this in her book entitled *Illness as Metaphor* (1979) when she describes how tuberculosis (TB) was considered to be the result of a "consuming" passion before its true cause was known. Romantic figures in literature were said to be suffering from TB because of a "romantic agony." Kafka was moved to write in 1917, as he died slowly from the disease, that "the infection in [my] lungs in only a symbol, the symbol of an emotional wound whose inflammation is called Felice" (Sontag, 1979, p. 43). These romantic notions of TB were due, of course, to a lack of knowledge of the illness. Sontag points out that syphilis was another dreaded disease during the 19th century that was *not* thought of metaphorically because everyone knew how one got it. Consequently, syphilis was not regarded as mysterious, only awful.

Not surprisingly, it became more difficult to speak of TB in a metaphorical sense as more was learned about it. By 1882 it was suspected to be a bacterial infection. However, it was not until 1939 that the Mycobaterium tuberculosius was identified and even later (1944) before streptomycin was introduced as an effective treatment. By 1952 isoniazid, an antibiotic, became the standard treatment for TB, and thoughts of the disease as being an expression of "diseased" love were abandoned.

Unlike TB, the origins of many behavioral disorders remain obscure. Consequently, their etiology lends itself to metaphorical speculation in place of fact. Given the different levels of physiological control and awareness discussed previously, one can see why this is easy to do. Nevertheless, some of our ignorance is giving way to an increased understanding of the nature of these problems. For example, one does not hear as much today about the family origins of schizophrenia (i.e., "the overcontrolling mother") as one used to (cf. McCord, Porta, & McCord, 1962). Apparently advances in explaining this disorder, at least in part, in terms of biochemical imbalances (cf. Snyder, Banerjee, Yamamura, & Greenberg, 1974) or other neurological dysfunction (cf. Seidman, 1983) make earlier explanations more difficult to maintain.

There is, of course, still much we do not know. Also, it is almost certain that all of the answers will *not* be found in biochemical or physiological explanations alone (Depue *et al.*, 1979; Engel, 1977). Nevertheless, there is much we do know about how the human body is organized and operates. Traditionally, much of this knowledge has remained apart from the common ground of psychological theory. Instead, psychologists have tended to fill in the gaps of their understanding of the *physio*logical components of behavior with *psycho*logical explanations. This is not necessary. The experimental literature in human physiology is abundant and often surprisingly relevant to problems concerning disordered behavior. The intention of this book is to explore some of this knowledge as it relates to the practice of behavior therapy.

Recommended Reading

Guyton, A. C. (1981). *Textbook of medical physiology* (6th ed.). Philadelphia: W. B. Saunders.

As a standard reference in physiology, the Guyton text is hard to beat. Easy to read and extremely comprehensive, this textbook has gone through more than six editions and has been translated into a half-dozen languages. It is said to be the most widely used text on medical physiology in the world. Guyton's influence and teaching will be evident throughout the present volume.

CHAPTER 2

Physiological Systems

The human body is made up of trillions of physiological systems, from intracellular systems operating on a molecular level to the highly developed central nervous system (CNS). In complexity and size, these systems range from those contained within the cell to those responsible for coordinating the activity of millions of cells. Yet, each shares the common purpose of regulating different aspects of the body's functions so that homeostasis is maintained.

Homeostasis

The term *homeostasis* is used to denote the maintenance of a stable set of conditions in which the cells of the body can function effectively. This is not a small achievement considering that the body is, by design, extremely unstable. Walter Cannon, the physiologist, put it best in his book *The Wisdom of the Body.*

> Our bodies are made of extraordinary unstable material. Pulses of energy, so minute that very delicate methods are required to measure them, course along our nerves. On reaching muscles they find there a substance so delicately sensitive to slight disturbance that, like an explosive touched off by a fuse, it may discharge in a powerful movement. Our sense organs are responsive to almost incredibly minute stimulations. Only recently have men been able to make apparatus which could even approach the sensitiveness of our organs of hearing. The sensory surface in the nose is affected by vanillin, 1 part by weight in 10,000,000 parts of air, and by mercaptan 1/23,000,000 of a milligram in a liter (approximately a quart) of air. And as for sight, there is evidence that the eye is sensitive to 5/1,000,000,000,000 erg, an amount of energy, according to Bayliss, which is 1/3,000 that required to affect the most rapid photographic plate. (Cannon, 1939, p. 19)

To the natural instability of the body, we must add conditions imposed on the body from without, those environmental challenges that

17

make the maintenance of homeostasis even more remarkable. For example, a person can tolerate a dry heat of 115 to 128 degrees Centigrade (239 to 261 degrees Fahrenheit) for a brief period without an increase in body temperature above normal. Yet, if the heat generated by 20 minutes of maximal muscular activity were not promptly dissipated, the albuminous substances in the plasma of our blood would become stiff, like a hard-boiled egg. This illustrates why the ability to maintain homeostasis under a wide range of conditions is necessary.

It is important, however, not to confuse homeostasis with "passivity" or with keeping things just the way they are. This would be true only if the maintenance of stability was a static process. But this is not the case, for things are forever changing as part of a "dynamic steady state"—an equilibrium of constantly interacting and inherently unstable biochemical systems (Schoenheimer, 1942). Consequently, maintaining homeostasis is very much an active, growth-producing process. The body must continually develop new competencies, new strengths to meet challenges, both old and new. Perhaps like Don Fabrizio in *The Leopard*, Giuseppe di Lampedusa's novel of 19th-century Italy in the midst of political and social upheaval, we must accept the irony that for things to remain the same, things must change (Lampedusa, 1958/1960). Or, as stated so eloquently by Cannon,

> When we consider the extreme instability of our bodily structure, its readiness for disturbance by the slightest application of external forces and the rapid onset of its decomposition as soon as favoring circumstances are withdrawn, its persistence through many decades seems almost miraculous. The wonder increases when we realize that the system is open, engaging in free exchange with the outer world, and that the structure itself is not permanent but is being continuously broken down by the wear and tear of action, and as continuously built up again by processes of repair. (1939, p. 20)

In short, the human body has developed a marvelous ability to regulate itself, automatically, under all sorts of conditions. And precisely because it is automatic, we seldom stop to reflect on it, unless, of course, the system breaks down. But the automatic regularity of the healthy body should not be seen as unimportant or trivial. It is, in fact, the foundation upon which all of our behavior is built.

Major Functional Systems

The Internal Environment

The more than 75 trillion cells that make up the human body function in an environment carried around by the body itself. Approximately

56% of the adult human body is fluid, of which two-thirds is found within the cells and the remaining third outside the cells. The latter, aptly termed extracellular fluid, provides the medium (the internal environment) in which the cells of our body live.

The extracellular fluid is kept in constant motion, rapidly mixed by the blood as it moves back and forth between capillary and cell. The plasma of the blood is part of the extracellular fluid system, just as is the fluid immediately surrounding each cell (the interstitial fluid). The circulatory system, as the name implies, keeps the extracellular fluid in motion. However, other fluid systems of the body, such as the lymphatic system, are important contributors to the process.

The reason why extracellular fluid is kept in motion is because every cell requires a constant and adequate supply of nutrients. We may not think of it as such, but oxygen is the most important nutrient of all. There is no nutrient that is more closely regulated in the body than oxygen. We can go for hours or even days without eating. We can modify our diets so that important vitamins are excluded and yet not experience any harmful consequences for weeks. We can even go without water for hours, but we cannot go without oxygen for more than a matter of minutes. Seven to eight minutes without oxygen will cause cells responsible for intelligent action in the brain to be damaged beyond repair.

The body's regulatory systems are designed to meet the cells' needs for oxygen before *anything* else. No other regulatory function in the body has a higher priority. However, oxygen is not the only nutrient required by the body, and other organ systems are available to regulate these needs. In addition to the lungs, which allow oxygen to be exchanged between air and blood, the gastrointestinal tract provides a necessary service by breaking down food and absorbing other nutrients into the blood stream. The liver (conveniently situated so that all blood from the intestines flows through that organ first) takes these raw materials and converts them into more usable forms. For example, the liver takes sugar (glucose) that is not needed by the body at that moment and converts it to glycogen to store for future use. Other systems, such as fat cells, the pancreas, and certain endocrine glands also play a role in regulating how nutrition for the cells is modified, stored, or used.

The metabolic breakdown of these nutrients creates waste products that must be removed. Although we are not apt to think of the lungs as part of the waste-removal system of the body, they are an important component of that system, for carbon dioxide is the most abundant end product of metabolism. The lungs are the place where excessive CO_2 is blown off. If it were not for the regulatory function of the lungs in maintaining a proper balance of CO_2 in the blood, severe acidosis or alkalosis would occur.

The other crucial organ system for disposing of waste products is the kidneys. The kidneys filter a tremendous amount of blood—in fact, the entire contents of the circulatory system every 3 to 4 minutes. The kidneys create a filtrate from the plasma of the blood and then reabsorb what is needed, such as glucose and sodium, while allowing metabolic end products to be excreted in the urine. The kidneys also play a crucial role in maintaining the acid-base balance of the body.

Up to this point we have talked about these internal regulatory systems individually. There is an obvious advantage for these systems to operate in harmony. For this to occur, there needs to be a method by which communication can occur between the systems already discussed.

There are two methods of communicating across internal regulatory systems—one neural and the other hormonal. In terms of the nervous system, it is probably more accurate to talk about nervous systems, for no single network of neurons is capable of doing all that is required.

The autonomic nervous system (ANS) is part of the regulatory system for the internal environment. Like the central nervous system (CNS), the ANS consists of nerves that sense information (afferents) and those that initiate action (efferents). Also, the ANS is divided into two branches—the sympathetic and the parasympathetic. The former is generally thought of as assisting the organism to prepare for action by anticipating demands on the internal environment before they occur and then facilitating the coordination of the organs in meeting these demands. The parasympathetic branch, on the other hand, is generally thought of in terms of its restorative function by which it helps the body in the process of recovery and repair.

As noted before, hormones provide another means for coordinating the activity of the internal systems. Located in the body are eight major endocrine glands that secrete chemical messengers. The hormones are transported in the blood throughout the body and help coordinate its function. Some hormones, such as epinephrine, simply augment the actions of the nerves, thus potentiating their effect. Other hormones act as special messengers, causing certain glands to secrete substances needed for the maintenance of bodily function. An example of the latter would be thyrotropin, which is released from the pituitary gland and travels through the blood to the thyroid gland, which in turn secretes thyroxin—a hormone that sets the tempo of all cellular activity.

The External Environment

The control systems we have discussed to this point regulate the internal environment. This regulation, of course, is necessary for the maintenance of life. But it is just as obvious that the cells in the internal environment would not long survive if the organism did not have some means of feeding, defending, and reproducing itself. These functions involve interacting with one's external environment.

The primary system for acting on the external environment is the musculoskeletal system. Approximately 40% of the body is skeletal muscle. This tissue not only provides the individual with the ability to move about in his or her environment but also provides structure and protection for the organs inside.

Connecting all of the skeletal muscles with the CNS is a network of nerves lying outside the spinal cord and called the *peripheral nervous system* (PNS). These nerves carry impulses from the various sensory receptors in the skin and joints of the body to the spinal cord and brain (afferent fibers) as well as transmitting signals from the brain and spinal cord, causing the muscles to contract (efferent fibers). Integration of these incoming signals and initiation of action takes place in the CNS itself.

Characteristics of Control Systems

Set Points

For homeostasis to be achieved, the various regulatory systems of the body must operate within certain very narrow limits. This is accomplished by anchoring their activity to a single, stable criterion—a set point. For example, the thousands upon thousands of complex biochemical reactions that occur every minute throughout the body occur optimally within a certain temperature range. Fortunately, the body has intricate means for regulating body temperature at a set point of between 37.0 and 37.1 degrees Centigrade (approximately 98 degrees Fahrenheit) so that these reactions occur under optimal conditions. The lowering of the body's core temperature a few degrees, say to 32 degrees Centigrade (approximately 90 degrees Fahrenheit), so disrupts the normal functioning of cells that the body's ability to regulate itself is impaired. If the core temperature is allowed to cool further to 28 degrees Centigrade (approximately 82 degrees Fahrenheit), all regulatory functions are lost, and death will follow. On the other hand, increases in body temperature are tolerated even less well. An increase of 4 degrees Centigrade to around 41 degrees (106 degrees Fahrenheit) is cause for alarm. An increase of another few degrees and lesions in the brain will appear with death occurring shortly thereafter if the process is not reversed (Guyton, 1981).

Temperature regulation is only one of the more obvious examples of how a set point operates. But virtually every regulatory system in the body is calibrated around some sort of set point. The level of sugar in the blood, the concentration of sodium ions in the interstitial fluid, the rhythm of firing of parts of the brain, all involve slight variations around some predetermined level. Even cells reproduce according to very definite regulatory rules that limit their growth to meet specific needs. Growth to a certain point will not be inhibited. But when that point is reached, cell division ceases. Failure to respond to this type of set point results in one of the most serious medical problems of all—cancer.

Negative Feedback

Most physiological control systems operate through a process of negative feedback. Negative feedback provides information to the regulatory system that is *counter to* or *against* (hence the term *negative*) the initiating stimulus. Therefore, negative feedback serves to drive a response back toward the set point. Thus, it can be seen that negative feedback is essential for maintaining homeostasis.

Negative feedback can be illustrated by again considering the regulation of body temperature. Heat sensors throughout the body appraise the hypothalamus of the body's temperature. These signals (feedback) allow the hypothalamus to make decisions concerning the cooling or heating of the body. If these sensors indicate a rise in body temperature, negative feedback will initiate a series of responses designed to lower body temperature. The vessels in the skin will become dilated, increasing the flow of blood to the periphery and thus cooling the body. If the temperature continues to rise, sweating will be stimulated. This allows for water to evaporate from the skin carrying heat away from the body. At the same time, other actions of the body that increase heat, such as shivering, are strongly suppressed.

The opposite sequence occurs when the body temperature begins to drop. Negative feedback will initiate responses to maintain body temperature, such as vasoconstriction of the peripheral vessels that conserves heat by directing blood away from the surface of the skin. If the temperature continues to drop, the hypothalamus will stimulate shivering. As the loss of heat continues, epinephrine and norepinephrine will be released to cause an immediate increase in the rate of cellular metabolism. If one is exposed to cold over a period of weeks, the hypothalamus, through the pituitary, will increase the levels of thyroxin and thus increase metabolism and heat production throughout the body.

Positive Feedback

Positive feedback accelerates change by stimulating responses in the same direction as the initiating stimulus. In other words, positive feedback drives a response further away from a set point. Again, using temperature control as an example, increased body heat becomes the stimulus, through positive feedback, for further increases in heat production. Obviously, a process such as this is very detrimental to the maintenance of homeostasis and thus is life threatening. That is why positive feedback for a physiological system usually occurs only when the system has lost its ability to self-regulate. Examples of this are seen during heat stroke, collapse of the circulatory system following a hemorrhage, or failure of one of the system's components, such as in the case of John Hunter's heart.

Keeping in mind that the maintenance of homeostasis is not a passive state, one can readily see that, in spite of the usual meaning of the word, "negative" feedback is not only desired but necessary for adequate functioning. It may be useful to remember that the self-righting capability of the human organism is based on the concept of *reversing excesses.*

Gain of a Control System

The gain of a control system is essentially an estimate of the effectiveness of that system in regulating change. Sometimes gain is referred to as the amplification of the system, the degree to which the system can "amplify" feedback, usually negative feedback, so as to exert its self-correcting influence. For example, experiments have shown that the temperature of an unclothed body changes approximately 1 degree Centigrade for every 25 degrees Centigrade change in the surrounding air. The feedback gain of the hypothalamus in regulating body temperature would then be estimated as 25—the amount of change if regulation were not to occur divided by the amount of abonormality that persists after corrective action has been taken (in this case, 25 divided by 1). According to Guyton (1981), this is a remarkably strong gain for a physiological control system.

The importance of the concept of feedback gain for our purposes is that different regulatory systems exhibit different degrees of effectiveness (i.e., differing feedback gains). Some systems are extremely powerful, such as the hypothalamic temperature regulatory system discussed previously. As it turns out, the more basic the regulatory system (i.e., the more involved it is with life-sustaining events) the more powerful its feedback gain. As noted earlier, the regulation of the delivery of oxygen to the tissues is a very powerful system. Other systems that are less immediately involved with the maintenance of homeostasis seem to exhibit less powerful feedback gain. Some systems, in fact, may be so removed from the more pressing demands of homeostasis that they exhibit little feedback gain at all. This may explain why viewing oneself as a failure can be maintained indefinitely without thoughts to the contrary, whereas the interruption of an adequate supply of oxygen will result in direct, compensatory responses almost immediately. Or, this may be why, as Lang has suggested, obsessive patients appear to be the victims of a positive feedback loop in which their behavior acts as the stimulus for further maladaptive responding (1979, p. 509).

Automaticity

As noted before, these regulatory functions are carried out, for the most part, outside the awareness of the individual. The most parsimonious reason for this is that there are simply not enough afferent (sensory) pathways available to apprise the brain of all that it could possibly know. In fact, it was argued in discussing the case of John Hunter that the transmission of all possible information is impractical as well as inefficient for the functioning of the body as a whole. Given the limited role of the conscious parts of the CNS in coordinating these responses, what makes the collaboration of these systems work is their *automaticity*.

Automaticity means that most regulatory systems of the body operate independently or at least quasi-independently of the higher centers of the CNS (recall the levels of control discussion in Chapter 1). In other words, they are "automatic." In fact, their automaticity is their strength, for they require little if any ongoing vigilance to insure their proper functioning. This is a decided advantage given that one does not have to "think" about making one's heart beat or setting in motion basic metabolic functions.

The automaticity of most of our regulatory systems is useful but imposes a certain handicap as well, at least from the perspective of the psychologist. Because these systems are so automatic, we are not aware of them and thus are likely to dismiss their importance. This may contribute to an overattention to conscious phenomena and to a tendency to ignore more basic systems.

It might be argued that, as psychologists, our interests do not reside with phenomena such as I have described; these matters are better left to physiologists or biochemists. Yet there can be no denying that these events provide a foundation for all behavior, conscious or not. And, when one considers how often the automaticity of their function is affected by things such as drugs, illness, or fatigue, it becomes apparent that these substrates to our conscious actions should not be ignored, even if they are normally automatic.

Systems Thinking

Complexity of the World

Everything in the world seems much more complex today than it was a few years ago. Knowledge has been expanding at a fantastic rate, outstripping our ability to keep up with it and posing new problems in terms of how one copes with it (Toffler, 1970).

One reason for this is the sheer amount of new information being generated by our own and related disciplines. It has been estimated that the number of scientific journals has doubled every 15 years, increasing many times over since the first journal was published over 300 years ago (D. J. Price, 1961). Also, it has been estimated that more than 90% of all scientists who ever lived are alive today (J. G. Miller, 1978).

Psychology is no exception. Not too many years ago a psychologist seeing a client had to deal with a dozen or so journals and master a base of knowledge that covered a handful of topics. This is not to say that the course of study was easy or that mastering this information was a trivial accomplishment. However, today one must add to that already sizable body of knowledge the information accumulated over several decades of research and practice. It is not that our colleagues 30 or more years ago had little to learn; the challenge today is that we have to learn so much more.

The Square Law of Computation

Another way to look at the extraordinary increase in complexity is to understand how complexity begets complexity. Every time a little knowledge is added to existing knowledge we have to readjust all of our calculations to take the addition of new information into account. In other words, new information often means looking at old information in new ways.

Weinberg (1975) illustrates this process by identifying three levels of analysis involved in describing the relationship between just two objects. First, one must calculate the behavior of the object in "isolation." That is, one must consider the particular characteristics of the object that affect its behavior apart from other influences. For example, the density and mass of a planet contribute to our understanding (calculations) of its behavior independent of other factors, such as the gravitational pull of another planet. Second, one must consider the "interaction" of the object with other objects. This statement attempts to quantify the effect of one object on another. An example might be calculating the effect of gravitational pull of one planet on the orbit of another. And finally, the third level of analysis takes into account the "field." This is a statement of how other objects in the environment would behave if the object of interest was not present. Again, an example would be calculating the movement of the other planets in the solar system if the planet under study was removed from it.

Psychologists interested in clinical phenomena are confronted with the same levels of analysis. For example, an isolation equation for a client would consider the client's past learning experiences that set him or her apart from everyone else. Interaction equations would attempt to take into account how the behavior of others affects the client's behavior and vice versa. And finally, a field equation would attempt to describe the client's environment, including important information such as opportunities for reinforcement and its potential for modification.

Actually, only one of these three levels of analysis is responsible for the remarkable increase in complexity as new information is added. With the addition of each new variable we must add a single isolation equation. These equations join the original field equation that remains unchanged. However, the number of interaction equations, according to Weinberg, increases exponentially so that for n variables we would need to describe 2^n relationships. Thus 2 variables generate 4 interaction equations, 3 variables 8, 4 variables 16, and so on. This is the square law of computation, which explains why things become so complicated so quickly.

The Science of Simplification

Psychologists have known for years that the human mind is limited in terms of its ability to process information (G. A. Miller, 1956). That, coupled with the square law of computation, suggests why it is so difficult to keep track of things when observing clinical phenomena. Consequently, some sort of simplification is necessary.

Rimm and Masters (1979) make this point in the first chapter of their text on behavior therapy. They argue that whereas simplification may keep us from explaining all human behavior, it is necessary from a practical standpoint. Simplifying assumptions allow us to get a handle on complex phenomena that in turn help us formulate models to increase our predictive power.

These authors use, as an example, Newton's formula for the distance traveled by free-falling bodies: $S = 16t^2$, where S is the distance fallen and t the elapsed time. Rimm and Masters point out that this formula can provide only an approximation because it fails to take into account many variables, such as air resistance and the shape, texture, and velocity of the object. In addition, use of a "constant" number (16) ignores the fact that this value varies depending on the distance of the object from the earth's center. Nevertheless, this simple formula provides considerable predictive power. Further, Rimm and Masters argue that had Newton started by trying to take into account every conceivable factor, he would have probably given up in frustration. In other words, the square law of computation would have made things too complex to understand unless certain assumptions had been made reducing the number of variables under consideration to a manageable few.

As Weinberg (1975) points out, simplification is at the heart of all science. Science does this in two ways. First, science consciously delimits the scope of its endeavor by focusing on those aspects of a problem it can adequately address. As Wigner (1964) noted in his speech accepting the Nobel Prize:

> Physics does not endeavor to explain nature. In fact, the great success of physics is due to a restriction of its objectives: it endeavors to explain the regularities in the behavior of objects. This renunciation of the broader aim, and the specification of the domain for which an explanation can be sought, now appears to us an obvious necessity. In fact, the specification of the explainable may have been the greatest discovery of physics so far. (p. 995)

A second way science goes about simplifying complex phenomena is through assumptions that are made concerning the nature of relationships between objects. For example, one frequent assumption is that objects in nature are related to one another in much the same way that parts of a machine operate.

Mechanical Simplification. From the beginning, the basic assumptions from the mechanical perspective

> implied the notion of a whole which was completely equal to the sum of its parts; which could be run in reverse; and which would behave in exactly identical fashion no matter how often these parts were disassembled and put

together again, and irrespective of the sequence in which the disassembling
or reassembling would take place. It implied that the parts were never significantly modified by each other, nor by their own past, and that each part once
placed in its approximate position with its approximate momentum would
stay exactly there and continue to fulfill its completely and uniquely determined function. (Deutsch, 1951, p. 230)

Weinberg (1975) illustrates the mechanical view of nature by also
referring to the work of Sir Issac Newton. In observing the heavens,
Newton was confronted with many thousands of objects, surely a phenomenon of great complexity. The square law of computation would
suggest that calculating the interactions between all of these objects
would require computations too numerous for even the largest and
fastest mainframe computer available today. Yet Newton was able to
solve this problem by making certain simplifying assumptions.

First, according to Weinberg, Newton decided that the influence of
most of the objects he could observe was insufficient to affect his point
of interest—the description of the orbits of the planets around the sun.
Second, because the mass of the sun is greater than the combined
masses of the other planets together, calculations not involving the
sun's mass could be ignored. Weinberg notes that the first assumption
resulted in a reduction in the number of equations by a factor of 100. The
second assumption reduced the number an additional 20 times. And
yet, Newton went even further. He observed that the dominant mass of
the sun allowed him to consider each planet in relationship to the sun
only, as a system separate from each of the others, thus reducing the
number of "interaction" equations dramatically. At this point, the
number of equations needed to be solved in order to get the answer was
manageable by one, albeit very able, individual of Newton's caliber.

As it turns out, all of Newton's assumptions were not completely
valid, for he missed a planet. And Newton was lucky. The solar system
lent itself to this type of simplification. Nevertheless, Newton was able
to make predictions that no one up to that point had been able to make.

Psychology has approached problems from the mechanical perspective as well. Some would argue that the operant learning paradigm
makes simplifying assumptions in this manner. Basically, the operant
model predicts that behavior can be increased or decreased by systematically varying its consequences (e.g., rewards). The arrangement of
these "parts" is seen as stable enough to make formal statements concerning the relationship between response and consequence (e.g.,
schedules of reinforcement). As in the case of Newton, the operant
paradigm has resulted in an increase in predictive power beyond that of
many other models. Indeed, its clear success in school, mental health,

retardation, hospital, and industrial settings would argue that this type of simplification has been worthwhile.

However, there are questions concerning the adequacy of the operant model to keep up with emerging knowledge of human behavior. One of the major challenges in this regard has focused on the operant model's ability (and the willingness of operant psychologists) to incorporate knowledge of physiological systems into its conceptual framework. Although it is true that the operant paradigm is often written "S-O-R-C," with the "O" representing "organismic variables" (Kanfer & Phillips, 1970), there is still some question as to how seriously biologically based, mediating variables are taken into account, particularly in terms of their interaction with stimulus settings, response topographies, and consequential events (Herrnstein, 1977). One of the most able proponents of operant psychology has stated: "The fact is that psychologists of learning have essentially ignored biological contributions to learning phenomena" (B. Schwartz, 1974, p. 192). As a result, operant psychologists assert that their "rules of learning" apply equally across species and stimulus settings. This assumption, termed the "equipotentiality premise," will be discussed at length in Chapter 4.

Statistical Simplification. Making the assumption that objects in nature are related to each other in a straightforward, mechanical manner is not the only type of simplification science can make in trying to deal with complex phenomena. Statistical manipulations of data provide a second approach.

Statistical simplification can be understood best by appreciating how it came about. Weinberg (1975) points out that Newton's great achievement was describing a system of perhaps 10^5 objects, of which he found 10 (the planets and the sun) of interest. Physicists in the 19th century were faced with a different problem. They were interested in the behavior of gases, such as molecules of air in a bottle. According to Weinberg, the differences between the problems facing Newton and these 19th-century physicists were three in number. First, the number of objects to be studied was larger, something along the magnitude of 10^{23} rather than 10^5. Second, they were not interested in 10 of these objects but in all 10^{23}. And finally, even if they had been interested in 10 of the total number they still would have had to study all 10^{23} molecules because they were pretty much identical and also in close interaction. As can be readily seen, the number of calculations required for such an understanding would be prohibitive, even by today's standards.

What these 19th-century physicists had going for them was the similarity of the 10^{23} molecules under study. A randomness of their interaction meant that the system was *sufficiently regular* to be studied statistically. In addition, the very largeness of the numbers of molecules strengthened the rationale for using statistical assumptions. It has been calculated that the probable error of a law of physics or chemistry is 1 divided by the square root of n: $(1/\sqrt{n})$, where n is the number of objects interacting to bring about that law. This is called the square root of n law or Schrodinger's law (Schrodinger, 1945). Consequently, if one were studying 10^2 molecules, the error of measurement would be 10%, which is rather high. If the same law were observed for 10^6 molecules, the error of measurement would decrease to .1% or to .001% if the system contained 10^{10} molecules. This direct relationship between the size of the sample and the stability of one's findings is, of course, one of the most basic assumptions of probability statistics as used in psychological research.

Fortunately for the 19th-century physicists, the basic prerequisites for statistical simplification were present when considering molecules of gas in a bottle. First, there was randomness. For gases, this is achieved naturally as the result of the similarity between molecules. In psychology, we impose a randomness of sorts by random assignment to groups. Second, these scientists were dealing with very large numbers. When studying molecules this is no problem. In psychology, it is only a problem if you cannot get enough subjects.

Psychology attempts to handle these requirements through the methodology of experimental design that is based on random assignment to groups and a relatively large number of subjects. This approach to studying psychological phenomena has been common but not necessarily successful in terms of increasing predictive power (Mischel, 1968). That may be because assumptions underlying statistical simplifications do not fit as well when dealing with human subjects. For example, randomness as imposed by the investigator is not the same as randomness resulting from the inherent properties of similar bodies interacting in a common field. Further, the numbers of objects studied in the physical sciences are great enough to allow for some rather stable generalizations. Most often in psychology, our numbers are small, and our results consequently are much more tentative.

Further, statistical simplification in psychology is based on what we *do not* rather than do know. For example, any number of variables unrelated to the research question are "controlled for" by randomly assigning a portion of the subjects to a no-treatment or attention-placebo condition. It is important to remember, however, that this does not mean that the variables controlled for do not have an effect. It merely allows one to partial out the amount of variance attributable to the treatment rather than that due to unknown sources of influence. In cases such as this, simplification is obtained but at a cost. Variables are excluded because we are ignorant of them, not because our models tell us which variables are important and which are not.

Summary. It can be argued that mechanical and statistical simplification both have their uses. The mechanical view appears to be useful for studying relationships between nonrandom objects of limited complexity. Consequently, mechanical models can deal with relationships between relatively few objects whose importance is known, such as the orbit of the planets around the sun. Weinberg refers to this phenomenon as exhibiting *organized simplicity,* and it may be analogous to situations in which salient environmental variables are identified as the primary determinants of a particular behavior. This notion can be illustrated if the degree of randomness and complexity of a phenomenon are plotted graphically, as in Figure 2.

The statistical view, on the other hand, is useful for studying objects that behave in a more or less random manner and that entail consider-

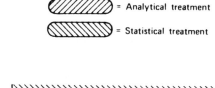

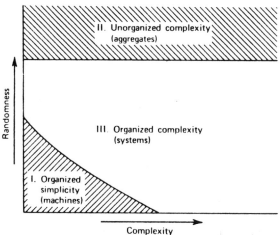

Figure 2. Methods of thinking with respect to different kinds of phenomena from *An Introduction to General Systems Thinking* (p. 18) by G. M. Weinberg, 1975, New York: Wiley. Copyright 1975 by John Wiley and Sons. Reprinted by permission.

able complexity due to the number of interactions involved. Molecules of gas in a jar are an example of this. Weinberg speaks of this type of phenomenon as displaying *unorganized complexity*. In psychology, the study of phenomena involving large numbers of subjects may be treated in this manner, although information may be lost in making actuarial statements of this type.

It may be, however, that the phenomena of greatest interest to psychologists who see clients fall in a third region—what Weinberg calls *organized complexity*. This is the region in which objects are sufficiently irregular (nonrandom) so that simplifying statistical assumptions cannot be made and yet that are of such complexity that mechanical models are insufficient. The interaction of individual human beings, each embracing a unique learning history and own biological makeup and with varied environments, may represent such a case. These are the types of phenomena that require a systems approach.

The Systems Approach

Definition. To this point we have used the term *system* without defining it. Weinberg defines a system as "a collection of parts, no *one* of which can be changed" (1975, p. 162). In other words, if one variable in a system is changed, at least one other variable in the system will be changed as well.

This view differs from the mechanical perspective described by Deutsch previously. With a machine, replacing one part may affect how the machine runs but will not change the characteristics of any of the other parts. For example, substituting a larger flywheel in an engine may make it run faster, but the nature of the interactions between the flywheel and the other parts of the engine will not change, although the other parts may run faster too.

The simplifying assumptions of statistics also do not take into account how changing one variable changes the properties of another. The unorganized complexity of phenomena suitable for this type of analysis is based on the assumption that all objects under consideration are similar enough to be considered random in their interaction. If changing one changes another, the very assumption upon which statistical simplification is based would be lost.

Systems thinking attempts to simplify things by taking into account both the complexity and the nonrandomness of a phenomenon. It does not assume that the behavior of diverse components of a system are sufficiently regular so that statistical averaging can be used to predict outcomes. On the other hand, the system's perspective recognizes that, for some phenomena, changing one object will invariably change the nature and characteristics of other objects in the system.

Characteristics of the Systems Approach. There are several characteristics of the systems approach that have direct implications for clinical practice. The first is that, because the nature of the relationships between components of a system is *interactional* (i.e., changing one variable changes another), studying a single variable in isolation may not tell us what we need to know about the behavior of the system as a whole. This does not mean that research that investigates one or two variables under highly controlled, laboratory conditions has no value for the clinician. It does, however, alert us to the possibility that when these same variables are operating within a complete, clinical system they may behave somewhat differently than expected or may be of much less importance overall than when seen in isolation (cf. Akins, Hollandsworth, & O'Connell, 1982; Akins, Hollandsworth, & Alcorn, 1983; Tucker, Shearer, & Murray, 1977).

Second, if one accepts the interactional nature of components in a system, then one might expect a single outcome to be *multidetermined.* This means that it is possible for a single response to be obtained by any one of several different pathways—in other words, to have multiple causes. This characteristic would suggest that models of human behavior emphasizing a single set of determinants may be inadequate (Bandura, 1977, p. 191). At the very least, the clinician should be suspicious of accepting models of human behavior that purport to explain complex clinical phenomena in simple, unidimensional terms, particularly when such an explanation cuts across a wide range of clients in many different settings.

Third, just as a single response may be multidetermined, changing one component in a system may result in *multiple outcomes.* This characteristic has obvious implications in evaluating treatment. The clinician does not assume a single outcome for a single intervention. Multiple changes as the result of modifying one aspect of the client's life are anticipated and planned for. As a result, the generalization or covariation of behavior following treatment is seen as a potentially predictable, not unexpected, phenomenon (cf. Kazdin, 1982).

In addition, we should note that systems are *dynamic* (i.e., they change over time). Improvement during therapy therefore is not expected to increase in a linear fashion with each session. Consequently, a single outcome measure at one point in time, even at the end of treatment, may be inadequate (cf. Gottman & Markman, 1978). Also the systems approach suggests that no single knowledge base is sufficient to deal with the complexity of human behavior (G. E. Schwartz, 1982c). Therefore, another aspect of the systems approach is its *multidisciplinary* nature. This suggests that psychologists need to be broadly trained and acquainted with several related disciplines from both the biological and social sciences in order to maximize their effectiveness with clients (Mahoney & Arnkoff, 1978; Wilson & Davison, 1969).

An Example of Systems Thinking

It is difficult to understand the physiology of human behavior without understanding systems thinking (G. E. Schwartz, 1982a, 1982c). Fortunately, physiologists have appreciated how a systems way of thinking adds to one's understanding of complex phenomena and have relied on it heavily. One of the foremost advocates of this approach has been Arthur Guyton. With his colleagues at the University of Mississippi Medical Center, Guyton has applied systems thinking to problems in cardiovascular physiology (Guyton, 1980; Guyton, Jones, & Coleman, 1973; Guyton, Taylor, & Granger, 1975). More specifically, this group of researchers has investigated the regulation of blood pressure as it relates to hypertension. Their model of the circulatory system is of interest to behavioral psychologists in that it provides a basis for understanding how behavior affects blood pressure. This in turn may lead to the development of more effective treatment strategies from a behavioral perspective (Hollandsworth, 1982).

The control of blood pressure, particularly as it relates to hypertension, provides a convenient way of comparing a mechanical perspective with a systems approach to the same problem because the current, most widely held model of hypertension found in the behavioral literature shares many characteristics of a mechanical view of things.

The Mechanical Model of Blood Pressure Regulation. Simply put, the mechanical model of hypertension in the behavioral literature has focused on the role of total peripheral resistance (TPR) in the establishment and maintenance of high blood pressure. The basis of this model is the equation: arterial pressure (AP) equals cardiac output (CO) times TPR ($AP = CO \times TPR$).

This equation, which relates three variables in an algebraic, noninteractive manner, means that AP is determined by the product of CO, which is the amount of blood pumped by the heart, and resistance to the flow of that blood throughout the entire circulatory system. Given the evidence that hypertensive patients usually exhibit normal levels of CO but increased TPR, many investigators have based their understanding of high blood pressure on an increase in TPR.

Over the years, as the complexity of hypertension has become better known, the number of variables that might affect this basic equation has increased. However, the focus on TPR as the final common mechanism for hypertension has been retained. For example, in the volume by Surwit, Williams, and Shapiro (1982) entitled *Behavioral Approaches to Cardiovascular Disease,* a dozen or more variables are identified as working together to establish hypertension. Nevertheless, just as all roads lead to Rome, all the pathways in their model lead to TPR as the final etiologic factor in hypertension. What is more important, however, is the fact that the addition of variables did not alter the manner in which they interacted. In other words, the model related each variable in a straightforward, additive sense, thus exhibiting characteristics of a mechanical view of hypertension.

There are, in fact, several good reasons for accepting this model of hypertension. For one, the data on CO and TPR obtained from patients with established hypertension support this view, as noted before. Another good reason is the work linking the defense–alarm reaction to increased peripheral resistance. As discussed in relation to John Hunter's death, when a person is alarmed, peripheral resistance and blood pressure increase, often dramatically, due to an increase in sympathetic activity. This has been termed a "pressor response" (Patel, 1977). And a related, but separate, reason for accepting the current view has been the success, with notable exceptions (e.g., Goldstein, Shapiro, Thananopavarn, & Sambhi, 1982), of some relaxation-based techniques in treating patients with hypertension. The success of this type of treatment would seem to support the emphasis on TPR because it is believed that relaxation has the effect of increasing blood flow to the periphery.

Limitations of the Mechanical Model. Although the mechanical model of hypertension has provided us with a useful set of simplifying assumptions, at the same time this understanding has certain important limitations that, after a certain point, may divert our attention from other meaningful aspects of hypertension that need to be understood when developing interventions for high blood pressure.

The major limitation of the mechanical model has been a tendency to look at single variables in relative isolation without taking into account, fully, the nature of the *interaction* among variables that combine to induce hypertension. This is not to say that investigators have not included many variables in their elaboration of the basic model or that they have not been sensitive to the pattern of physiological responses necessary to cause high blood pressure. There has been, however, a tendency to think of these variables in a simple, additive sense without taking into account the complex interactions that are reported in the physiological literature.

An example of the problem of viewing variables individually is the assumption, inherent to the mechanical model, that CO and TPR are independent. This is an important assumption because attributing an increase in AP to increased TPR presumes that CO is not reduced at the same time. In other words, AP is increased because TPR is increased, whereas CO is maintained at the same level. However, it can be demonstrated in a number of ways that CO and TPR are very much interdependent and, further, that as TPR increases, CO decreases (Guyton, 1980). Starling (1918) pointed out over 80 years ago that the heart is like a sump pump that pumps out all of the blood that enters it within, of course, certain limits. This concept is still accepted today. If the amount of blood returning to the heart is reduced, CO will be diminished accordingly. Because TPR is a major determinant of how much blood flows through the system (in other words, the greater the resistance the lower the blood flow), TPR plays a major role in determining the level of CO. (Taking into account the interactional aspect of variables is, of course, a major characteristic of the systems approach.)

Autoregulation. What complicates the picture further is the likelihood that the major determinant of TPR over the long run is not, contrary to the behavioral literature, the ANS. There is another, major variable that affects both TPR and CO. This is the phenomenon of autoregulation, which we have mentioned before.

It may be remembered that autoregulation is the property of tissue to adjust the perfusion of that tissue to a level that matches the tissue's need for nutrients, primarily oxygen (Cowley, 1980). This means that the arterioles, which are the single greatest contributor to TPR, automatically dilate when blood flow is reduced so as to keep the delivery of oxygen and other nutrients uninterrupted, or, under conditions of overperfusion, constrict to adjust blood flow to the level of need. Although there is still debate as to how this might occur, such as whether the process is mediated by a metabolic by-product or directly by the concentration of oxygen in the blood, the important point is that the phenomenon is not neurally mediated.[1]

---

[1]There are actually several hypotheses that attempt to explain the regulation of blood flow at the local tissue level. The metabolic theory proposes that either a decrease in the concentration of oxygen in the blood or a decrease in the pH of the blood causes vasodilation. A myogenic theory has resulted from the observation that vascular smooth muscle relaxes when transmural vascular pressure is reduced. Whatever the case, the autoregulatory response appears to be closely linked to the delivery and utilization of oxygen. What is unclear is whether oxygen *per se* or some metabolic end product, such as carbon dioxide, hydrogen, potassium, adenosine, or some other metabolite, moderates vascular tone at the local level (Cowley, 1980).

The adherents of the mechanical model would point out that the ANS has a powerful affect on the constriction and dilation of blood vessels. There is no question that neural, that is autonomic, control of the vasculature is quick and effective. But it is also short-lived. It's role appears primarily to be that of buffering sudden changes in blood pressure due to minute-to-minute demands on the circulatory system, as is encountered when one stands up. Constriction of a vascular bed due to increased sympathetic activity is poorly sustained over time (Korner, 1974). Not only that, certain aspects of autonomic control, such as the baroreceptors, are known to adapt within a few days to new pressure levels and thus cease to play a role in the long-term regulation of blood pressure (Guyton, 1980). On the other hand, autoregulation has little effect in the short run. It responds more slowly, but over a period of days its effects become even more powerful.[2] This understanding that regulatory feedback gains differ over time (i.e., are *dynamic*) is yet another characteristic of a systems approach.

A way to emphasize the interaction of these variables is to remind ourselves that the circulatory system is, at any given instant, a closed system.[3] Blood pumped in to the high-pressure side of the system must be available from the low-pressure side. If resistance increases so as to impede the flow of blood into the low-pressure side, then less blood is available for CO. In fact, if resistance was to become infinitely high, CO would theoretically drop to zero. Consequently, whether TPR is increased by sympathetic discharge or by autoregulation, CO must be maintained or even increased in the face of increased resistance if an elevation of blood pressure is to be sustained.

[2]The reason that autoregulation increases its effect over time is because a prolonged alteration in the perfusion of tissue results in more or less permanent changes in the structure of the vascular beds supplying that tissue (Cowley, 1980). One such change under conditions of overperfusion, for example, is a thickening of the arteriolar wall so that the diameter of the vessel is decreased. The accumulative strength of autoregulation means that relatively small increases in CO can result in proportionally much greater increases in arterial pressure, what Guyton refers to as a "quantitative cascade" (Guyton, 1980). For example, it is estimated that a long-term increase in CO of only 8% can induce a 40%, chronic increase in AP. This is yet another example of how viewing these variables as interacting simply in a additive fashion can be very misleading.

[3]The circulatory system, of course, is not "closed" in a literal sense. The capillary membranes are highly permeable to almost any substance smaller than the size of albumin molecules. This means that water, nutrients, and electrolytes can pass freely from the blood into the interstitial spaces. However, we can still speak in terms of a "blood volume" because a balance of hydrostatic and colloid osmotic forces allows the circulatory system to maintain a volume of fluid (plasma) separate from that of the surrounding interstitial spaces. A detailed look at the dynamics of the body fluids can be found in Guyton, Taylor, and Granger (1975) or in Guyton's *Textbook of Medical Physiology* (1981).

Long-Term Regulation of Blood Pressure. How can this occur? Increased sympathetic stimulation to the heart will not do it. Making the heart a better pump will not increase CO, unless there is an increase in the supply of blood for the heart to pump. However, one way to increase CO in spite of increased TPR is to increase blood volume. An increase in blood volume increases the amount of blood returning to the heart.[4] This one factor alone will sustain an increase in CO in spite of increased resistance, thus maintaining blood pressure at an elevated level.

How blood volume is regulated becomes central to our understanding of the long-term regulation of blood pressure. The apparent answer lies with the kidneys[5] (Guyton, 1980). The kidneys are the one organ system charged with maintaining the fluid balance of the body. Over the past 30 years Guyton and his colleagues have studied the role of the kidneys in the long-term regulation of blood pressure for this reason. What they propose is that the kidneys operate most efficiently at a set pressure level (a *set point*) in terms of their ability to excrete sodium and water from the body. If this set point is raised, the kidneys retain fluid until blood volume is sufficient to raise blood pressure to that level.[6]

---

[4]More specifically, the amount of blood returning to the heart (venous return) is determined by a pressure gradient between the average pressure level in the circulatory system (mean circulatory filling pressure) and the pressure at the right atrium (where blood reenters the heart). With the exception of those individuals with diseased and weakened hearts, the pressure at the right atrium is usually 0 mm Hg, whereas the mean circulatory filling pressure normally is 7 mm Hg. An increase in blood volume without a corresponding expansion of the capacity of the circulatory system means that the average pressure throughout the system is increased accordingly. Thus, increased blood volume increases the pressure gradient for venous return.

[5]Blood volume is proportional, to the point of edema, to the amount of extracellular fluid in the body. This is because water is freely exchanged between the circulatory system and the interstitial spaces, as noted before. Extracellular fluid volume, in turn, is determined by the amount of sodium in the body because sodium ions are responsible for 90 to 95% of the osmolality of the extracellular fluid. The osmolality of the extracellular fluid is tightly regulated. When osmolality increases, we drink more fluids, and the kidneys excrete more sodium. However, when osmolality drops, we reduce our intake, and sodium is conserved. Thus when we talk about regulating extracellular fluid volume, which determines blood volume, we are talking about the regulation of sodium, which is handled entirely by the kidneys.

[6]Basically, the kidneys function by filtering a very large amount of fluid and then reabsorbing 99% of the filtrate. Because of this, slight changes in the rate of reabsorption can have a dramatic effect on the amount of fluid excreted. For example, a 1% decrease in reabsorption from 99 to 98% effectively doubles the amount of fluid excreted. And because water passively follows the active reabsorption of sodium in the renal tubules, sodium conservation or excretion determines fluid balance. Consequently, factors that either facilitate or impede the reabsorption of sodium from the renal tubules will reestablish the set point

Pressure in excess of the set point will cause the kidneys to excrete fluid until the pressure levels are in balance once again. This process, which illustrates the concept of *negative feedback,* is much slower than the regulation of blood pressure by the autonomic nervous system. However it operates, with autoregulation, in an accumulative fashion over time so as to exhibit a very powerful effect (feedback gain).

To put all of this together in a more meaningful way, the development of hypertension starting with changes in renal functioning would proceed as follows. A resetting of the set point of the kidneys in an upward direction would lead to an increase in blood volume, which in turn would increase CO. The increased CO would, initially, account for the increase in AP. Over a period of several days to 2 weeks, autoregulation at the tissue level would occur in response to the increased CO. As the effect of autoregulation became more pronounced, CO would decline. However, AP would be maintained given the increase in TPR due to autoregulation. This higher level of AP would be important to allow the kidneys to continue to excrete sodium and fluid efficiently.

Given this basic understanding of renal functioning, there are three basic ways by which sympathetic activity can affect urinary output (i.e., raise the set point of the kidneys). These include a direct neural effect on sodium reabsorption, an effect on renal hemodynamics so as to modify the physical forces involved in sodium reabsorption, and an effect on the secretion of various hormones that alter sodium reabsorption. More specifically, increased sympathetic outflow has been shown to increase the reabsorption of sodium by affecting its transport in the proximal tubules of the kidneys independent of hormonal or hemodynamic changes (Gottschalk, 1979). Also, other investigators have demonstrated that changes in renal plasma flow and glomerular filtration rate following sympathetic nerve stimulation results in increased sodium reabsorption that can not be explained by direct or hormonal effects (Hermansson, Larson, Kallskog, & Wolgast, 1981). And finally, the link between increased sympathetic nerve activity and the renin–angiotensin system, a potent sodium conserver, has been well established (Davis & Freeman, 1976).

Work by Light, Obrist, and their associates at Chapel Hill has provided evidence that these physiological mechanisms may come into play under conditions of psychological stress (Light, Koepke, Obrist, & Willis, 1983). Selecting a group of young men with a family history of hypertension, these researchers found that both sodium and fluid excre-

---

either upward or downward, respectively (notice the direction of change given the effect on reabsorption).

tion were significantly reduced under conditions involving competitive mental tasks. In addition, the degree of fluid retention was "directly related to the magnitude of heart rate increase during stress, suggesting common mediation by way of the sympathetic nervous system" (p. 429).

The identification of a common pathway in the establishment of hypertension has implications for psychological treatments in this area. For example, the implication of the ANS may explain why interventions designed to reduce sympathetic activity, such as relaxation training, appear to alleviate high blood pressure, at least in the short run (Agras & Jacob, 1979; C. B. Taylor, 1980). Nevertheless, the distinction between short- and long-term regulation encourages us to look at these data somewhat differently. Single assessments of blood pressure, for example, would seem inadequate, and careful, continuous monitoring of blood pressure over a 24-hour period would seem necessary to demonstrate the effectiveness of these procedures (e.g., Agras, Taylor, Kraemer, Allen, & Schneider, 1980). In addition, identifying the kidneys as a major contributor to chronic elevations in blood pressure suggests that a variety of nonpharmacological treatments, such as the reduction of sodium intake and other life-style changes, should be considered in addition to stress management. Confusing short-term changes with long-term regulation, however, has tended to provide the latter with more status than perhaps it deserves. Although the mechanical model has provided some useful insights in terms of how hypertension operates, the limitations of this view can be clarified as our knowledge of the circulatory system increases. It is hoped that this example illustrates how approaching the problem from a different perspective—a systems approach—adds to the sophistication of our learning and the depth of our understanding.

Recommended Reading

Weinberg, G. M. (1975). *An introduction to general systems thinking.* New York: Wiley.

> There are many introductions to systems thinking available today. It is possible that Weinberg's book will be seen as dated or perhaps too generic by those who have a special interest or expertise in systems theory. Nevertheless, for the general reader, this book will provide a broad overview that may be just what he or she is looking for.

CHAPTER 3

Central Nervous System

Psychologists have a special interest in the central nervous system (CNS), particularly the "gray matter," that thin layer of neocortical cells only 2 to 5 mm deep in which our most highly developed capabilities reside. Our cerebral cortex allows us to hear, taste, smell, feel, and see. In addition, it puts all of these sensory inputs together in meaningful ways. This is where we "know" things and form our "thoughts." Further, the neocortex allows for the most delicate control of our finest muscles, notably those in our hands, feet and face. And finally, the neocortex, particularly that part that is located in the very frontmost part of the brain, is where we make plans, contemplate the future, render judgments, set priorities, solve problems, and organize long sequences of behavior. It is little wonder, then, that the cerebral cortex, with all that it allows us to do, plays such a prominent role in our models of human behavior.

In some ways, one might think of the cerebral cortex as an "enlightened monarch," ruling our world within and without. Other physiological systems are seen, from this perspective, as secondary in importance to neocortical control and as operating at its command. For many psychologists, the state of the body is, for all intents and purposes, the state of the neocortex. Nevertheless, there is more to life than higher cortical control. It is possible that some psychologists unnecessarily limit their understanding of human behavior by neglecting important aspects of bodily function that occur in regions apart from the gray matter of the brain.

An alternative view of human behavior sees the body as a "democracy" in which the neocortex rules at the pleasure of other, more basic regulatory systems. As long as these systems are running smoothly (recall the concept of "automaticity" discussed in Chapter 2), the cerebral cortex is free to follow its own pursuits, free to do its own thing, so to speak. However, when one or more of the more basic systems becomes disordered, such as during a panic attack, the dominance of the neocortex in directing behavior is compromised. Yet, if the more basic, survival-oriented functions regain their normal automaticity, the neocortex can resume control.

The Triune Brain

One does not have to go very much below that thin layer of neocortical cells to find structures designed to direct complex physiological responses apart from neocortical control. In order to understand why basic structures play such an important role in directing our behavior we might acknowledge our evolutional heritage. As Paul MacLean has put it:

> In order to appreciate where we are going, we must first look back in time to see where we have been . . . . Man puts so much emphasis on himself as a unique creature possessing a spoken and written language that, like the rich man denying his poor relatives, he is loath to acknowledge his animal ancestry. In the last century it almost killed him to admit his resemblance to apes, but the time is approaching when he must say "uncle" and admit to having far poorer relatives! (1973, p. 7)

MacLean has proposed that the human brain is actually a composite of three distinct brains, each different in structure and chemistry yet interacting and functioning as a single organ. Organized around a neural chassis that provides a foundation for all CNS activity, these separate brains are said to be stacked one on top of the other and apparently represent different points in the phylogenic (i.e., evolutionary) development of the CNS.[1]

Supporting the three brains is the *neural chassis* that includes the spinal cord and areas in the brain stem responsible for the most fundamental aspects of body regulation, including respiration, circulation and the wake–sleep cycle. If these are the only areas left intact, an animal will continue to live but with a severely limited range of activity. An animal that has been lesioned just above the brain stem, for example,

---

[1]Some students of the brain might object to MacLean's topographical divisions and argue that the integrated nature of all brain activity prevents us from making this type of simplification. Although recognizing the interactive complexity of the CNS (a point to be developed more completely later in the chapter), we can use MacLean's concept as a heuristic device here (e.g., Restak, 1984). The appropriateness of making simplifying assumptions such as this was discussed in the previous chapter.

can still perform basic movements, such as chewing, biting, growling, and hissing; display exaggerated postural reflexes, such as standing; and exhibit some sleep–waking behavior (Kolb & Wishaw, 1980, p. 132). These are the basic units of behavior around which more complex responses are built.

An animal that has to rely on the neural chassis alone, however, could not survive in anything less than an artificial environment. To live in the "real" world, an animal must be capable of behaviors that allow for the acquisition of food, defensive maneuvers, and reproduction. This is where the first component of the triune brain comes into play. The *reptilian brain*, as MacLean calls it, is said to have been developed over 100 million years ago and accounts for aggressive and certain stereotypic behaviors. Surrounding the neural chassis, the reptilian brain consists of the midbrain, interbrain, and basal ganglia portions of the endbrain.

MacLean emphasizes the ritualistic nature of behaviors associated with the reptilian brain. "The reptilian brain seems hidebound by precedent. Behaviorally, this is illustrated by the reptile's tendency to follow roundabout, but proven, pathways, or operating according to some rigid schedule" (p. 10). Thus animals operating with this brain alone, such as our reptilian ancestors, are able to survive independently, but survival is based more on genetically programmed information and habit rather than learning through an interaction with the environment. For example, an animal can still engage in voluntary movements after being lesioned above the diencephalon. However, these motor responses are poorly directed and lack adaptive flexibility.

Reptiles have only a rudimentary cortex. Early mammals, however, appear to have developed a more elaborate cortex around the structures encompassed by the reptilian brain. It should be noted, however, that the cortex referred to here is not the wonderful neocortex discussed at the beginning of the chapter. This is a primitive cortex that lies beneath the younger and more highly developed cerebral cortex. This cortical material corresponds to what we call the limbic system and was evolved, apparently, to allow for more purposeful behavior than was possible with the reptilian brain alone. In addition, this "old" cortex, which MacLean calls the *paleomammalian brain*, is largely responsible for organizing complex patterns of visceral responses in support of the behaviors resulting from an interaction with the external environment.

With the development of the paleomammalian brain, primitive mammals were able to move beyond the repetitious, programmed movements characteristic of the reptiles. This capability, however, was not based on the logic of a highly developed gray matter. Learning at this level resulted from a system of rewards and punishments "experienced" by the limbic system. Thus, an animal with an intact limbic system is able to link voluntary movements to appropriate stimuli well enough to maintain itself in simple environments.

The brain capable of reading, writing, and doing arithmetic is said to have come some 50 million years later and is represented by the great mass of cells on the surface of the cerebral hemispheres. This is what MacLean calls the *neomammalian brain*. An animal with an intact neocortex cannot only do all that has been described before but can perform sequences of movement in organized patterns as well as respond to complex patterns of sensory stimulation. In more highly developed mammals, such as the human being, the ability to initiate long sequences of purposeful behavior and to anticipate needs is even more obvious.

The new brain is also much more externally oriented than the old cortex. "It seems to thrive on change, presumably because nature designed it to come up with new ideas and solutions" (MacLean, 1973, p. 19). The external orientation of the neomammalian brain can be compared to the somewhat more internal orientation of the other two, older brains. This may explain the tendency of the former to act, at times, like the "bewildered onlooker," as discussed in Chapter 1. In fact, MacLean has suggested that, on occasion, our neocortex often may be "all out of step with our animal brains" (p. 18).

In summary, the triune brain is composed of three components, each active, each important, and each concerned with different aspects of our behavior. To use MacLean's terms:

> In the popular language of today, these brains might be thought of as biological computers, each with its own peculiar form of subjectivity and its own intelligence, its own sense of time and space and its own memory, motor, and other functions. (p. 8)

There may be some human activities, such as doing mental arithmetic, that rely almost entirely on the neomammalian brain alone. But most problems that behavior therapists are called upon to work with represent a coordinated pattern of responses involving all three components of the triune brain.

Structure and Function of the Central Nervous System

Overall Organization of the CNS

An overview of the CNS is presented in Table 1, which is organized in three columns. The left-hand column corresponds to MacLean's tri-

Table 1. Anatomy of the Human Brain

Triune division	Mammalian division	Structures
Neural chassis	Mylencephalon (spinal brain)	Fourth ventricle Medulla oblongata Cranial nerves IX-XII
	Metencephalon (across brain)	Pons Cerebellum Cranial nerves V-VIII
Reptilian brain	Mesencephalon (midbrain)	Cerebral aqueduct Central gray Reticular formation Tegmentum Tectum Cranial nerves III-IV
	Diencephalon (between brain or interbrain)	Third ventricle Thalamus Hypothalamus Cranial nerve II

	Telencephalon (endbrain)	Basal Ganglia
		  Caudate nucleus
		  Putamen
		  Globus pallidus

Paleomammalian brain	Telencephalon (endbrain)	Lateral ventricles
		Limbic system
		  Amygdala
		  Hippocampus
		  Cingulate gyrus
		  Septum
		Cranial Nerve I

Neomammalian brain	Telencephalon (endbrain)	Cerebral hemispheres
		  Sensory cortex
		  Associational cortex
		  Motor cortex

une division of the brain as discussed before. Most textbooks organize the mammalian brain using a topology similar to the one represented in the second (middle) column. In the right-most column are several structures of the CNS to be discussed later.

The Packaging of the CNS. The CNS is covered by tough, connective tissue consisting of three layers. These are called the *meninges.* The outermost layer, the *dura mater,* is a tough, relatively thin layer next to the bone of the skull and spinal column. Immediately beneath the dura mater is a soft, spongy layer called the *arachnoid.* Between the arachnoid and the third layer is a gap called the *arachnoid space,* filled with *cere-*

brospinal fluid. Cerebrospinal fluid is similar in composition to blood plasma (the fluid of the blood minus the white and red blood cells). Beneath the arachnoid space is the third layer, the *pia mater.* The pia mater follows the contours of the nervous tissue more closely than the dura mater, separating the two layers widely in places.

The ventricles are spaces or cavities within the brain filled with cerebrospinal fluid. They are connected to each other and with the arachnoid space by a series of small openings and canals. This network provides a medium in which the CNS actually floats. This helps cushion the brain and protects it from damage caused by sudden movements.

The Spinal Cord. The tissue surrounding the *central canal* of the spinal cord, which is part of the ventricle system, is gray. This means that the white, fatty material that provides electrical insulation around the axons of many nerves in the CNS, *myelin,* is absent. Myelinated nerves transmit signals much more rapidly than smaller unmyelinated nerve fibers. However, the absence of a myelin sheath around the axon allows for cross-talk between nerves. In some parts of the CNS this is desired because it facilitates the integration of information. The cerebral cortex, for example, consists mostly of unmyelinated fibers and is thus referred to as "gray matter."

The remaining portions of the spinal cord are white matter, consisting of myelinated nerve fibers. As would be expected, these nerve tracts are concerned primarily with the transmission of information to and from the brain. There are two major *ascending* pathways carrying sensory information to the brain. The first of these, the *dorsal column,* is located directly between the dorsal horns of the gray matter. The second, the *spinothalamic pathway,* is positioned as two separate bundles of nerves toward the outer wall of the spinal cord. The different characteristics of the two transmission systems will be discussed later in the chapter.

There are several *descending* fiber tracts carrying motor (efferent) signals from the brain. The most important of these are the *corticospinal tracts,* which carry information from the pyramid-shaped cells in the motor cortex and thus are part of the *"pyramidal" motor system.* These fibers, located on each side of the lateral horns or the gray matter, carry messages that control fine-motor movements. There is also an efferent system involving pathways from structures such as the cerebellum and basal ganglia. These tracts, part of the *"extrapyramidal" system,* are located in the white matter beyond the lateral and ventral horns and control gross-motor movements of which we are generally unaware as well as coordinate complex responses initiated by the motor cortex. The different functions of the two major, motor systems will be discussed in more detail shortly.

The Neural Chassis

The spinal cord ends in the region of the second lumbar vertebra where it narrows and branches into *spinal roots* forming the *cauda equina,* or "mare's tail." At the other end it enters the skull through a large opening called the *formen magnum.* As we begin our discussion of the brain itself, it will be helpful to refer to Figure 3.

Mylencephalon (Spinal Brain). At the top of the spinal cord is the *medulla oblongata.* The medulla serves primitive visceral reflexes, such as the regulation of heart rate, blood pressure, and respiration. At the medulla, the central canal expands to become the *fourth ventricle.* The medulla is also where 4 pairs of cranial nerves (IX through XII) leave the CNS. All together, 12 pairs of cranial nerves exit from the base of the brain and serve both afferent (sensory) and efferent (motor) functions in the upper shoulders and head regions. Two of the nerves at the level of the medulla (the *glossopharnygeal* [IX] and the *hypoglossal* [XII]) are concerned with sensations and movements of the tongue as well as swallowing. The *accessory* nerve (XI) controls shoulder movements, turning of the head, and voice production. And finally, the *vagus* (X) courses its way down into the chest and abdomen, innervating many important organs, including the heart, lungs, stomach, small intestine, and colon.

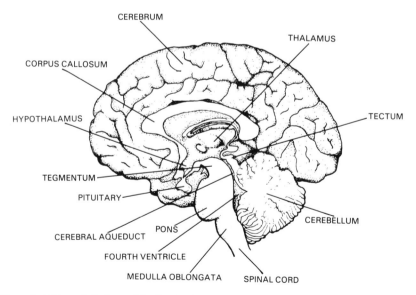

Figure 3. Midsaggital view of the brain. From *Human Physiology* (p. 160) by E. B. Mason, 1983, Menlo Park, CA: Benjamin/Cummings. Copyright 1983 by Benjamin/Cummings Publishing, Corp. Adapted by permission.

The vagus is responsible for more than 85% of the activity of the parasympathetic branch of the autonomic nervous system.

Metencephalon (Across Brain). The "across brain" consists of two major components—the *pons* and the *cerebellum,* which lie just above the medulla. The pons plays a very important role as a relay station between the cerebral cortex and the cerebellum. In fact, a major portion of the pons is taken up with nerve tracts (called *peduncles*) for this purpose. In addition, the pons serves important respiratory functions as well as containing nuclei (the *pontine nuclei*) that mediate deep and rapid-eye-movement (REM) sleep. The reticular activating system, which we will discuss shortly, has many fibers in the area of the pons. This system is important in activating the sleep–wake cycle.

The *cerebellum* is the most important structure of the extrapyramidal motor system. The "silent" area of the brain, it monitors and makes corrective adjustments in motor activities initiated by other parts of the brain, primarily the motor cortex. It is especially important in controlling balance between agonist and antagonist muscles during rapid changes in body position. The cerebellum compares the intentions of the motor cortex with the actual status of the body. It does this by monitoring inputs from the motor cortex and sensory inputs from the muscles and joints at the periphery.

Four additional cranial nerves exit the CNS from the metencephalon. Three of the four, the *abducens* (VI), the *trigeminal* (V), and the *facial* (VII), have efferent roles in eye movement, chewing, and facial expression, respectively. The trigeminal also carries sensory information from the face, nose, and mouth. Taste sensations are carried by the facial nerve, whereas the *acoustic* nerve (VIII) carries information concerning hearing, balance, and change of motion. These cranial nerves are the last structures we will discuss in relation to the neural chassis.

The Reptilian Brain

Mesencephalon (Midbrain). At the pons, the fourth ventricle narrows into the *cerebral aqueduct.* Surrounding the cerebral aqueduct is an area called the *central gray.* The central gray is where strong rage or fear reactions are elicited when it is stimulated. If, for some reason, it is destroyed, the subject is impaired in the ability to display defensive-aggressive behaviors.

The central gray is in close association with the *reticular formation.* This extensive network of cells continues into the midbrain. The reticular formation is involved with motor control, arousal, attention, and wakefulness. It has both an excitatory and inhibitory effect on the extrapyramidal system as well as being responsible for maintaining consciousness. Its role in activating the cerebral cortex via its interaction with the thalamus will be discussed shortly.

To either side of the central gray are two large bodies of nuclei that take on a red color when stained. These are the *red nuclei* that are an important link in the flow of information from the cerebellum to the motor neurons in the spinal cord. As part of the extrapyramidal motor system, the red nuclei are also concerned with forward and backward deviations from the body axis and are thus important in maintaining upright balance. Another area, the *substantia nigra,* lies near the red nuclei and appears to be a motor-relay station for the basal ganglia, thalamus, and the reticular formation. Together with the red nuclei, this area is called the *tegmentum.*

Two pair of colliculi, referred to as the *inferior* and *superior colliculi,* make up the *tectum* or "roof" of the midbrain. The former acts as a relay station for all auditory information from the ear to the auditory cortex. Several auditory reflexes are integrated at this point, leading to the interesting possibility that lesions beyond the colliculi enable a subject to exhibit a startle reflex in response to an unexpected, loud noise but be completely unaware of having heard a thing. The superior colliculi play a role in sight by providing automatic scanning movements when following objects passing across the visual field.

Two more pairs of cranial nerves exit at the level of the mesencephalon. The *oculomotor* (III) and the *trochlear* nerves (IV) innervate the muscles of the eyes and are concerned with eye movements. The oculomotor, in particular, is able to control the eyelid, pupil size, and accommodation (focusing) of the lens.

Diencephalon (Between Brain). The two major components of the diencephalon are the thalamus and hypothalamus. The *thalamus* is the "inner chamber" of the brain that mediates a majority of neural inputs to the cerebral cortex. Some thalamic nuclei relay sensory signals to specific areas of the neocortex, whereas other nuclei project diffusely to widespread regions of the neocortex and to other thalamic nuclei. The latter are responsible for a generalized level of arousal in the cerebral hemispheres and operate through the reticular activating system. Still other thalamic nuclei project the specific areas of the neocortex but do not relay sensory information. These nuclei are believed to function in the focusing of conscious attention.

The thalamus also mediates aggressive-defensive behavior by linking the hypothalamus to the limbic system, which we will discuss later. In addition, the thalamus participates in higher cognitive processes, such as learning and memory, through its interplay with associational areas of the neocortex. It accomplishes this by activating various areas of the neocortex, making them receptive to the input of information, the integration of these signals, and the initiation of responses. The role of the thalamus as a central, preconscious, "executor" of the brain can not be overemphasized.

Operating in close association with the thalamus is the *hypothalamus*. Sometimes referred to as the "head ganglion" of the autonomic nervous system, the hypothalamus is the major output pathway for the limbic system. The hypothalamus sends its signals in two directions, downward through the brain stem mainly into the reticular formation of the mesencephalon (the midbrain), the pons, and the medulla, and upward to many areas of the cerebrum, especially the anterior thalamus and limbic cortex. It directly affects cerebral cortical function through the activation or inhibition of the reticular activating system. Also it serves several vegetative functions, such as the regulation of body temperature, thirst, and hunger. In addition, it has a role in sexual expression and defensive-aggressive behaviors.

A major output mechanism for the hypothalamus is the *pituitary gland*. The pituitary is the most important endocrine gland in the body. Its anterior portion produces six very important hormones plus several less important ones, whereas the posterior portion produces two additional ones. Hormones secreted from the anterior portion control bodily growth, basic metabolism, rates of chemical reactions throughout the body, milk production, and sexual receptivity. The posterior portion secretes hormones important to water conservation and regulation of milk flow during suckling.

One pair of cranial nerves originates from the diencephalon, but it is a major one—the *optic* nerve (II). As the name indicates, the optic nerve transmits signals from the retinae to the primary visual cortex. This pair of nerves transmits information from the 125 million rods and 5.5 million cones in each retina to the visual cortex that requires many fibers (approximately 900,000 each as counted with the light microscope).

Telencephalon (Endbrain). The final structures associated with the reptilian brain are the *basal ganglia*. These are very large regions of gray matter lying to either side, above, and in front of the thalamic nuclei. The basal ganglia essentially consist of three structures—the *caudate nucleus, putamen,* and *globus pallidus*. In addition, the substantia nigra, and major portions of the thalamus, reticular formation, and red nucleus operate in close association with these areas and are thus part of the basal ganglia system for motor control. Some of these structures are illustrated in Figure 4.

The basal ganglia act to inhibit or excite motor tone throughout the

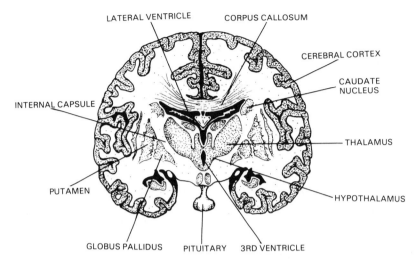

Figure 4. Cross-section view of the brain. From *Human Physiology* (p. 157) by E. B. Mason, 1983, Menlo Park, CA: Benjamin/Cummings. Copyright 1983 by Benjamin/Cummings Publishing, Corp. Adapted by permission.

body, regulate gross intentional movements, and provide a background of motor tone for intended movements. In addition, they are responsible for many subconscious stereotypic or even unlearned programs of movement either functioning alone or in close association with the cerebral cortex. More specifically, the caudate nucleus and putamen (together called the *striate body*) help control gross, intentional movements of the body that we perform unconsciously. The globus pallidus, on the other hand, provides background muscle tone for intended movements.

Unlike the cerebellum, the basal ganglia can initiate sequences of patterned responses. It is believed that many overlearned motor responses (i.e., stereotypic behavior patterns) become programmed in the basal ganglia. When the appropriate occasion arises, these programs can be run off and completed on their own without further direction from the motor cortex. On many occasions, signals from the motor cortex initiate these sequences of behaviors. On other occasions, however, commands from the hypothalamus and limbic system may set a course of action in motion.

The putamen and globus pallidus are located to either side of the thalamic nuclei. However, there is another structure between the thalamus and the basal ganglia. This is the *internal capsule,* a large mass of heavily myelinated fibers that transmit signals between the neocortex and other parts of the CNS. It should be kept in mind that major portions of the brain do nothing more than pass messages from one area or structure to another.

In summary, three areas of the brain, the midbrain, the interbrain, and portions of the endbrain, all make up what MacLean refers to as the "reptilian brain." Some of the most important structures that comprise this brain are the thalamus, the hypothalamus, and the basal ganglia. These structures allow for complex patterns of behavior affecting both the internal and the external environments.

The Paleomammalian Brain

As noted earlier, the "old" cortex of the paleomammalian brain is represented neuroanatomically by the limbic system. Surrounding the reptilian brain, the limbic system is responsible for a wide range of responses involving vegetative functions, fear and punishment reactions, sexual drives, and overt rage and fighting responses. Some of the structures we usually associate with the limbic system are the *amygdala, hippocampus, cingulate gyrus, septum* as well as parts of the thalamus and hypothalamus. The inclusion of the latter suggests the close connection the limbic system has with the reptilian brain. In fact, one could consider the limbic system as a primitive cortex for the reptilian brain, operating in much the same way that the neocortex serves as an extension of experience for the paleomammalian brain. The limbic system is represented in Figure 5.

The *amygdala* is a large complex of nuclei located in the tips of the temporal lobes. There are several divisions of the amygdala. One is involved with the sense of smell (olfaction). Another major division is concerned with visceral responses. When stimulated, this portion evokes feelings of rage, fear, and sexual arousal. Some believe that the amygdala mediates defensive-aggressive behavior by integrating and directing the activity of the more primitive emotional centers of the midbrain, the thalamus, and hypothalamus. This area may be the center for the fight–flight response,

Extending behind the amygdala is the *hippocampus*. The hippocampus plays an important role in the consolidation of memory and, in opposition to the amygdala, may dampen affective intensity. The hippocampal regions join to form the *cingulate gyrus*. This structure, which runs along the top of the corpus callosum, is where emotional feelings such as fear and anger are experienced. Through its many connections with the thalamic and prefrontal cortical areas, this primitive cortex is also closely associated with defensive-aggressive behavior. The *septal*

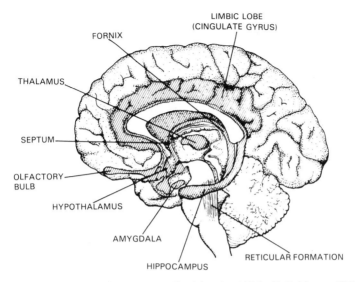

Figure 5. The limbic system. From *Human Physiology* (p. 161) by E. B. Mason, 1983, Menlo Park, CA: Benjamin/Cummings. Copyright 1983 by Benjamin/Cummings Publishing Corp. Adapted by permission.

area, which separates the diverging horns of the lateral ventricles, has been found to be one of the most important reward centers of the brain.

Another important part of the limbic system is the last cranial nerve—the olfactory nerve (I). This cranial nerve was noted historically for its connection to the limbic system. As a result, it was thought that the limbic cortex was designed to process olfactory information, leading to its being termed the *rhinencephalon* (Kolb & Wishaw, 1980). Later it was discovered that the limbic system had many functions, only one of which is olfaction. Nevertheless, the directness of the connection between olfaction and this primitive cortex, the only sensation that is not relayed through the thalamus, suggests the primitive nature of this basic sense.

The Neomammalian Brain

A huge mass of heavily myelinated fibers beyond the limbic system takes up a major portion of the remaining volume of the hemispheres. In fact, millions of fiber tracts radiate from the corpus callosum. This mass of fibers is called the *corona radiata* and consists of nerves spreading from the internal capsule to the cerebral cortex. This is the "white matter" that underlies the "gray matter." At the ends of these fibers is the neocortex, with which we began our discussion of the CNS.

The cerebral cortex is marked by many ridges (convolutions or *gyri*) and furrows (fissures or *sulci*). A large furrow, the *central fissure,* extends vertically almost in the middle of the brain and provides a dividing line between the *frontal lobes* and the *parietal lobes* to the rear. Another large furrow, the *lateral fissure,* separates the *temporal lobes* below it from the rest of the brain. And finally, the *occipital lobes* occupy the rearmost area of the hemispheres.

More important than the physical division of the brain into four lobes is the division of the neocortex into its basic, functional areas. The *sensory cortex* allows for the sensation of simple stimuli as well as special sensory functions, such as vision and hearing. Secondary sensory areas adjacent to primary sensory areas allow for higher order perceptual processing. The primary and secondary areas for vision are found in the occipital lobe, whereas hearing is located in the temporal lobe. A large band of sensory cortex is located immediately behind the central fissure and is concerned with somatic sensation, such as touch and pressure. There is a similar arrangement in the *motor cortex,* which lies just in front of the central fissure. The primary motor area provides for fine-motor control via the pyramidal system.

Another major region of the neocortex, the *associational cortex,* links the input and output systems described previously. There are two areas of associational cortex that are particularly important. First, a *general interpretative area* (often called *Wernicke's area*) lies on the upper side and to the rear of the temporal lobe where the parietal, occipital, and temporal lobes come together. This means that visual, somatic, and auditory associational areas converge so that higher order interpretations, called *cerebrations,* can be made. In right-handed persons, this area is almost always in the left hemisphere. This is the area where "thoughts" occur. If it is damaged, things do not make sense. For example, if the stream of visual experiences passing into the area is blocked, a person could see words on a printed page and even know that they are words but not be able to interpret their meaning (Guyton, 1981).

A second important associational area is the *prefrontal area,* which lies forward of the motor and premotor cortex in the frontal lobe. This area is particularly important for both the sequencing and elaboration of thought. The former is important for keeping mental functions directed toward a goal, such as in carrying out long chains of related behaviors. The latter function enables a person to engage in many abstract tasks, such as making predictions about the future, formulating plans, delaying impulses until further sensory information is received, considering consequences before motor actions are initiated, solving complicated problems requiring logic, and responding to ethical and moral considerations. It is this highly developed prefrontal area that corresponds to what we consider to be intellectual activities. Needless to say, other mammals, such as the dog and cat, do not enjoy the benefit of a prefrontal cortex. Their cerebral cortex is concerned almost entirely with sensory and motor functions.

Another interesting associational area of the neocortex deals with the recognition of faces. A brain abnormality (called *prosophenosia*) occurs when a person has extensive damage on the underside and to the middle of the occipital and temporal lobes. In cases such as this, the person may be able to do almost anything a normal person can, including all of the complicated mental tasks described previously, but not be able to recognize faces.

Before leaving the neocortex, its relation to the more basic structures discussed earlier must be noted. All areas of the neocortex have direct afferent and efferent connections with the thalamus. The connections are in two directions, from the thalamus to the neocortex and then back to the same area of the thalamus. If any of the connections are cut, cortical function in the affected areas becomes almost entirely abrogated. "Therefore, the cortex operates in close association with the thalamus and can almost be considered both anatomically and functionally to be a large outgrowth of the thalamus" (Guyton, 1981, p. 685). The thalamus, in short, acts as a control center that can call forth stored information, channel sensory signals to appropriate parts of the brain, detect sensations before they reach the neocortex, and initiate prefrontal lobe activity.

Functional Systems of the CNS

Although helpful in some ways, detailing the functions of various brain structures can be dangerous, for it may lead one to think that different behaviors are located in different parts of the brain. This is the concept of "localization" and was very popular in the latter part of the last century as neurologists were able to draw "functional maps" of the cerebral cortex. The problem, however, is that no single behavior is the result of a single group of neurons. As noted by Luria (1973),

> mental functions, as complex functional systems, cannot be localized in narrow zones of the cortex or in isolated cell groups, but must be organized in

systems of concertedly working zones, each of which performs its role in a
complex function system, and which may be located in completely different
and often far distant areas of the brain. (p. 31)

Luria illustrated this concept by referring to a frequently observed
neurological disorder, *apraxia* (when a patient is unable to manipulate
objects in certain ways). Initially it was thought that a lesion in the area
of the parietal lobe was responsible for this problem. Further investigation, however, revealed that the same disorder would result from lesions in any of three different parts of the brain. (Recall the interactional
and multidetermined characteristics of systems discussed in Chapter 2.)
This is because the manipulation of objects with one's hand requires
several different capabilities that together form a functional system.

More specifically, if the brain is unable to receive information concerning the position of the joints or the tone of the muscles, apraxia will
occur. This would result from a lesion that prevents the reception of
afferent impulses from the arm and hand. However, even if sufficient
afferentation is present, apraxia will still occur if the brain is not able to
calculate the necessary spatial coordinates by which the hand is placed
in three-dimensional space. This problem (spatial apraxia) is due to an
inability to integrate the afferent signals that are received. And finally, a
lesion in the basal ganglia may disrupt the ability of the pyramidal motor
system to perform the manipulation smoothly, even if the kinesthetic
afferents are being received and integrated appropriately (Luria, 1973,
pp. 34–38).

It can be seen that Luria's example involves all three functional
areas of the neocortex discussed previously—sensory, integrative, and
motoric. These systems and the relationships between the various structures of the brain that go to make up each are presented in Figure 6. Also
included is the environment, which is the source of most of our stimuli,
and overt behavior, which is how we influence the environment.

Starting with the sensory system, it will be noted that there are four
types of sensors, each designed to assess different aspects of one's environment, both internal and external. *Proprioceptive* sensation apprises
the brain of the physical state of the body and includes information
concerning tension of the muscles and tendons, angulation of the joints,
and deep pressure from the bottom of the feet. The *visceral* sensors have
the same function but for the internal organs. Sensations transmitted to
the brain from the viscera include pain, fullness, and sometimes the
sensation of heat. These sensations are similar to those assessed by the
exteroceptive sensors except, of course, the latter detect their information
from the surface of the skin. Additional exteroceptive sensations would

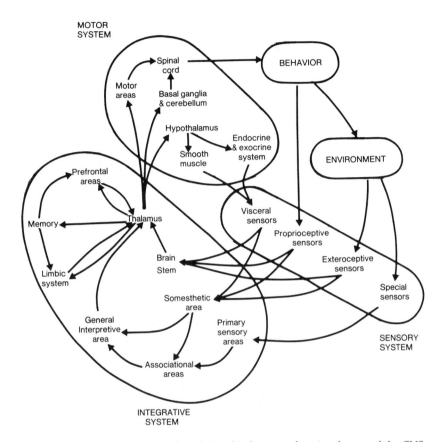

Figure 6. Schematic drawing of the relationship between functional areas of the CNS.

include touch, pressure, heat, and cold. The final group of sensors are the *special* sensors, which includes vision, hearing, taste, and smell.

Messages from the special sensors travel directly to their primary sensory areas. Somesthetic sensations, on the other hand, use a dual system for the transmission of signals, as noted earlier in our discussion of the spinal column. The *dorsal column* pathway is relatively fast (35 to 80 meters per second) and sends very discrete signals because of its heavily myelinated fibers. In addition, it has few synapses in the brain stem and sends its signals directly to conscious portions of the cerebral cortex. The second system, the *spinothalamic* pathway, is slower (1 to 30 meters per second) and sends diffuse signals because there is much cross-talk between its unmyelinated fibers. In addition, there are many termination points for this system in the brain stem (the pons and medulla) and midbrain. Consequently, this system is concerned more with autonomic reactions. Not surprisingly, the dorsal system sends messages of high localization and gradations of intensity. The spino-thalamic system, on the other hand, sends more generalized messages such as crude touch, pressure, tickle, and sexual sensations. An example of how the two systems work together can be appreciated if you have ever placed your hand under very hot water from a faucet. The sensation of water running over the surface of the skin is felt noticeably sooner than the perception of pain.

As noted in the Figure 6, signals reaching the primary sensory areas of the neocortex are transduced (i.e., organized into fewer signals) and passed on to the associational areas, including the general interpretative area. Recalling the intimate relationship between the thalamus and cerebral cortex, these signals, which now have been interpreted, may be passed along to other portions of the neocortex for elaboration. In addition, many pathways connect directly to the limbic system for processing on an affective level. Also, the prefrontal areas may become involved in the process as discussed earlier. In addition, memories from various areas may be retrieved. In other cases, however, responses may bypass prefrontal involvement and move directly to the output system.

Signals from the motor cortex are coordinated and corrected by the extrapyramidal system involving both the basal ganglia and cerebellum. Patterns of signals are then transmitted down the spinal cord to various muscle groups. The resultant overt behavior will, in turn, start the process over again in two ways. First, the behavior itself will cause a change in proprioceptive sensation. Second, changes in the environment due to overt-motor activity will be sensed via the exteroceptive and special sensory groups. In addition, other components of the motor system include contraction of smooth muscles in the internal organs as well as secretions by endocrine glands in many parts of the body. These outputs will be detected, in part, by the visceral sensors. Thus the cycle is completed.

Summary

We began this chapter by discussing two basic views of the importance and role of the neocortex in directing behavior. One position saw the cerebral cortex as the dominant force in this process; the other emphasized the supportive and permissive role of more basic systems throughout the body. In this chapter we have favored the latter view by emphasizing the hierarchical organization of the brain and describing neocortical functioning in terms of its ties to more basic structures.

For example, the most basic component necessary for intellectual processing is the reticular activating system (RAS). Divided into two parts, the RAS is responsible for generalized wakefulness as well as conscious activity by activating specific areas of the neocortex. The essential role of the thalamus also has been discussed. Not only does the thalamus direct the RAS in its stimulation of the neocortex, but it also determines which thoughts will be stored for future use and which are retrieved from memory.

The prefrontal areas, the site of our most elaborate intellectual capabilities, also are unable to function independently of the more basic structures. This region is essentially a short-term memory area that holds memories that have been "dumped" temporarily for comparison with incoming signals. This process has been likened to the operation of random access memory (RAM) in a computer or calculator that holds information temporarily while solving problems. Thus the program that directs prefrontal activity is not found in the neocortex itself but in more basic structures, particularly the thalamus. The thalamus, in turn, is a central, integrative unit for the other major components of the CNS.

The point of all of this is that a "thought" cannot direct behavior independently of what else is going on with the body. Events that affect the body as a whole will invariably affect the thinking process as well. This explains why everyday occurrences such as illness, fatigue, or drug and alcohol use, have such noticeable effects on our ability to think clearly.

Recommended Readings

Luria, A. R. (1973). *The working brain: An introduction to neuropsychology.* New York: Basic Books.

> A classic work on brain systems, this reference is technical yet easy to read. For the general reader the first part, "Functional Organization and Mental Activity," should prove most useful.

Kolb, B., & Whishaw, I. Q. (1980). *Fundamentals of human neuropsychology.* San Francisco: W. H. Freeman.

> This is an introductory text to neuropsychology. As with the two other texts listed next, the illustrations, reading level, and examples make it suitable for the general reader.

Carlson, N. R. (1977). *Physiology of behavior*. Boston: Allyn & Bacon.

Probably in a more recent edition by now, this text has been used with success in a number of courses for students not specializing in physiological psychology. The students report liking the relaxed writing style and clear examples.

Mason, E. B. (1983). *Human physiology*. Menlo Park, CA: Benjamin/Cummings.

This book is for physiology what the Carlson text is for physiological psychology. Of the three texts selected here, Mason's book probably has the best illustrations, three of which were adopted for inclusion in the present volume.

PART II

Basic Issues

Part I—Preliminary Concepts—introduced two major points. First, it was suggested that there are many levels of physiological control, some of which we are aware and some not. Second, it was proposed that the manner in which these levels interact can best be understood in terms of systems thinking. The resultant view of behavior does not allow us to think in terms of single cause–effect relationships. Rather, behavior is seen as involving the complex interaction of many factors, the relative importance of which depends on the nature of the response, the individual's physical makeup and past experience, and the situational context in which it occurs.

Part II—Basic Issues—is broadly organized around the theme of triple response modes. Chapter 4 (Nature and Nurture) will attempt to provide a background for this heuristic device by discussing the interaction of innate and acquired contributions to behavior. The triple modes themselves will be the topic of Chapter 5, whereas the manner in which each mode interacts with the others will be discussed in Chapter 6 (Biofeedback). Part II concludes with a chapter in which some of these concepts developed are applied to one of the most elusive of psychological constructs—emotion.

CHAPTER 4

Nature and Nurture

In 1972 Martin Seligman and Joanne Hager published a collection of readings along with their comments entitled *Biological Boundaries of Learning* (Seligman & Hager, 1972). In this work Seligman and Hager seek to accomplish two things. First, they question the widely held assumption that learning principles derived in the laboratory are equally valid across species and are unaffected by the particular stimulus, response, or reinforcer under investigation. Second, they offer an alternative hypothesis ("preparedness") to explain much of the data that seemed at odds with traditional learning theory. In support of their position, Seligman and Hager assert that "animals, man included, learn some things easily, others only painstakingly, and still others not at all" (p. 463), and they propose that these differences have a biological basis.

The question of whether there is a biological predisposition to learn some things more easily than others is not new. John Locke, a British philosopher of empiricism, saw the mind as a tabula rasa, an empty tablet, upon which experience etches its lessons. In contrast, Immanuel Kant, a German proponent of nativism, proposed that the mind contributes to the way in which we classify and organize our experiences and that this ability is genetically determined rather than the product of experience.

In the earlier part of this century psychology was caught in the debate between those who emphasized the importance of instincts for human behavior (e.g., William McDougall) versus those who saw environmental factors as having a prepotent influence (e.g., J. B. Watson). Although the two positions are not mutually exclusive (Eysenck, 1982), Watson interjected behaviorism into the controversy by adopting an extreme environmentalistic position. "According to Watson, the child is at birth equipped with nothing but the structure of its body and a few elementary unlearned responses" (Bergmann, 1956). Although he was not, according to Eysenck (1982), as radically environmentalistic as others have held him to be (for Watson claimed that certain emotions such as fear, love, and rage were largely instinctual), he did place behaviorism firmly in the "nurturist" camp. As Cravens (1978) notes:

> Before 1917 it was difficult to find any psychologist who questioned the instinct theory. By 1922 it was almost impossible to identify more than a handful of psychologists who still accepted the human instinct theory as a legitimate category of scientific explanation. (p. 191)

Around the same time, but independently, Pavlov adopted a similar position. In his *Lectures on Conditioned Reflexes* (1928), Pavlov proposed that all stimuli are equivalent in their ability to elicit a conditioned reflex.

> If our hypothesis as to the origin of the conditioned reflex is correct, it follows that any natural phenomenon chosen at will may be converted into a conditioned stimulus . . . Any visual stimulus, any desired sound, any odour, and the stimulation of any part of the skin, whether by mechanical means or by the application of heat or cold. (Vol. 1, p. 86)

Thorndike, the father of instrumental conditioning, also proposed that the process of conditioning is similar across species. In 1911 he wrote:

> If my analysis is true, the evolution of behavior is a rather simple matter. Formally the crab, fish, turtle, dog, cat, monkey and baby have very similar intellects and characters. All are systems of connections subject to change by the laws of exercise and effect. (1911/1970, p. 280)

And perhaps most importantly, B. F. Skinner emphasized the equivalence of learning across species when he wrote:

> Pigeon, rat, monkey, which is which? It doesn't matter. Of course, these species have behavioral repertoires which are as different as their anatomies. But once you have allowed for differences in the ways in which they make contact with the environment, and in the ways in which they act upon the environment, what remains of their behavior shows astonishingly similar properties. (Skinner, 1959, p. 374)

The Equipotentiality Premise

The assumption that principles of learning derived in the laboratory using infrahuman subjects are generalizable to natural settings and to other species, including human beings, has been termed the "equipotentiality premise." This position assumes further "that the particular stimuli, responses, and reinforcers one chooses to study will not have a determining influence on the outcomes one obtains" (B. Schwartz, 1974, p. 184). In short, conditioning, whether operant or respondent, is not affected by biological limitations imposed by species membership or sensory-integrative specialization.

Seligman and Hager (1972) question this assumption by citing a series of papers in which John Garcia and his colleagues studied taste aversion in rats. In one study, rats were exposed to taste and audiovisual stimuli paired with nausea induced by radiation. The results indicated that taste but not audiovisual cues became aversive. In a companion experiment, they paired the same two stimuli with electroshock. In this study, only the audiovisual stimulus became aversive, whereas the taste cues did not (Garcia & Koelling, 1966). The authors conclude:

> It seems that given reinforcers are not equally effective for all classes of discriminable stimuli. The cues, which the animal selects from the welter of stimuli in the learning situation, appear to be related to the consequences of the subsequent reinforcer. (p. 124)

Another interesting aspect of the two studies is the long delay between the presentation of the stimulus and the unconditioned response (nausea). Classical conditioning theory predicts that it is not possible for conditioning to occur under these circumstances because "delays of the order of 3 to 45 sec have a deleterious effect upon learning in a wide variety of experimental situations" (Garcia, Ervin, & Koelling, 1966, p. 121). It was found, however, that taste aversion could be conditioned with delays of up to 75 minutes.

Garcia proposes that neurological "hard wiring" of the central nervous system (CNS) accounts for these anomalies (Garcia, McGowan, & Green, 1972). All stimuli are not equivalent, it is suggested, because their reception and integration depend on the particular receptor that transduces the physical energy from sensory inputs and the central mechanisms that handle the incoming signals. In support of this contention, they cite Konorski (1967) at length.

> The function of the afferent systems is to provide the brain with information concerning the external environment in which the organism is situated and the feedback generated by its own activity. The well-being of the organism requires that this information should be highly selective, picking up particular combinations of elements of the external world and neglecting the other ones . . . this selectivity is provided by convergence of messages arising in particular elements of the receptive surface upon particular neurons (units) of higher levels of a given system, and by inhibition of those messages which are incongruent with the stimulus pattern representing these units. Since the stimulus-patterns impinging upon each afferent system belong to various

categories of various aspects of the events of the external world, each category having a different significance for the organism, these systems must be endowed with powerful sorting mechanisms distributing the message delivered by the receptors to particular aggregates of units (centers or fields) for their proper utilization accomplished by associative systems. This is why each afferent system not only has a hierarchical structure but also is amply ramified, forming different hierarchies for different categories of stimuli. (pp. 507–508)

In the case of taste aversion, Garcia and his colleagues propose that because food absorption takes time, the visceral centers in the CNS have been specialized to handle long interstimulus intervals. Further, it is suggested that taste information is handled differently than sensorimotor information, such as shock to the foot. Sensorimotor information appears to affect immediate motor responses (such as approach and eating behavior), whereas taste information is tied to visceral activity.

Seligman and Hager suggest that taste aversion learning may be so basic, so innate, that it does not involve systems associated with cognition, such as conscious expectations, attention, and information seeking. To support this interpretation, they include three additional studies. In one, rats formed taste-poisoning associations under deep anesthesia (Roll & Smith, 1972). In another, Nachman (1970) found that electroconvulsive shock, which commonly disrupts learning, did not disrupt taste-aversion associations. And finally, Best and Zuckerman (1971) found that a neurosurgical technique, which ordinarily disrupts fear conditioning (cortical spreading depression), also failed to disrupt taste-aversion learning.

Seligman and Hager (1972), like others (e.g., Rozin & Kalat, 1972), propose that the biological basis for learning is a product of evolution. "Learning is only one of many ways that an animal adapts to its environment, and that the form learning takes will invariably reflect the real selective pressures that evolution has exerted on its species" (p. 65). In support of this inference, they include a study by Wilcoxon, Dragoin, and Kral (1971) that suggests that quail learned to avoid water associated with illness more on the basis of visual (i.e., the color of the water) than taste cues. Rats, on the other hand, learn to avoid water that is flavored. Seligman and Hager propose that "unlike the nocturnal rat, birds are visual feeders and they are prepared to associate colors with illness over long delays, while ignoring contiguous tastes" (p. 463).

Moving to other species and different types of learning, Seligman and Hager also include articles that suggest that rats have difficulty learning to groom themselves to avoid a loud noise (Bolles & Seelbach, 1964); that pigeons are so "prepared" to peck lighted keys that they do so even when it is unrelated to the presentation of grain (P. L. Brown &

Jenkins, 1968); and that they will continue to do so (after they have acquired this response) even when it prevents reinforcement (Williams & Williams, 1969). Other articles present data that suggest that dogs are unable to learn to move one paw over the other for food if the signal consists of different tones coming from the same place but are able to do so if the tones differ only in location. However, dogs readily learn whether to move a paw or not to move it if the tones are different but come from the same place (Dobrzecka, Szwejkowska, & Konorski, 1966). Seligman and Hager suggest that the direction of an auditory cue is "prepared" to control the direction of responding (i.e., to move one paw before another), whereas differences in tone are more prepared to control a "go-no go" response (i.e., to move a paw or not).

The Preparedness Hypothesis

All of this led Seligman and Hager (1972) to conclude that animals, including human beings, are "prepared" to learn some things, not prepared to learn others, and even "counterprepared" to learn still others (see also Seligman, 1970).

> It is a truism that an organism brings to any experiment certain equipment and predispositions either more or less appropriate to the situation. It brings specialized sensory and response apparatus with a long evolutionary history which has modified it into its present appropriateness or inappropriateness. Often forgotten is the fact that in addition to sensory motor apparatus, the organism brings associative apparatus which also has a long and specialized evolutionary history. This specialization may make certain contingencies easier to learn about than others, more difficult to forget, more readily generalizable, and so on. (1972, p. 3)

The concept of preparedness is not new. Eysenck (1982) notes the similarity of preparedness to Thorndike's concept of "belongingness" (Thorndike, 1935), a similarity that Seligman and Hager also acknowledge. The hypothesis is also similar to ideas expressed by G. Stanley Hall in his study of fears almost 90 years ago.

> There is a peculiar prepotent quality about some of these fears that suggests some ancient origin, and points to the persistency of cells or protoplasm rather than to the more formed and therefore more transformable tissues of later stages. (1897, p. 245)

According to Seligman and Hager, preparedness occurs along a continuum. At one end, behavior that is learned quickly and that displays a strong resistance to extinction would be considered to be an example of a highly prepared response. These behaviors are seen as being primarily instinctive or reflexive in nature. At the other end, behaviors that suggest little if any learning after repeated opportunities to learn or that extinguish rapidly are considered to be unprepared or even counterprepared. In short, prepared responses "may be expected to be (a) very rapidly acquired, (b) very slowly extinguished, and (c) not mediated by cognitive activity" (Ohman, Erixon, & Lofberg, 1975, p. 41).

For Seligman (1971), many human phobias are an example of a highly prepared response. Their resistance to extinction is well known. Also, the persistence of phobias after the client is intellectually aware of their irrationality is seen as further evidence of their preparedness.

Partial support for Seligman's position has been reported in a series of laboratory studies coming out of the University of Uppsala in Sweden using human subjects. Although it was found that electrodermal responses could be rapidly conditioned to electroshock for a wide range of stimuli, it was also found that responses paired with prepared stimuli, such as angry faces (Ohman & Dimsberg, 1978) or spiders and snakes (Ohman, Eriksson, & Olofsson, 1975), are much more resistant to extinction than those paired with unprepared stimuli, such as flowers or mushrooms (Ohman, Frederikson, Hugdahl, & Rimmo, 1976). Further, it was found that instructions indicating the termination of shock fail to affect the conditioning process, supporting the noncognitive aspect of the hypothesis (Ohman, Erixon, & Lofberg, 1975).

Application of the preparedness hypothesis to clinical problems other than phobias includes the selection of an unconditioned stimulus (UCS) for use in aversive control procedures. Wilson and Davison (1969), for example, question the use of electrical stimulation rather than nausea-producing chemicals in the treatment of alcoholics. Although an electrical UCS can be delivered with greater temporal contiguity than an emetic, a condition favored by classical conditioning theory, it is suggested that a human preparedness for associating taste cues with visceral discomfort should favor the latter. A. A. Lazarus (1968) reports in a case study that an alcoholic responded much better (i.e., stopped drinking) when electric shock paired with the alcohol was dropped in favor of a foul-smelling mixture of smelling salts. Lamon, Wilson, and Leaf (1977) also found that stronger gustatory aversions could be conditioned with nausea than with electric shock. Although other data do not support this distinction (e.g., Evans & Busch, 1974), the literature on pretreatment emesis in cancer patients receiving chemotherapy (cf. Redd & Andrykowski, 1982) attests to the clinical relevance of a readiness in humans to form taste aversions.

Criticisms of the Preparedness Hypothesis

In spite of its attractiveness, the preparedness hypothesis has numerous problems. One of the major ones is its circular nature (Ohman, Eriksson, & Olofsson, 1975; B. Schwartz, 1974). Preparedness is usually defined by the rapidity with which a response is learned. (Associations that are learned rapidly are prepared, whereas those that are not are unprepared.) However, one verifies that a response is prepared using the same criterion, namely the rapidity with which it is learned.

One can break the circularity of this reasoning if the preparedness of a response can be verified independently of how it was defined in the first place. For example, B. Schwartz (1974) argues that Bolles's (1970) notion of species-specific defense reactions (SSDRs), defined in the laboratory under experimental conditions, might be verified by observing the defensive behaviors of the species in its natural environment.

In the case of preparedness, however, its dependence on evolution as an explanatory construct poses a problem. Because evolution is open to many interpretations (i.e., although agreeing that evolution has occurred, theorists often disagree on *how* it occurred), it is difficult to predict which stimuli should be prepared in an evolutionary sense. The vagueness of phrases such as *the survival value of behaviors*, for example, presents problems when placing stimuli into "prepared" and "unprepared" categories, often resulting in arbitrary and unreliable distinctions (Delprato, 1980, p. 89).

Also problematic for the preparedness hypothesis are several alternative explanations for the data upon which it is based. Probably the most compelling of these concerns the preexperimental history of the organism. This position states that learning that has occurred prior to the experiment can account for the preference for one response over another in the laboratory. In the case of taste aversion, for example, Testa and Ternes (1977) suggest that the taste stimuli are simply more novel than the auditory and visual stimuli. Because the rat is familiar with sights and sounds but unfamiliar with novel tastes, the superiority of taste stimuli for conditioning can be accounted for by this fact alone.

The same reasoning can be applied to human subjects demonstrating a preference for certain stimuli over others when conditioned to electric shock. Bandura (1977) notes:

> In everyday life, houses and faces are repeatedly correlated with neutral and positive experiences as well as with negative ones, whereas references to snakes are almost uniformly negative. Differential rates of extinction are more likely to be due to differential correlates here and now than to snake bites suffered by a few ancestors generations ago. (p. 76)

The inability to control for the preexperimental history of subjects is not the only methodological question that has been raised. For example, comparative psychologist M. E. Bitterman (1975) suggests that the superiority of taste versus visual stimuli in establishing aversion with a long stimulus response delay is more likely due to the lingering of the gustatory cues in the mouth or to the reinstatement of cues when the animal regurgitates after becoming ill than to a biological preference for one stimulus over the other. The visual cues (i.e., lights), it is argued, lack the temporal constancy of the taste stimuli and thus are not favored. In response, Garcia, Hankins, and Rusiniak (1976) cite numerous studies that ostensibly controlled for these variables, but Bitterman (1976) remains unconvinced. A lengthy reply to Bitterman by Revusky (1977), however, led Delprato (1980) to conclude that "it does not appear that taste-aversion phenomena can be easily disregarded on straightforward methodological grounds such as those suggested by Bitterman" (p. 85).

Another methodological criticism deals with the limitations of the methodology itself. This criticism raises the question of whether one can adequately test the equivalency of behavior across different species using the same experimental design.

> The fact that a phenomenon known in one animal fails to appear with a second animal does not prove, of course, that it does not occur at all in the second animal. . . . The failure . . . is significant only on the assumption that the conditions under which the animals have been compared are indeed equivalent, an assumption which is difficult to justify. How, for example, are rats and fish to be made equally hungry? Or how is the incentive value of food pellets for rats to be compared with that of *Tubifex* worms for goldfish? (Bitterman, 1975, p. 702)

In other words, the biomechanical properties of different species will favor certain responses over others meaning that the anatomical features of a species will make certain responses easier to perform than others, regardless of centrally mediated learning preferences. These naturally occurring behaviors thus confound attempts to sort out what is predisposed biologically for learning and what occurs as a natural product of the organism's interaction with its natural environment. For example, Bolles (1970) argues that only SSDRs are rapidly learned as avoidance responses. This argument, however, can be reduced to the question of which behaviors occur most frequently naturally, because "behaviors that are not SSDRs simply do not occur; hence they cannot be reinforced. If one could somehow induce them, however, they would be learned as rapidly as SSDRs" (B. Schwartz, 1974, pp. 190–191).

A final set of criticisms of preparedness focuses on the inconsistent or partial empirical support the hypothesis has received. As noted earlier, the Uppsala experiments with human subjects failed to find evidence for the acquisition component of the theory, although the resistance to extinction and noncognitive aspects were demonstrated. Levis and Malloy (1982) as well as Delprato (1980) point out that Seligman himself was not successful in finding experimental evidence for his construct. Rachman and Seligman (1976), for example, summarize the unsuccessful treatment outcomes for two patients with reportedly "unprepared or perhaps even counterprepared phobias" (p. 335). One patient in this report evidenced a powerful fear of chocolate whereas the other "complained of an excessive fear of vegetables and plants, particularly their leaves" (p. 336). These certainly seem to be fears for which little adaptive significance exists. From a clinical standpoint, however, one may question the etiology of these unusual fears and suspect that they may be the product of some other, pathological condition, such as a thought disorder, rather than conditioning.

In a second study, De Silva, Rachman, and Seligman (1977) surveyed 69 phobic and 82 obsessional patients over a 5-year period. Although finding that a majority of the phobias and obsessions were "prepared," they failed to find a systematic relationship between preparedness and the therapeutic outcome, severity, intensiveness of treatment received, or age of onset. However, the selectivity of the subjects is cited as a possible explanation for the failure to observe differences within this clinical population. It is argued that an examination of fears among a large, random sample of people might demonstrate the relationship of preparedness to variables such as severity and age of onset. Nevertheless, these studies raise questions regarding the usefulness of the concept of preparedness in clinical settings.

Instinct and Human Behavior

The criticisms leveled at the preparedness hypothesis have left this notion somewhat less attractive than it once was. Nevertheless, the more basic question concerning a biological contribution to learning remains. Refuting a particular explanation (preparedness) for a specific disorder (phobias) does not logically confirm the alternative position (the equipotentiality premise). The more enduring contribution of Seligman and Hager's book may be its reintroduction of the possible role of instinct in human behavior. As noted by B. Schwartz: "The studies in the Seligman and Hager book, and others as well, have made it clear that we can ignore biological contributions to learning no longer" (1974, p. 192).

Ethology

Seligman and Hager's view that organisms may be biologically prepared to learn some things more readily than others was heavily influenced by the tenets of ethology. Ethology is concerned with

> the study of behavior from the zoological viewpoint. It concentrates
> on . . . its biological causes, its survival value for the species, its probably
> evolutionary origin and history, its relationship to ecology, and its develop-
> ment during an animal's entire life. (*Encyclopedia Americana*, 1985; Vol. 10,
> p. 632)

The modern roots of ethology go back almost 100 years and are particularly strong in Europe.

Unlike most psychologists, ethologists are interested in the *differences* in learning across species. As Tinbergen (1969) has summarized it:

> The student of innate behaviour, accustomed to studying a number of differ-
> ent species and the entire behaviour pattern, is repeatedly confronted with
> the fact that an animal may learn some things much more readily than
> others. That is to say, some parts of the pattern, some reactions, may be
> changed by learning while others seem to be so rigidly fixed that no learning
> is possible. In other words, there seem to be more of less strictly localized
> "dispositions to learn." Different species are predisposed to learn different
> parts of the pattern. So far as we know, these differences between species
> have adaptive significance. (p. 145)

Examples of species-specific behavior were discussed earlier in this
chapter. One of the most interesting findings in this area comes from the
work of Wilcoxon, Dragoin, and Kral (1971) with rats and pigeons. It will
be remembered they found that Bobwhite quail learn to avoid flavored
water after one trial when illness is induced by a drug one-half hour
later. Unlike the rat, however, quail also learn to avoid unflavored water
that has been darkened by vegetable dye. They concluded that visual
cues are more salient than taste cues for this species. Seligman and
Hager went on to assert that "we would expect this from the natural
history of these organisms: birds are largely visual feeders (Brower,
1969), while rats, as a nocturnal, burrowing species, rely heavily on taste
and kinesthetic senses" (1972, p. 251).

Psychology and ethology, however, have had little to say to each
other over the years.

> Ethologists were not much interested in problems related to learning and,
> though they recognized that their animals could learn, they generally ig-
> nored or eliminated this fact from their theories and experiments. Experi-
> mental psychologists, on the other hand, were almost exclusively interested
> in learning. (Manning, 1972, p. 22)

There seem to be several reasons for the distance between the two. For one, the two disciplines generally conduct their studies in different settings—ethologists in the field and psychologists in the laboratory. Also, as noted before, ethologists are more interested in species-specific differences in learning than psychologists who are interested in similarities in learning across species. And finally, ethologists are interested in the "structure" of learning, the ways in which behavior is ordered, whereas psychologists emphasize behavior itself with little or no regard for the nature of internal structures. In short, "the two disciplines have different underlying assumptions, which lead to different research methods, which yield different sets of data, and ultimately, different conclusions" (B. Schwartz, 1974, p. 183).

Perhaps this is the way it had to be. Skinner (1938) made certain simplifying assumptions when he began his study of animal behavior; he rejected a methodology that entailed what he called "botanizing" in order to focus on behavior itself. This decision yielded a set of powerful empirical generalizations that have had a far-reaching impact, and it can be argued that these advances could not have been made without making these simplifying assumptions. Nevertheless, the issue of a biological basis to learning remains an important topic for further research, particularly in the areas of language development (e.g., Chomsky, 1968, 1975; Lenneberg, 1967; Skinner, 1957) and intelligence (e.g., Furth [Piaget], 1969; Kendler, 1963; Sameroff, 1971; Skinner, 1950).

Instinct

As noted earlier in the chapter, psychologists in the early part of this century, before Watson's influence, considered instinct as an important aspect of behavior. Instinct is defined as "the innate aspect of behavior that is unlearned, complex, and normally adaptive" (*American Heritage Dictionary of the English Language*, 1976, p. 680). Aubrey Manning, in his introductory text to ethology (1972) (a portion of which is included in Seligman and Hager's book) identifies two characteristics of instinct.

> First, that it consists of rigid, stereotyped patterns of movement which are very similar in all individuals of a species; . . . Secondly, instinctive patterns can often be evoked most readily by very simple stimuli. (p. 18)

Instinct appears to be related to two basic, biological variables, life span and size. Short-lived organisms, such as insects, depend very little on learning. In fact, given the brief span of a few weeks of life, it appears that most if not all insect behaviors are well programmed. There simply is no time to "learn" from an ongoing interaction with the environment. Relatively long-lived organisms, however, require greater flexibility to survive in a more variable world and also have more time in which learning can occur (Manning, 1972).

A second variable seems to be body size. Highly developed learning requires a relatively large amount of brain tissue. In very small animals, the cortex necessary to devote to this purpose is not there. As one progresses up the phylogenetic ladder, there is an increase in the amount of neural matter available for learning (Bitterman, 1965). The end result is that flexibility, which is characteristic of learning rather than instinct, increases with phylogenetic complexity and development. Consequently "simpler organisms profit less from experience than more complex ones. Similarly, infantile behavior is far more rigid [i.e., less complex] than adult behavior" (B. Schwartz, 1974, p. 195).

Where does this leave human beings in terms of instinctual behavior? Has the adult human advanced so far that the contribution of instinct to behavior is essentially nonexistent? Many psychologists, including some of the most notable learning theorists, would seem to say so.

> Evidence that learning in lower species operates under severe biological constraints does not mean that human learning is also governed by event-specific mechanisms. Because of both the advanced human capacity to symbolize experience and limited inborn programming, humans are capable of learning an extraordinary variety of behaviors. . . . Under such diverse and highly variable conditions of living, generalizable mechanisms of learning, that rely heavily upon experiential organization of behavior, have a greater evolutionary value than do fixed inborn mechanisms, except in the regulation of rudimentary biological functions. (Bandura, 1977, pp. 73–74)

Behavior as a System

From the systems view presented in Chapter 2, thinking of instinct and learning in an either/or fashion (i.e., some behaviors are instinctual, whereas others are the product of learning) would appear unnecessary. It may be more productive to emphasize the *interaction* of genetic and environmental contributions to behavior (cf. Plomin, DeFries, & McClearn, 1980).

This possibility, interestingly enough, has its advocates in both camps. Concerned with what he considers to be an arbitrary instinct/learning dichotomy, Lenneberg (1969) observes:

> Everything in life, including behavior and language, is interaction of the individual with its milieu. But the milieu is not constant. The organism itself

helps to shape it (this is true of cells and organs as much as of animals and man). Thus, the organism and its environment is a dynamic system and, phylogenetically, developed as such. (p. 641)

Delprato (1980) echos similar sentiments when he offers a developmental perspective as an alternative to viewing behavior as either "innate" or "learned." Citing theorists such as Hebb (1958), Kuo (1967), and Schneirla (1972), Delprato asserts that "behavior is the product of an ever-evolving, dynamic interchange between the organism, through which genetic effects operate, and its internal and external environment" (p. 95). Declaring that a response is "not conditioned" does not imply that it is, therefore, "innate." Rather, behaviors are seen as "the result of the organism's developmental history that begins at conception, in which genetic and experiential factors always fully participate" (p. 97).

This interactive emphasis shares much in common with the concept of reciprocal determinism advanced by Bandura (1977).

In the social learning view of interaction, . . . behavior, other personal factors, and environmental factors all operate as interlocking determinants of each other. The relative influences exerted by these interdependent factors differ in various settings and for different behaviors. There are times when environmental factors exercise powerful constraints on behavior, and other times when personal factors are the overriding regulators of the course of environmental events. (pp. 9–10)

Although Bandura's "personal factors" are more cognitive than physiological, the role of one's genetic makeup in affecting life experiences, particularly during the early years, is well established (Erlenmeyer-Kimling, 1972; J. L. Fuller, 1973). For example, there is

ample evidence that humans differ from each other in temperament and receptivity to environmental stimulation from earliest infancy, presumably as a function of genetic differences or the interaction of genetic and parental factors (Berger & Passingham, 1973; Hersh, 1977). (Erlenmeyer-Kimling, 1979, p. 392)

To put it in other words, the regulation of physiological events on many different levels throughout the body is always active and always interacting with our more conscious intentions so as to influence both the quantity and quality of our behavior. Although John Hunter's death was offered as an example of this process, the physiological contributions to behavior are not limited to responses that are life threatening. Essentially everything we do calls upon the cooperative and supportive activity of our most basic physiological systems (cf. Rodin, 1985).

An example of a more commonly encountered interaction of a basic physiological response with other aspects of our behavior can be found by observing what happens to the adrenal glands when we are excited. The adrenal glands sit on top of the kidneys. An important part of the glands, the *adrenal medulla*, is actually a specialized extension of the sympathetic branch of the autonomic nervous system (Guyton, 1981). As such, it operates like a sympathetic ganglion, except that it secretes epinephrine and norepinephrine. These powerful neurotransmitters, released from the medulla in times of emergency, travel through the circulatory system and thus affect structures throughout the body, including the reticular activating system, the internal organs, and the reward and pleasure centers of the brain. Their effect is exactly the same as direct sympathetic stimulation except that it is greatly prolonged and much more pervasive. As such, this single physiological response provides a basic tone for the body's behavior. Consequently, the adrenal response has been implicated in many problems of clinical interest, including anger, fear, phobias, skill deficiencies, and sexual dysfunction.

In many ways, responses associated with the regulation of our internal environment share much in common with what we normally consider to be instinctual (i.e., programmed) behavior. For example, they are "unlearned, complex, and normally adaptive." Further, they are in accord with the two characteristics of instinct described by Manning (1972). First, these responses, such as the adrenal response to danger, are highly programmed and similar among members of a single species, including human beings. Second, these responses can be evoked by very simple stimuli. Thus, from a physiological perspective, the programmed aspects of behavior may deal less with making our way in the external environment and more in terms of the regulation of our internal environment.

The nature–nurture debate can be summarized, therefore, as the interaction of many factors. Bandura (1977) emphasizes an interaction between the environment and personal factors that are primarily cognitive in nature. Ethologists, such as Manning (1972), stress an instinctual (i.e., programmed) contribution to this interaction. Delprato (1980) and others, such as B. Schwartz (1974), focus on the role of learned behaviors in this process.

From a systems perspective, none of the these elements are mutually exclusive. The contribution of each is determined by many factors, such as the setting and the nature of the task. Thus, one can consider behavior as encompassing aspects of all three components—cognition, programmed responses, and behavior. Although called by different names, this tripartite system of analyzing our interaction with the environment has gained some popularity under the rubric of "triple modes of responding" (e.g., Bellack & Hersen, 1977; Lang, 1971, 1977a). This will be the topic of the next chapter.

Recommended Reading

Plomin, R., DeFries, J. C., & McClearn, G. E. (1980). *Behavioral genetics: A primer.* San Francisco: W. H. Freeman.

This book provides a good introduction to biology–behavior interactions. In spite of a common misperception, behavioral genetics does not try to explain how genes determine behavior but rather focuses on how the environment influences the expression of one's genetic inheritance. This primer gives a good overview of an area that is becoming increasingly important.

CHAPTER 5

Triple Modes of Responding

A tea and rubber plantation in the tropical forests of central Ceylon would seem an unlikely place to begin a discussion of behavioral assessment. Yet, this was the location in 1944 for a well-organized and comprehensive program that set in motion a process that led to one of the more popular notions in behavioral assessment today.

Actually, this assessment station (Camp K) was part of a larger program established by the U.S. Office of Strategic Services (the OSS) during World War II to select recruits for commando-type operations behind enemy lines (OSS Assessment Staff, 1948). Assessment stations were set up in several locations in the United States (California, Maryland, and Washington, DC) as well as in China, India, and Ceylon. These stations were staffed by a diverse collection of professionals interested in human behavior, including

> clinical psychologists of various persuasions, animal psychologists, social psychologists, sociologists and cultural anthropologists, psychiatrists who had practiced psychoanalysis according to the theories of Freud, of Horney, and of Sullivan, as well as psychiatrists who were unacquainted with, or opposed to psychoanalysis. (p. 26)

Theoretical differences, however, took a back seat to the exigencies of war. The task was straightforward—try to predict behavior of men and women in the unpredictable and demanding circumstances of combat behind enemy lines. The time available to accomplish this task was severely limited.

What emerged was an assessment procedure that was light on theory and heavy on practicality. This emphasis on determining what was required to accomplish the job and designing a method to assess these qualities resulted in a "multiform" strategy that included "a rather large number of procedures based on different principles" (p. 28). For example, the assessment package in Ceylon included an interview to obtain a relevant history of the recruit, several nonverbal intelligence tests, a sociometric evaluation to determine interpersonal relations, problem-solving projects administered in small groups, and a number of tasks designed to assess technical skills, such as map reading, use of the compass, and close-combat proficiency.

The new approach to assessment was not forgotten after the war. In 1956, Richard Walk sought to demonstrate the predictive validity of one of the OSS assessment tasks—a mock parachute jump from a 34-foot tower. In particular, Walk was interested in whether the self-report of subjective fear for airborne trainees just prior to their practice jumps would predict successful completion of the training program. In addition, he asked a group of trainees to report on certain "psychosomatic" reactions in the jump tower, such as a pounding heart, shortness of breath, sweaty hands, and an upset stomach. In short, Walk assessed three different components of this fear-evoking situation, subjective feelings, physical reactions, and actual performance.

A few years later Lang and Lazovik were looking for dependent measures to use in their study of systematic desensitization (Lang & Lazovik, 1963; Lazovik & Lang, 1960). As it turned out, their biggest problem was deciding what fear was.

> Our analysis of this question led to the conclusion that the concept of fear (or anxiety) is associated with three measurable behaviors: verbal, motor, and somatic. The verbal aspect of fear is clearly illustrated by the patient's statement, "I am afraid." It is also revealed in disturbances of speech pattern or verbal recall. The main motor component is simple avoidance. The individual who is afraid of heights requests a hotel room on the first floor. A hooded rat, shocked previously in the black compartment, jumps a barrier into the white enclosure. The motor component may also show itself in failures of coordination or "displacement behavior." The third relevant sector of behavior involves the muscular and autonomic substrate of fear. Distress is betrayed by alterations in respiration, cardiac rate, and blood pressure, and by a decrease in skin resistance and an increase in electromyographic levels. (Lang, 1964, p. 41)

To assess the verbal component of fear, Lang and Lazovik (1963) used the 10-point scale developed by Walk (1956) in his study of parachute trainees. The motor component was assessed by the actual avoidance of the phobic object, which in this case was a tame, 5-foot pilot black snake. Assessment of the third, "somatic" component was not actually accomplished in the 1963 study but was pursued concurrently in related studies using the polygraph (Lang, Geer, & Hnatiow, 1963; Lang & Hnatiow, 1962).

The major strength of this assessment approach was its multidimensional nature, the need for which Lang emphasized.

> No one of these behaviors is fear. A particular sector may give out a false
> lead. Thus, an individual may say he is unafraid, while his manifest avoid-
> ance behavior and heightened somatic activity send a different message. On
> the other hand, disturbances in somatic activity may be a function of emo-
> tional states other than fear or organic disease. Even avoidance behavior does
> not constitute a completely reliable estimate of fear, if no account is taken of
> the other activity just described. Ideally, all three sectors should be evalu-
> ated. (1964, pp. 41–42)

This approach to the study of fear or anxiety was consistent with
earlier efforts by psychophysiologists to discover patterns of "somatic
reactions" to stress (Ax, 1953; Lacey, 1950) and was shared by several
other important investigators during the mid-1960s (e.g., Paul, 1969;
Spielberger, 1966). Albert Ellis (1968), for example, also categorized
"emotional disturbance" during this period into three major headings
that corresponded to Lang's description of the three components of fear.
"Perceptual-cognitive" factors, according to Ellis, included the manner
in which individuals perceived or thought about themselves and the
world around them and was assessed by self-report. His "emotional and
motivational" factor specifically included reactions of the autonomic
nervous system. His final factor, "motor and habituation" responses,
involved dysfunctional motor habits. In commenting on Ellis's categories, Hans Strupp added that "all forms of psychotherapy use all three
in different combinations" (Strupp, 1968, p. 95).

By the 1970s, the method of assessment based on the triple modes
was well established (Borkovec, 1976; Lang, 1971) and had become the
standard upon which the study of systematic desensitization was based
(cf. van Egeren, 1971). The relationship between the different modes
soon became a subject for investigation in its own right with particular
interest in the conditions under which the three dimensions corresponded closely (synchrony) or differed widely (desynchrony) (Hodgson & Rachman, 1974; Rachman & Hodgson, 1974). The emergence of a
separate literature devoted specifically to behavioral assessment further
strengthened the tripartite view as a central concept for the investigation
of behavioral disorders in general (Ciminero, Calhoun, & Adams, 1977;
Cone & Hawkins, 1977; Hersen & Bellack, 1976; Lick & Katkin, 1976).
And with the more recent interest in health psychology,

> A research strategy, involving simultaneous assessment of psychological,
> behavioral and physiological measurements is recommended in light of the
> "whole body" nature of the stress response. (Baum, Grunberg, & Singer,
> 1982, p. 217)

The Triple Modes

Defining the three modes in a manner so that meaningful distinctions can be made between them is not as easy as may first appear. Over the years, different investigators have defined each mode in terms of their own research interests or theoretical biases. For example, the "physiological" mode (Bellack & Hersen, 1977) means "biological" to some (van Egeren, 1971), "emotional and motivational" to others (Ellis, 1968), and "covert behavior" to still others (Hersen, 1973). This lack of uniformity across theorists can also be seen in references to the "cognitive" mode. Some writers have emphasized the subjective, experiential nature of this mode (e.g., Ellis, 1968; van Egeren, 1971), whereas others, focusing more on the manner in which it is usually assessed, have stressed its verbal characteristics (e.g., Hersen, 1973; Lang, 1977a).

Motoric Mode

Definition. Of the three modes, the motoric is perhaps the easiest to define. Essentially, all writers on the subject agree that the motoric mode refers to overt behavior. This rubric includes avoidance responses (Lang, 1971), motor habits (Ellis, 1968), and interpersonal skills (Twentyman & McFall, 1975). The thread running through the various uses of the term is the *instrumental* nature of these behaviors. That is, the motoric mode generally deals with behaviors that are positively (e.g., social skills) or negatively (e.g., avoidance responses) reinforced. As such, this mode seems to deal with problem behaviors that are most appropriately viewed from an operant perspective. For the purposes of the chapter, the *motoric mode* will be defined as *overt responses of the musculoskeletal system, including actual behavior and level of muscle tone.* (The reason why the latter component is included here rather than as part of the physiological mode will be discussed shortly.)

Example. The literature on social skills provides examples relevant to all three modes (Eisler & Frederiksen, 1980; Kelly, 1982). In terms of the motoric mode, social interactions require performance of skilled behaviors involving both verbal and nonverbal components. Some of the verbal behaviors include asking questions, expressing opinions appropriately, sharing one's feelings, or making a request. Nonverbal components include eye contact, appropriate affect, speech fluency, and vocal characteristics (Hollandsworth, Kazelskis, Stevens, & Dressel, 1979).

Because one usually has to "think" about what one says in social interchanges, one might be tempted to label these expressive behaviors as "cognitive" events. Yet, these responses must be as automatic as possible so that a person can think about "what" to say rather than attending to "how" he or she is saying it. Consequently, training in social skills focuses heavily on the practice of overt behaviors so that they may be overlearned and thus become automatic. In fact, there is some evidence that too much cognitive involvement (i.e., too much attention to one's behavior) may actually interfere with the ability to perform these responses effectively (Salmoni, Schmidt, & Walter, 1984; Sandifer & Hollandsworth, 1981). Therefore, the actual performance of social skills is seen as representative of the motoric rather than cognitive mode.

Physiological (Autonomic) Mode

Definition. When most psychologists use the term *physiological*, they are referring to the autonomic nervous system (ANS). Hersen (1973), for example, referred to this mode as *covert behavior*, a term very much in keeping with the role of the ANS in the regulation of the internal environment (see Chapters 1 & 2). Also Albert Ellis's (1968) discussion of the "emotional and motivational factors" includes the feeding, fighting, and reproductive role of the ANS.

The problem with the term *physiological* is its broadness. Physiology is "the science dealing with the functions of living organisms and their parts" (*American College Dictionary*, 1958, p. 915). Thus the motor system, the ANS, as well as the central nervous system, are legitimate subjects for physiological investigation. The use of the term by psychologists to describe a single mode may tell us more about boundaries between disciplines than about the identifying characteristics of a particular mode. For the same reason, the use of the term *biological* (e.g., van Egeren, 1971) is also unsatisfactory. It would seem more appropriate to refer to the "physiological" mode or "somatic" mode, as Lang and Lazovik described it in 1963, as the *autonomic mode.*

Another definitional issue concerns the inclusion of muscle tension as part of the autonomic mode. Lang wrote of a "muscular and autonomic substrate of fear" in 1964 (p. 41), with the musculoskeletal component measured by changes in electromyographic (EMG) activity. Including muscle tension as part of the "physiological" mode can be supported by two lines of reasoning. First, EMG activity is usually measured with a polygraph in a manner similar to the measurement of other variables associated with autonomic activity. Second, certain types of EMG activities, such as in facial displays, are closely related to the expression of affective experience (Fridlund, Schwartz & Fowler, 1984). This type of response, as well as more basic posturing in preparation for fight or flight, are automatic (i.e., reflexive) and possibly tied directly to autonomic responsivity (e.g., Zuckerman, Klorman, Larrance, & Spiegel, 1981).

Neither reason, however, would seem sufficient to include EMG activity as part of the autonomic mode. First, assessment methodology by itself is not a legitimate basis upon which to assign responses to different modes (a point to be discussed shortly). Second, evidence of a relationship between certain patterns of EMG activity and the ANS does not mean that both are representative of the same mode. In fact, there is ample evidence to suggest that muscle tone is not a very good index of autonomic arousal, although under some circumstances certain aspects of this response may be related to the ANS.

Relating the musculoskeletal system to autonomic activity goes back almost 50 years to Edmund Jacobson (1938) who gave us deep-muscle relaxation. It has been proposed that by controlling muscle tone one can "thereby affect, indirectly, autonomic and cortical functioning as well" (Budzynski, 1977, p. 437), which provides a basis for the use of EMG biofeedback in the treatment for stress-related disorders (Gaarder & Montgomery, 1977; Stoyva, 1977). Over the past 20 years, however, since Lang included muscle tension as a component of his "somatic" mode, there has been considerable research in this area. Several investigators now believe that muscle tone is not representative of autonomic activity generally (e.g., Burish, 1981). In fact, studies involving EMG recordings suggest that the level of muscle tone has little bearing on the degree of generalized relaxation, muscular or autonomic (Carlson, Basilio, & Heaykulani, 1983; Fridlund, Cottam, & Fowler, 1982; Fridlund, Fowler, & Pritchard, 1980).

These data suggest that it might be best to think of EMG responses, including even its more programmed components, as another index of musculoskeletal activity (i.e., motoric mode) rather than as part of the autonomic mode. Consequently, the *autonomic mode* will be defined for our purposes as *internal regulatory activity, including vegetative functions such as hormonal and other biochemical regulation, as well as visceral responses of organs such as the heart and stomach.*

Example. Returning to the social skills example, the autonomic component of social interactions focuses on a subset of responses that may enhance or interfere with the performance of motor skills that do exist. A dry throat, excessive perspiration, or shortness of breath, for example, may interfere with social skills in at least two ways. First, one's awareness of this activity may affect social performance by focusing attention inwardly rather than on the other person. Second, the responses may interfere with performance directly by preventing normal vocal expression or by revealing unintended affect.

Cognitive Mode

Definition. The cognitive component of the triple modes was defined initially by Lang (1964) as verbal statements of one's subjective experience (e.g., "I am afraid"). This emphasis on the self-report of one's feelings has been generally accepted (van Egeren, 1971). Hersen (1973), for example, refers to this mode as the "verbal (attitudinal)" component of fear. Ellis (1968), however, extends his "cognitive factor" to include perceptual factors by proposing that individuals are biased by past experience to see what he or she "thinks" he or she should see. Meichenbaum (1977a), on the other hand, has emphasized the role of self-statements in organizing and directing behavior. And yet others focus on problem solving as one of the most important contributions of cognition to behavior (Goldfried & Goldfried, 1975).

At the risk of oversimplification, one might define the cognitive mode as those "person" variables that *mediate* the relationship between stimulus and response. This view emphasizes the role of cognitive events in affecting behavior through selective attention, personal evaluation, self-instructional guidance, or problem-solving strategies. Some behavioral theorists argue that focusing on mediational events such as these is unnecessary and even misleading (e.g., Wolpe, 1976a, 1976b). On the other hand, others have welcomed the extension of behavioral constructs to include cognitions as long as the resultant formulations are subjected to the same criteria as other explanations of behavior. The latter view requires that any consideration of a cognitive contribution to behavior be evaluated in terms of its empirical yield, just as other theories concerned with more observable phenomena (Mahoney & Arnkoff, 1978, p. 713).

One problem with the broad definition, however, is the tendency for people to use it so loosely that it includes *everything*. It can be said, for example, that cognitive events mediate essentially all behavior in which a clinician is interested. Nevertheless, some activities are clearly less cognitive than others. For example, reflexes, overlearned motor responses, and most of the programmed activity of the ANS are carried out with little if any mediation (as the term is used here to denote a manipulation of information). These responses appear to be organized in such a way that they can be performed automatically. This has obvious advantages because it frees us up to think about things of which we need to be aware, such as novel experiences and pressing problems. Although awareness of the more conscious aspects of behavior may be involved in the early stages of learning, once a behavior is well established, the "cognitive" components appear to assume less importance (Meichenbaum, 1977a).

Still, some authors insist that any response, motoric or autonomic, is basically a cognitive event (e.g., Moates & Schumacher, 1980; Murray & Jacobson, 1978). Equating cognition with CNS activity generally, however, is of little use clinically because of its overinclusiveness. By explaining everything, it explains nothing. It will be argued later in the chapter that the triple modes approach is useful because it allows the practitioner to make assessments that are finer grained than is possible using diagnostic criteria only. Claiming that all problems can be attributed to a common, cognitive mechanism may gloss over meaningful distinctions and thus work against the concept of differential treatment in spite of the clear movement of clinical practice in that direction (e.g., Paul, 1969; Rachman & Wilson, 1980; Strupp, 1978).

Although the issue of what constitutes cognition will be explored more fully in Chapter 7 (Emotion), for the purposes of this chapter the cognitive mode will be defined more broadly than verbal reports of subjective states yet more narrowly than the primary causative factor for all behavior. More specifically, cognition will be viewed as encompassing mediational events (between stimulus and response) that act upon (i.e., manipulate) information in some way. This mediation may involve subjective evaluation, self-direction via private talk, planning, decision making, or other forms of abstract symbol manipulation. To put in other terms, the *cognitive mode* will be defined as *private mediational events, including subjective experience and use of one's intellectual facilities* (broadly defined).

Example. Cognitive factors have always played an important role in social skills training. From the beginning, the "right" of individuals to express their opinions and feelings was emphasized (Alberti & Emmons, 1974). These beliefs are usually discussed in treatment and often codified in the form of a mandate, such as the "Assertive Human Rights" (M. J. Smith, 1975). Self-instruction also plays an important role as a training tool (Kelly, 1982), as do several other cognitive strategies (Rathjen, Rathjen, & Hiniker, 1978). In addition, misattributions or faulty assumptions have been identified as posing problems for the socially deficient individual and are treated using various cognitive restructuring techniques in conjunction with specific training for performance (Lange & Jakubowski, 1976).

Summary

Since Lang's original formulation over 20 years ago, the tripartite approach to assessing behavioral problems has been expanded considerably to include a wide range of disorders in addition to fears and anxiety. Some of these include obsessions and compulsions (Rachman & Hodgson, 1980), depression (Craighead, 1980), social interactions (Ost, Jerremalm, & Johansson, 1981), chronic pain (Kincey & Benjamin, 1984), headache (Philips, 1980), alcohol use (Abrams, 1983), and even pretreatment emesis for cancer patients receiving chemotherapy (Nicholas & Hollandsworth, in press) as well as many others.

For our purposes the motoric mode has been equated with overt behavior, just as Lang defined it over 20 years ago. However, it has been suggested that muscle tone as indicated by EMG activity is more accurately included under this mode than as part of Lang's "somatic" component. On the other hand, Lang's use of a somatic mode to cover visceral responses has been maintained. This dimension, which is referred to as the physiological mode by most, has been renamed the autonomic mode for our purposes to emphasize its relationship to the ANS. And finally, the subjective aspect of the cognitive mode has been expanded beyond reports of personal experience to include other cognitive events such as self-talk and problem solving. Taking motor activity to mean behavior, the overall result of this classification scheme is what one might term the *ABCs of responding*—autonomic, behavioral, and cognitive.

Criticisms of the Triple Modes

Attempting to define the triple modes emphasizes the arbitrary nature of categorizing responses along three dimensions. Consequently, the triple modes perspective has many critics, one of the most vocal of whom is Gary Schwartz. Schwartz's position is that the division of human behavior into three modes is not only arbitrary but misleading.

> Verbal response, behavior, and physiology are *all* psychobiological processes, and separating them into these particular three categories confuses levels of analysis (from behavior to physiology and endocrinology to neurology). "Verbal" output is a psychobiological process which bases its activity to a large extent on conscious processes (both cognitive and somatic). "Behavioral" output is also a psychobiological process (which should more aptly be classified as *non*verbal behavior), which is not dependent on subjective experience. "Physiological" output is really the first level analysis of both verbal and nonverbal behavior. Saying that "physiology" often does not correlate with "behavior" implies that physiology and behavior are separate. It is accurate to say that certain behaviors do not covary with other behaviors, or certain physiological responses do not covary with other physiological responses, under specific conditions. (G. E. Schwartz, 1978, p. 71)

Schwartz's criticism points to several problems. For one, there is the obvious problem of delineation. What is included under one mode but not another? The question whether EMG activity is an index of the autonomic or the motoric mode is an example of this problem. Another problem concerns the possibility that responses in which clinicians are interested represent much more than simply the expression of three modes, individually or in combination. Schwartz refers to this idea as the "emergent property" of behavior.

> The concept of pattern here refers not simply to the isolated viewing of combinations of processes, but rather goes beyond the individual components making up the pattern to recognize the novel, interactive, or emergent property that patterns acquire. Simply stated, the whole may have properties that are qualitatively and/or quantitatively different from the sum of parts, yet it may be dependent upon the organization of its parts for its unique properties. (G. E. Schwartz, 1978, pp. 71–72).

These criticisms are compelling. Yet, triple modes of responding has not only survived but prospered over the 20 years since it was introduced. The reason may lie in the fact that *any* conceptualization of human behavior has limitations and that there are different uses for different models of behavior. Given what the triple modes view of things is asked to do, it seems to do it very well. In short, triple modes has as many strengths as it has weaknesses.

One strength, for example, is that triple modes is *simple*. It requires little in the way of prerequisite knowledge and makes intuitive sense. As a result, clinicians pick up on it quickly and incorporate it easily into their practice. (Recall the need for making simplifying assumptions as discussed in Chapter 2.) Although it can be argued that oversimplistic views of human behavior are harmful, it is also common knowledge that if a view is not easily accessible it will fail to be adopted widely, regardless of its merits.

Another advantage of triple modes is that it is *practical*. It reflects the realities of clinical assessment. Reality dictates that all assessment techniques impose a structure of their own. We talk to, observe, and, on occasion, monitor our clients with instruments. Each measure by its very nature is limited. The practitioner's problem is how to select and integrate multiple sources of assessment data, each of which offers only partial information. A triple modes view of things provides a rationale for doing this. In fact, the "multimodal" aspect of assessment has been endorsed so frequently as to have become an established research desideratum (Bergin & Lambert, 1978; Rachman & Wilson, 1980; Strupp, 1978).

Lang and Schwartz joined battle over this very issue. Lang, supporting a "practicalist" position, stated that "it is not a knowledge of chemistry which guides the chef to a good bouillabaisse, but knowing which fish to use and how to cook them" (1977b, p. 863). Schwartz noted in response that "although clearly the average chef need not know chemistry to cook a fish well, it is still possible, if not likely, that understanding the underlying chemistry will improve the trial and error means by which such cooking is approached and taught" (1978, p. 73).

It is hard to argue against Schwartz's assertion. The value of understanding psychobiological principles underlying treatment techniques provides a basic reason for writing the present volume. But still there is the issue of utility. Elegant conceptual models may be of little use in some settings because they are too complex for the "average chef" or because they are simply too unwieldy to apply. These models may have great value in directing research or in developing new treatment strategies. Nevertheless, the most elegant models are not always the best. Inevitably, at some point theory must be translated into practice.

Schwartz, himself, does not escape this reality. After criticizing Lang for the practical approach, and after presenting his own model of self-regulation, Schwartz proposes that anxiety is best viewed as having *two dimensions*—one cognitive and the other somatic. In spite of an elaborate theoretical basis (cf. Davidson, 1978; Davidson & Schwartz, 1976; G. E. Schwartz, Davidson, & Goleman, 1978), Schwartz and his colleagues end up having to make similar, simplifying assumptions. Yet, even with a more elaborate theory, their cognitive-somatic hypothesis cannot be seen as superior to the triple modes in terms of its empirical fruit (Kirkland & Hollandsworth, 1980; Lehrer, Schoicket, Carrington, & Woolfolk, 1980; Warrenburg, Pagano, Woods, & Hlastala, 1980; Woolfolk, Carr-Kaffashan, McNulty, & Lehrer, 1976; Woolfolk, Lehrer, McCann, & Rooney, 1982; Zuroff & Schwartz, 1978).

In short, no one has a monopoly on truth, and what works for one man (or woman) will not necessarily work for another. Triple modes of assessment has its problems as discussed previously. But it also has provided a useful way of conceptualizing clinical disorders for over 20 years. This would speak to its viability as a heuristic device, until a better alternative makes an appearance. As long as the triple modes way of viewing things is presented as a tentative and even flawed construct with specific uses and definite limitations, then one need not apologize for its simplicity or practical applicability.

Triple Modes Assessment

Originally, each of the three modes was identified by the particular method used to assess it. Thus, verbal reports were linked to cognitions, observation meant motoric events, and the use of instruments related to autonomic activity, such as heart rate or skin resistance. However, defining the triple modes in this manner can be misleading, for there is no reason to limit a particular mode to a particular assessment method. In practice, one method is often used across modes. Self-report, for example, is used to gather information about past behavior and autonomic activity as well as subjective states (Bellack & Hersen, 1977).

The application of different assessment methods across three modes can be visualized as a simple 3 × 3 matrix, such as presented in Table 2. The familiar pairings of self-report with the cognitive mode, observation with the motoric mode, and instrumentation with the autonomic mode fall along the diagonal. It might be said that the diagonal represents the *preferred* method by mode combinations. However, it also can be seen that useful combinations exist for all nine cells of the matrix.

Self-Report

Self-report, the first method to be discussed, has a history as old as psychological assessment itself. Verbal accounts of past and current experience, for example, provided a foundation upon which the interpretative therapies, such as psychoanalysis, were built. In fact, almost all psychological therapies see client reports as an important source of information, although they differ in terms of how this information is used (Linehan, 1977).

Traditionally, self-report has been used to assess subjective experience. Walk (1956), for example, had airborne trainees rate their feelings of fear just before a practice jump. Wolpe's (1973) Subjective Anxiety Scale, which ranges from 0 ("absolutely calm") to 100 ("the worst anx-

Table 2. Examples of Measures Characteristic of Different Mode-by-Method Combinations

Response mode	Assessment method		
	Self-report	Observation	Instrumentation
Cognitive	Subjective Anxiety Scale	Block-design test (WAIS)	Electroencephalogram
Motoric	Assertion Inventory	Behavior checklist	Posture prompter
Autonomic	Autonomic Perception Questionnaire	Heart sound auscultation	Electrocardiogram

iety you have ever experienced, or can imagine experiencing"), is used to determine the level of discomfort the client is experiencing during systematic desensitization. In addition, self-report has been used to assess personal attitudes and opinions. The Semantic Differential Technique (Osgood, Suci, & Tannenbaum, 1957), which has subjects rate other persons or things using pairs of adjectives, such as "good/bad," "active/passive," or "hard/soft," is an example of this use of self-report.

Self-reports have also been used to assess self-talk and problem-solving ability. One study used a video recorder to monitor subjects taking a test of mental abilities and then played it back afterward in an attempt to elicit their self-instructional, test-taking strategies (Hollandsworth, Glazeski, Kirkland, Jones, & Van Norman, 1979). In a related study, subjects were presented with individual items from the same test (using a slide projector), asked to respond, and then prompted to report what problem-solving strategies they used in arriving at their answer (Glazeski, Hollandsworth, & Jones, in press).

Self-report techniques are used to assess the occurrence of motoric responses as well. Self-monitoring, for example, is widely used to record the occurrence of specific behaviors. Also, most of the self-report measures of assertive behavior provide examples of the use of self-report for assessing motor responses. Assertion inventories, such as the Adult Self-Expression Scale (ASES; Gay, Hollandsworth, & Galassi, 1975), focus on the frequency of specific behaviors. For example, an item from the ASES asks: "Do you freely volunteer information or opinions in discussions with people whom you do not know very well?" Another measure, the Assertion Inventory (Gambrill & Richey, 1975), asks the client to respond to items such as "ask a favor of someone," in terms of response probability as well as the degree of discomfort engaging in such a behavior entails. This measure thus gleans information concerning both the cognitive (i.e., subjective) and motoric modes.

In terms of the autonomic mode, there have been many attempts over the years to assess physiological responsivity using a self-report methodology (Hastrup & Katkin, 1976; Ikeda & Hirai, 1976; Stern & Higgins, 1969). The Autonomic Perception Questionnaire (APQ) was one of the first to be developed (Mandler, Mandler, & Uviller, 1958) and has been widely used (e.g., Hollandsworth & Jones, 1979; Jones & Hollandsworth, 1981). Subjects are asked on the APQ to report their awareness of responses such as increased heart rate, rapid breathing, cold hands, dry throat, or upset stomach when they are anxious. In spite of the limited success of this and other measures as a predictive assessment technique, there is continued interest in the use of self-reports to monitor autonomic activity (e.g., Waters, Cohen, Bernard, Buco, & Dreger, 1984).

Thus the self-report method of assessment is capable of eliciting information across all three modes. The degree to which this information coincides with other modes is of interest in itself. When using self-report, however, it must be remembered that the information obtained with this method can be affected by numerous variables unrelated to the problem for which the client was referred. Some of these considerations would include the demand characteristics of the assessment situation, the client's level of awareness, and the availability of events such as problem-solving strategies and autonomic activity for introspection (cf. Nisbett & Wilson, 1977).

Observation

The use of observers to collect data has a long and fruitful history as well (Wildman & Erickson, 1977). Observational data, for example provided a basis for the child development movement of the 1920s and 1930s. This is not surprising given that infants and small children have limited self-report capabilities. Although the early studies relied on parents' descriptions of their children's behavior (called "baby biographies"), the limitations of informal and nonobjective observations such as these were quickly realized. As a result, attempts to improve the methodological rigor of observational data made an early appearance (e.g., Arrington, 1932).

Observation has been invariably linked to overt behavior. In their cataloging of behavior checklists, Walls, Werner, Bacon, and Zane (1977) list 166 instruments, almost half of which rely on direct observation. (Most of the remainder involve verbal reports of current or past behavior.) Some of the behaviors covered by checklists using direct observation include social skills, language development, motor skills, work performance, self-management skills, and behavior problems.

As the matrix suggests, observation does not have to be limited to the motoric mode. Direct observation can also be used to assess cognitive functioning, such as occurs when performance tasks are used in intelligence tests or neuropsychological evaluations (Boll, O'Leary, & Barth, 1981). More than 20 of the checklists noted previously are designed to assess a wide range of cognitive and conceptual skills. Measures such as these, which infer cognitive function from observations of performance, are particularly useful when dealing with populations deficient in verbal skills, such as retarded individuals.

Direct observation can also be used to assess the autonomic mode, such as when one feels one's pulse or listens to heart sounds. The key here is that the observer, not the subject or an instrument, generates the data. Even the use of a stethoscope does not make a difference because the observer is still the one who senses the response and records his or her findings. Also, observation can be used to assess autonomic activity when it results in some type of externally observable outcome. Examples might include perspiring, flushing, or hyperventilating as well as disturbances in sleep patterns (Borkovec, 1982; Monroe, 1967).

Instrumentation

The use of instruments to measure psychophysiological responses goes back almost a hundred years. In 1888, a French physician, Féré (1888/1976), noted that when a weak electrical current was applied to a patient's forearm, the resistance of the skin to the current was systematically related to different emotional stimuli. This was termed the "psychogalvanic response," now more commonly referred to as the galvanic skin response (GSR; Lang, 1971). This interesting property of the skin to reflect internal (i.e., autonomic) events was exploited in the first half of this century by Darrow (1932) who used a glass plate to record the formation of sweat droplets. About the same time, Wendt (1930) devised a mechanical system for recording the knee-jerk reflex, providing a forerunner to the polygraph.

Advances in the ability to detect and amplify signals following World War II greatly hastened the development of the polygraph. Soon mechanical, electrical, thermal, optical, chemical and even magnetic transducers were being used to detect various aspects of bodily function (Rugh & Schwitzgebel, 1977). These signals were amplified, transduced, and recorded so that physical records of this activity could be analyzed. Today the polygraph is used to record a wide number of responses, including but not limited to anal sphincter pressure, blood pressure, muscle tension, eye movement, brain wave activity, electrodermal responses, gross motor movement, posture, heart rate, micturition, penile erection, respiration, stomach motility, and salivation. In addition, instrumentation can be used to measure biochemical and/or metabolic activity, such as plasma catecholamine levels or oxygen consumption, which is representative of autonomic activity (e.g., Hollandsworth, Gintner, Ellender, & Rectanus, 1984; Morrell & Hollandsworth, in press).

It can be readily seen that although many of these responses are subsumed under the autonomic mode, several are not. Thus the use of instruments is not limited to monitoring autonomic responses, such as heart rate, and can be extended to measure motoric activity as well (Tryon, 1984). One example of the use of an instrument to record motor behavior involves a mercury switch, which operates on the basis of gravity, and a pocket calculator (Sanders, 1980). This device is strapped to the leg of a chronic pain patient and is activated when the patient stands upright. When the patient is lying in bed, the mercury switch is closed, and time does not accumulate on the calculator. Motor activity, an important dependent variable in the treatment of chronic pain patients (Fordyce & Steger, 1979), can thus be closely monitored with this simple instrument. Another example would be Barry Dworkin and Neal Miller's posture prompter for patients suffering from idiopathic scoliosis (Dworkin, 1982; N. E. Miller, 1981). This device detects relaxation of the spine from a straightened position and signals the patient to make the appropriate musculoskeletal correction.

The application of instrumentation to cognitive events is perhaps best illustrated by the electroencephalogram (EEG). Differential patterns of EEG activity have been linked to the direction of attention (e.g., Davidson, Schwartz, & Rothman, 1976) as well as imaginal focus (e.g., Davidson & Schwartz, 1977). In an area more relevant to clinical concerns, Carter, Johnson, and Borkovec (1984) measured EEG activity in subjects experiencing chronic worry. Compared to controls, the worriers displayed significantly more overall cortical activation, as measured by parietal alpha, especially during a demanding cognitive task (internal math).

Summary and a Word of Caution

In short, the method of assessment is not restricted to a particular mode. Although some methods are more commonly linked to one mode than another, all three methods of assessment provide different views of the same mode, just as the different modes provide different perspectives of the same response.

Before leaving our discussion of triple modes assessment, a word of caution is in order. Although this approach may strengthen one's assessment procedures by expanding the range of variables to be considered, at the same time interpretation of the assessment data becomes correspondingly more complex. This can pose numerous problems (Peterson, 1984). For example, an increase in the number of measurements resulting from a triple modes assessment increases the probability of chance findings. This, in turn, can lead to an emphasis on a few variables that best fit one's preconceptions while ignoring other variables that fail to support this view. Another problem is the use of broad, modal labels that may blur important distinctions between measures falling within a single mode.

Although there are no simple answers to this problem, Peterson (1984) has suggested that the use of multivariate statistics can be helpful in sorting out the relative contribution of multimodal measures. Further, she advocates a weighting of outcome criteria based on an *a priori* determination as to which mode is logically most important given the particular nature of the problem at hand. For example, overt motor behavior may be of primary concern during certain medical procedures, such as lumbar punctures or bone marrow aspirations, for which movement can cause both tissue damage and pain. In other instances, the experience of subjective anxiety may be the most appropriate target if this response is interfering with the patient's willingness to participate in a treatment program. Whatever the case, it is clear that the triple modes approach is not a quick and easy solution to one's assessment problems. If anything, it calls for an even greater appreciation for the complexity of human behavior than has been required in the past.

Implications for Treatment

Triple modes emerged as the result of a need for more comprehensive assessment. Although the triple modes approach to assessment appears to have earned its wings, its application to questions of treatment is less established. Nevertheless, the literature does hint at some interesting possibilities. More specifically, the triple modes view of things may allow us to observe different patterns of responses within diagnostic categories. These "profiles," in turn, may provide the basis for differential approaches to treatment (Lang, 1977a).

It has been known for some time that the responses of diverse physiological systems respond differently under the same conditions. An interesting example of this is the concept of "schizokinesis." In a series of studies by Gantt and his colleagues, it was found that the motor system and the ANS display different characteristics when being conditioned to the same stimulus (Brogden & Gantt, 1942; Newton & Gantt, 1960; Royer & Gantt, 1966). More specifically,

> In the study of the cardiac components of the conditional reflex to food or to pain we saw that the cardiac conditional reflex formed rapidly, usually before the motor or the salivary and often after one reinforcement by the unconditional stimulus (Gantt, 1953). Not only did it form first, as a rule, but it generally was much more resistant to extinction. Often the cardiac conditional reflex might continue for several years after the motor or the salivary component had been extinguished by active efforts for extinction. The respiratory conditional reflex behaves in this respect more like the cardiac conditional reflex than like the specific salivary or motor components. The fact that

the cardiac conditional reflex may continue while the other components are
absent led to the concept of schizokinesis, a split between the more general
functions as the respiratory and the cardiovascular and the specific ones.
(Gantt, 1966, pp. 61–62)

Similar distinctions may be relevant to certain human disorders as
well. Ost and his colleagues (Ost, Johansson, & Jerremalm, 1982) classified 34 claustrophobic, psychiatric outpatients as being behavioral or
physiological reactors on the basis of their responses in a test situation.
The patients were randomly assigned to either a "behaviorally oriented"
treatment (exposure), a "physiologically oriented" approach (progressive relaxation), or a waiting-list control condition. Although both
treatment groups were significantly better after eight individual sessions
than those on the waiting list (as determined by self-report, avoidance,
and heart rate measures), the exposure treatment was more successful
with the behavioral reactors, whereas the relaxation treatment favored
the physiological responders. Treatment gains were maintained at a 14-
month follow-up. These findings were similar to those from an earlier
study by the same group of investigators involving the treatment of
social fears (Ost, Jerremalm, & Johansson, 1981).

However, the idea that diagnostic categories can be broken down
into subgroups on the basis of modal responses has not received uni-
form support (e.g., Sartory, Rachman, & Grey, 1977). Ost and Hugdahl
(1983) also failed to find a predicted pattern of responses with agoraphobics. Investigating the proposal by Rachman (1977) that fear can be
acquired in three ways (direct conditioning, vicarious learning, or provision of information), these investigators hypothesized that agoraphobics
reporting a conditioning basis for their fears would demonstrate greater
responsivity on the autonomic mode than those who acquired their fears
vicariously. Drawing data from a group of 80 agoraphobic patients, they
failed to find the anticipated relationship. Although the overwhelming
majority of these subjects (81%) attributed the onset of their phobias to
conditioning experiences, a significant proportion of these subjects
scored higher on the subjective than on the autonomic component of the
assessment. Although an earlier study of claustrophobics by the same
two investigators did not agree with these findings (Ost & Hugdahl,
1981), a more recent study involving blood and dental phobics replicated
these results (Ost & Hugdahl, 1985). Another study (Ost, Jerremalm, &
Jansson, 1985) with agoraphobics also failed to support the earlier finding (i.e., Ost et al., 1982), suggesting that treatments tailored to patient
"profiles" may not be the answer.

Other data, however, suggest that desynchrony across modes holds
promise in the prediction of treatment outcomes (Vermilyea, Boice, &

Barlow, 1984). More specifically, agoraphobic patients were assessed prior to receiving a treatment that involved *in vivo* exposure and self-instructional coping strategies. Patients who began with the highest levels of heart rate responsivity during a behavioral walk were most likely to evidence improvement on a composite measure of outcome. The prognostic potential of psychophysiological measures such as heart rate is also supported by the past, extensive research by Lang and his associates on the integration of affective responses (Lang, Levin, Miller, & Kozak, 1983).

Some investigators have suggested that, at least in treating agoraphobics, the issue of desynchrony is confounded by its variation over the course of treatment. Mavissakalian and Michelson (1982) propose that "change starts with behavioral and clinical measures followed by psychophysiological measures of which psysiological [sic] responsivity has the longest lag" (p. 347). For example, it is not uncommon to observe meaningful behavior change (i.e., increased freedom of movement) before the client reports the elimination of subjective distress or evidences decreased autonomic responding. Vermilyea *et al.* (1984) suggest that the failure to distinguish patients according to their response patterns and subsequently averaging data across subjects also accounts for the inconsistent findings.

Whatever the case, the evidence for the utility of a triple modes approach to differential treatment is uncertain. The data that do support this notion are in keeping with the view that diverse physiological systems exhibit different characteristics under similar conditions. These data are also congruent with theories, such as "preparedness," that highlight a biological contribution to learning. (Recall the discussion of the equipotentiality premise in the preceding chapter.) On the other hand, the complex, interactive nature of human problems may obscure these differences in a clinical setting. Whatever the case, the idea of modal variation as a guide to differential treatment is a concept of some promise but whose time has not yet come.

Mode by Treatment Interactions

With this caution in mind, one can turn to the treatment literature for guidelines in selecting appropriate interventions for problems involving specific modes. Contingency management, for example, is often the treatment of choice for problems involving overt behavior (Kazdin, 1980). Phobias exhibiting a strong autonomic component, on the other hand, seem more tractable to interventions based on some form of desensitization (Wolpe, 1973) or controlled exposure (Marks, 1978), whereas problems of a more cognitive nature are often most successfully treated using procedures based on an understanding of how information is processed (Mahoney, 1974).

Although specific treatments may be targeted for specific modes, it is common for a client to present a problem heavily loaded on one mode that is symptomatic of disregulation involving another mode. Consequently, if a person presents with high levels of autonomic activity, one does not necessarily assume that he or she has been classically conditioned and thus requires desensitization.

Table 3 is an attempt to illustrate how problems presenting along one dimension might be conceptualized as involving a dysfunction more characteristic of another mode. As an example, anxiety is generally seen as involving all three modes. One verbally reports subjective discomfort, which is often experienced in conjunction with increased autonomic discharge (i.e., heart palpitations) and impaired or avoidant motor performance (Spielberger, 1966). Although there may be agreement between modes (synchrony), it is also possible that a further assessment will reveal some degree of desynchrony. It is the finer discrimination between modes that points to a differential treatment process.

Problems along the Autonomic Dimension. For example, a therapist might be struck by a client's high levels of autonomic responsivity. Further assessment might reveal that this activity, although subjectively perceived as quite aversive, does not appear to be caused by maladaptive cognitions, such as ruminations of peril, fearsome imagery, or excessive self-standards or expectations. In fact, the client may report being "frozen" with fear and unaware of any particular cognitions at all (e.g., Hodges & Hollandsworth, 1980). Also, this reaction may be most evident in relatively few situations linked to one another logically, such as increased perspiration and rapid heart rate around small animals,

Table 3. Examples of Clinical Problems Presenting as One Mode but Symptomatic of the Dysfunction of Another Mode

Presenting mode	Dysfunctional mode		
	Autonomic	Motoric	Cognitive
Autonomic	Phobic reaction	Reactive anxiety	"Free-floating" anxiety
Motoric	Impaired social skills	Deficient social skills	Underutilized social skills
Cognitive	Medically based worry	Worry about deficient skills	Worrisome thoughts

whether they be rats, stuffed toys, or kittens. In a case such as this, one may tentatively conclude that the problem is a phobic disorder, in which case any number of treatments based on *in vivo* or imaginal exposure might be selected (Marks, 1978).

In another case, however, the situations related to excessive autonomic reactivity may require the performance of a behavior involving complex motor skills. Examples would include making a speech before an audience or interacting with someone of the opposite sex. In this situation, the motor involvement would alert the therapist to the possibility that he or she is dealing with "reactive anxiety" in which the excessive autonomic activity is the reasonable consequence of deficient motor skills. In other words, the reaction may be realistic given that the demands of the task exceed the competence of the individual. As a result, treatment would focus on rectifying the skills deficit rather than reducing the level of autonomic responsivity directly through some sort of desensitization procedure (e.g., Hollandsworth, Glazeski, & Dressel, 1978).

Yet another client might present the same degree of autonomic reactivity but also be assessed as having good performance skills. Although it is, of course, possible that the autonomic response is interfering with the use of these skills, it may be found with further assessment that the client is engaging in a number of maladaptive cognitions. For example the client may be mislabeling another's behavior, derogating his or her own performance, or exaggerating the negative valence of some outcome. Beck refers to these problems as "automatic thoughts" (Beck, 1976) that can result in anxious (or depressive) reactions on their own. Treatment in this case might be directed toward providing experiences that contradict these maladaptive cognitions as well as logically disputing them in a manner similar to that employed in rational-emotive therapy (Ellis & Grieger, 1977).

Problems along the Motoric Dimension. Using this basic approach, one can work through the remaining six cells in Table 3. The presenting problem may be, for example, difficulties in performing an appropriate behavior, such as a withdrawn child's interacting with peers at school (Clarizio & McCoy, 1983). A functional analysis might reveal that other children have teased or in other ways failed to reinforce the child's attempts to join in. On the other hand, the child may handle interactions in an awkward manner, thus setting the stage for rejection. In either case, the problem would be seen as falling along the motoric dimension and could be approached by either restructuring the environment to provide appropriate reinforcers for the child's efforts to make friends or by enhancing the child's interpersonal skills so that social reinforcers that do exist can be accessed (cf. Kelly, 1982; O'Connor, 1969).

In another case, a child might have appropriate social skills and enjoy warm relationships with peers but have extreme difficulty in other interpersonal situations, such as speaking in front of the class (e.g., Hosford, 1969). The problem in this case might be excessive autonomic reactivity to specific stimuli that interferes with the performance of an established motor skill. Treatment therefore might proceed by reducing this reactivity, perhaps through some sort of desensitization procedure for the child (Koeppen, 1974). This approach would assume that existing contingencies are appropriate for the performance of intact skills and that the acquisition of further skills is not necessary.

On the other hand, the child might have adequate verbal and interactive skills, be free of disabling anxiety, and yet remain socially withdrawn as a result of an unreasonable expectation of rejection. In this case, additional skills training might add little if the child is afraid to utilize these competencies. Gottman, Gonso, and Rasmussen (cited in Meichenbaum, 1977a) dealt with this type of problem by "inoculating" a child against possible rejection using a coping self-statement sequence developed by Meichenbaum and Goodman (1971). This "cognitive" intervention for a "motoric" problem is integrated with other components, including some skills training. The cognitive intervention, in this example, is used to facilitate the performance of a motor skill.

Problems along the Cognitive Dimension. Sometimes the major presenting problem deals with the nature of one's cognitions themselves, such as ruminations, faulty problem solving, or worrisome thoughts. These cognitive events are problematic because they can disrupt behaviors or cause excessive autonomic responding. For example, research on insomnia led Tom Borkovec and his colleagues to study "worry" (Borkovec, Robinson, Pruzinsky, & DePree, 1983). They found that worriers were distinguished most from nonworriers "by their reported uncontrollability of cognitive intrusions once worrying was initiated" (p. 9).

Although intrusive cognitions might be treated "cognitively," as through stimulus control instructions (Borkovec, Wilkinson, Folensbee, & Lerman, 1983) or thought stopping (Wolpe, 1958) (although the latter has little empirical support [cf. Mahoney & Arnkoff, 1978]), the therapist would be remiss not to explore a possible motoric or autonomic contribution to a client's worries. For example, there are many reasons for insomnia other than intrusive thoughts (Borkovec, 1982). It is possible that the chronic ingestion of a hypnotic medication, alcohol, or other CNS depressant over time is disrupting the client's sleep patterns. The resultant fatigue and distress over the loss of sleep might provide a more or less realistic basis for the client's worries. Cognitive restructuring in a case like this without checking out the possible physiological basis for the problem would be ill advised.

In a similar manner, there could be a motoric basis for worry as well. A client might worry excessively about an upcoming job interview. It is tempting to treat a problem like this with reassurance, information, and statements designed to increase the client's "self-image." If, however, the client does not have the prerequisite motor skills for handling this demanding and complex performance task, information and moral support will fall short (Hollandsworth, Dressel, & Stevens, 1977).

Summary. Table 3 and these examples illustrate a process of assessment that proceeds as much with the active exclusion (i.e., ruling out) of intervention strategies as with discovering the "right" one. This, of course, is in the best tradition of the scientific method with its emphasis on choice points (Platt, 1964) and multiple working hypotheses (Chamberlin, 1965). Although falling short of providing a comprehensive model for treatment selection, the triple modes approach, nevertheless, may offer some basic guidelines for thinking through complex clinical problems in this manner.

Clinical Examples

Problems with Anger Control

The inability to control angry outbursts is a problem with serious consequences (Novaco, 1976, 1977, 1978). Ray Novaco (1975) has conceptualized anger as an emotional response to provocation that involves all three response modalities. Central to his formulation is the cognitive mode consisting of attributions and expectations that affect the way in which one interprets a confrontational situation. Depending on the nature of these cognitions, another's statements, facial expression, or behavior may be seen as evidence of threat, ill will or rejection.

Cognition appears to play a major role in determining how a person handles confrontation as well. Consequently, Novaco uses Meichenbaum's stress-inoculation model (Meichenbaum, 1977a) in his treatment approach. This model relies heavily on self-instructions to direct behavior in more adaptive ways. For example, self-instruction is used to monitor and then dispute unreasonable expectations or assumptions so that another's behavior is not misunderstood or distorted. In addition, self-instruction appears useful in training the client to engage in more adaptive problem-solving skills that might lead to a successful resolution of the conflict situation.

The central role of cognition in anger does not lead Novaco, however, to view this mode as acting alone. He acknowledges the contribution of all three. The autonomic mode, for example, is seen as priming or exacerbating one's anger. Increased activity of the ANS, a predictable and programmed response to threatening situations (see Chapter 1), provides a basis for tension and agitation that may interact synergistically with cognitive misappraisal. It is important to be aware of this process early in the sequence of events so that steps can be taken to interrupt, as much as possible, the automatic progression of a defense/alarm reaction. Calming self-talk may help, but more somatically oriented techniques, such as muscle relaxation or breathing exercises, may be more useful.

The motoric mode is also important. Novaco sees both withdrawal and aggression as contributing to problems in anger control. The former may perpetuate the conflict because disagreements are seldom resolved in this manner. A more appropriate strategy might be to provide the client with the motor skills to handle interpersonal situations more effectively, such as in a more assertive rather than aggressive manner (Heisler & McCormack, 1982; Hollandsworth, 1977, 1985b). The same would be true if one's agitation leads to aggressive behavior that serves as a provocation. These responses also might be retooled into more appropriate ways of expressing one's frustration or disagreement (Hollandsworth & Cooley, 1978; Woolfolk & Dever, 1979).

In summary, problems with anger control can be seen as resulting from a synergistic interaction of all three modes. Targeting one for change without taking into account the contributions of the other two would seem short-sighted. This does not mean that all three components are equally important in all cases. Rather, the approach is to conduct a comprehensive assessment that determines the relative contribution of each. Thus, treatment might include some combination of self-instructional training for misattributions and faulty reasoning, somatic strategies for reducing autonomic reactivity, and skills training for interpersonal behaviors. It also should be noted that interventions directed toward one mode may affect responses related to another. Self-instructional training, for example, should aid in the performance of effective assertive behaviors. Also, physical strategies, such as controlled breathing, may serve as useful attention-focusing or distraction techniques, thus alleviating the subjective component of the response (McCaul & Malott, 1984).

Depression in the Elderly

Depression is regarded as one of the two most frequent problems of geriatric populations (Levy, 1981a). It also has been estimated that a large proportion of elderly persons living in the community evidence difficulties associated with social isolation and poor social adjustment

(Bennett, 1973). A therapist eager to deal with depression in an elderly person might jump in where it seems most convenient. For many, this would mean "working through" the feelings of loneliness associated with the loss of loved ones and friends. By focusing on the subjective component of the problem, however, the well-intended service provider might miss the boat entirely. Depression in old age is a complex phenomenon with many possible causes, only some of which are cognitive.

Depression, for example, can be the result of deteriorated or disordered physiology, which is common among the aged. Reduced olfactory and gustatory sensation can affect eating patterns and thus induce malnutrition (Sherwood, 1973; Stare, 1977). Levels of digestive enzymes may be reduced, thus affecting the ability of the body to utilize nutrients that are consumed. Alterations in the synthesis, storage, release, or utilization of neurotransmitters accompanying age might provide an even more parsimonious explanation for depression in this population (Lipton, 1976). In addition, infections or physical disorders that are found more frequently in this group can induce depressivelike symptoms that may be difficult to distinguish from depression of a more psychological nature (Epstein, 1976; Levy, 1981a).

Musculoskeletal deterioration can also cause problems apart from the phenomenology of growing old. Physical infirmity, related to the aging process, may hinder motor activity, even in the well-nourished and otherwise healthy client. Decreased mobility can significantly impact activity levels and social interaction, thus contributing to a sense of isolation or helplessness. In addition, because retirement calls for a range of behaviors that are perhaps unfamiliar to a patient accustomed to a work setting, there may be the need to provide direction and training in the acquisition of motor skills for tasks more adaptive to the new role.

The cognitive mode is also important. However, this dimension involves more than subjective grief or despair over the loss of one's companions. Libow (1977), for example, has estimated that from 5 to 15% of all persons over 65 living in the community and anywhere from a quarter to a half of those living in institutions show significant signs of senile dementia. Some of the affective and information-processing problems in the elderly are due to this type of disorder. Acute brain syndromes, for example, can result in restlessness, confusion, or anxiety and result from medical conditions such as heart failure, infections, malnutrition, toxic substances, or head injury (Butler & Lewis, 1977). Other cognitive problems stem from chronic brain disease resulting from either cellular atrophy or changes in the cerebrovascular system (Levy, 1981a).

Treatment of the depressed geriatric client would follow a comprehensive assessment along all three dimensions. (Such an assessment would naturally involve appropriate medical personnel). The environment and the client's physical ability to ambulate in it would be an obvious consideration in determining whether the depressive state could be treated through increased access to reinforcing events such as other people or a wider range of activities. The possible medical basis for a host of problems, including those involving the cognitive mode, would also be a primary concern.

This does not mean, of course, that the depressed client's subjective experience would be neglected. Emotional support and attention to the feelings of growing old would play an important role in the overall treatment program (Levy, 1981b). But, as with the example of anger control mentioned previously, no one component would be isolated from the others. If, as G. E. Schwartz (1978) suggests, psychobiological problems (such as depression in the geriatric patient) are the emergent properties of complex systems, then one must have multiple explanations and multiple strategies for treating these disorders. The notion of triple modes of responding may provide a useful, if simple, guide for undertaking these considerations.

Recommended Readings

Ciminero, A. R., Calhoun, K. S., & Adams, H. E. (Eds.). (1977). *Handbook of behavioral assessment*. New York: Wiley.

Cone, J. D., & Hawkins, R. P. (Eds.). (1977). *Behavioral assessment: New directions in clinical psychology*. New York: Brunner/Mazel.

Hersen, M., & Bellack, A. S. (Eds.). (1976). *Behavioral assessment: A practical handbook*. New York: Pergamon.

These works are standard references in the area of behavioral assessment. Published almost 10 years ago, they remain current in terms of providing a good overview of the theoretical and methodological underpinnings of this assessment approach. Because assessment issues today are usually incorporated within chapters dealing with specific disorders, these volumes are useful in that they allow the reader to apply the triple modes broadly across problem areas.

Rachman, S. (1978). *Fear and courage*. San Francisco: W. H. Freeman.

There are very few works organized specifically around the concept of the triple modes. A notable exception is this exploration of fears, phobias, and feats of valor. Written for the general public, this book is as interesting as it is informative.

CHAPTER 6

Biofeedback

"Biofeedback is interacting with the interior self." So wrote Barbara Brown in her popular book on brain–body interactions more than a decade ago (1974, p. 1). What her definition lost in specificity it made up for in capturing the new direction this area provided for psychology. Biofeedback and other innovative therapies of the 1960s and 1970s championed the self-regulating potential of human beings and renewed an interest in "mind over matter." The title of Barbara Brown's 1974 book illustrates the point nicely—*New Mind, New Body: Biofeedback, New Directions for the Mind*.

The interest in voluntary control of internal events and the wave of research it spawned were important to furthering our understanding of how the human body works. Although the enthusiasm of the movement led to some remarkable breakthroughs, in the process we also learned that there were limits to our awareness and that the ability to control internal events is not as powerful as some had hoped. Thus, paradoxically, biofeedback broke new ground while reminding us of our limitations at the same time.

An interesting example of this paradox is the "voluntary-but-unconscious" regulation of visceral responses. In an investigation of cardiac awareness, we came across it quite unexpectedly (G. E. Jones & Hollandsworth, 1981). The study concerned differences between subjects who routinely engage in aerobic exercise (runners) as compared to more sedentary individuals in terms of their ability to monitor their heart rate. It was proposed that aerobic exercise serves as a natural biofeedback procedure so that exercisers should be more aware of their heart rate than those who do not exercise (Hollandsworth, 1979).

We found that male runners were, in fact, better at discriminating between actual and false heart rate feedback than sedentary, male subjects. No differences, however, were found for females. After the experiment, each subject reported what strategy he or she used for detecting heart rate. The subjects also estimated how good they were on the discrimination task.

Actual performance scores on the experimental trials identified those subjects who were either good or poor detectors of heart rate. Using these scores, the subjects were divided into three groups in terms of their discriminatory ability—high, medium, and low. The debriefing sheets were then given to two independent raters with all identifying information removed. The raters were asked to use the subjects' self-reports to categorize them into three groups on the basis of their perceptions of awareness. Interrater agreement for the two extreme groups (high and low) was 100%. However, the correspondence between subjects placed in either group based on their self-reports and their status in terms of actual performance was only 33% (at chance levels). Apparently, many good perceivers thought they were bad and vice versa. In other words, a majority of subjects on this awareness task were unaware of how they actually did.

This finding is congruent with earlier observations that have found that subjects can control cardiovascular activity without being aware of how they do it. In two studies by D. Shapiro and his colleagues (Shapiro, Tursky, Greshon, & Stern, 1969; Shapiro, Tursky, & Schwartz, 1970) subjects were trained using feedback to increase or decrease blood pressure. To control for instructional effects, they were not told which bodily function they were to manipulate nor the direction (i.e., increase or decrease) of the change desired. Although the subjects were able to increase and decrease blood pressure significantly more than a control group receiving random feedback, "postexperimental questionnaires revealed that subjects were not aware they had actually controlled their blood pressure, nor did they realize the direction their pressure had changed" (G. E. Schwartz, 1973, p. 667).

This finding is similar to that reported by H. D. Kimmel (1974) in his work on the instrumental conditioning of the galvanic skin response (GSR).

> Ninety-eight percent of the [200] subjects interviewed in our laboratory report no awareness that *anything* they might have done during the conditioning session was correlated with the delivery of reinforcement. (p. 329)

In a like manner Blanchard, Scott, Young, and Edmundson (1974) asked subjects who had been trained to control their heart rate how they did it.

Surprisingly, "subjects who showed good control and subjects who showed poor control both reported using the same strategies" (Blanchard & Epstein, 1978, p. 37).

In short, although biofeedback extended the possibilities of voluntary control over many responses once assumed to be more or less automatic, at the same time it revealed that much of what goes on inside us is outside conscious awareness. The degree to which we can be made aware of what our bodies are doing and the manner in which we attempt to influence this process is the subject of the present chapter.

Biofeedback

Biofeedback resulted from the merger of two, established paradigms in experimental psychology—Pavlovian or respondent ("classical") conditioning and Skinnerian or operant conditioning (Birk, 1973; G. E. Schwartz & Beatty, 1977). The former is applied widely to the conditioning of autonomic (i.e., visceral) responses, whereas the latter deals with observable behaviors directed by the musculoskeletal system.

Tradition and choice dictated a certain distance between the two approaches to learning. Pavlov, a physiologist, chose to study the autonomic nervous system (ANS). Consequently, the responses that interested respondent conditioners had a certain reflexive or "automatic" quality about them, such as the salivation of a dog when presented with meat powder. Operant psychologists, on the other hand, were interested in overt behavior and thus responses of the musculoskeletal system that are more flexible, more varied, and certainly more observable.

Operant psychologists explicitly avoided the "black box" of the body. This did not mean that Skinner and his colleagues did not appreciate what respondent conditioners had to say. To the contrary, Skinner was an admitted admirer of Pavlov (Skinner, 1966). Nor was Skinner unaware of physiological contributions to behavior. While at Harvard he had, after all, worked in Walter Cannon's laboratory.

The reason why operant psychologists avoided applying their methods to the study of autonomic responses was twofold. First, Skinner felt that theorists interested in physiological and neurological explanations of behavior, including Pavlov himself, drew inferences too quickly and thus separated themselves prematurely from their data. Second, Skinner asserted that although knowledge of physiological events might fill in certain gaps (1974, p. 215), it "will not make the relation between stimulus and response any more lawful or any more useful in prediction and control" (1953, p. 54). Nevertheless, attempts to control more basic, physiological responses using operant techniques made an appearance. And interestingly enough, the first problem approached in this manner was a *motor* response that was *unobservable*.

Following World War II physicians used sensitive equipment to monitor very slight electrical potentials generated by muscles that had lost their ability to respond as a result of a cerebrovascular accident (i.e., stroke) or other neurological impairment (Andrews, 1964; Marinacci & Horande, 1960). These "myoelectric" messages were translated into acoustic or visual signals, such as popping noises on a loudspeaker or spikes on a cathode ray oscilloscope. During an electromyographic (EMG) examination, the physician would ask the patient to try to alter these signals. The fact that patients could often control these myoelectric signals without being able to produce an observable response served to stimulate the use of instrumentation in conjunction with operant procedures for rehabilitation purposes.

Another development that encouraged a merging of the two paradigms was a growing interest in autonomic activity as a target response in and of itself. Autonomic conditioning had been implicated in the development of psychosomatic disorders for some time (Gantt, 1953). However, the respondent approach had focused on the reflexive nature of this type of learning (as the title of a primary journal in this area, *Conditional Reflex,* suggests) and showed less interest in how autonomic responses might be controlled voluntarily. Nevertheless, in 1962, Shearn reported data that suggested that subjects could learn to increase their heart rate in order to avoid a mild electric shock. This was accompanied in the literature by a series of studies by Lang and his colleagues who used continuous visual feedback to train subjects to stabilize their heart rates (Hnatiow & Lang, 1965; Lang, Sroufe, & Hastings, 1967). About the same time, other investigators were claiming to demonstrate operant control over diverse responses, such as alpha rhythms in brain wave activity (Kamiya, 1969), fluctuations in skin resistance (GSR acitivty; Fowler & Kimmel, 1962; Kimmel & Hill, 1960; Kimmel & Kimmel, 1963), and blood pressure (Shapiro *et al.,* 1969).

By the late 1960s the ability of individuals to control responses previously thought to be involuntary was enthusiastically prophesied. The manner in which one could go about this was based on combining operant principles, such as shaping and reinforcement, with increasingly sophisticated instrumentation. The former provided the conditions under which learning could optimally occur, whereas the latter contributed the technology necessary to detect and amplify the responses to be controlled.

Definition

Specifically, biofeedback is "the application of operant conditioning methods to the control of visceral, somatomotor, and central nervous system activities" (Shapiro & Surwit, 1979, p. 45). Over time, however, biofeedback has come to assume a wider meaning, for the possibility that learning can affect "involuntary" physiological responses has broader implications. Birk (1973), for example, relates this potential to the treatment of medical disorders generally. By cutting across the mind–body dichotomy, the new field has introduced the possibility of learning to control one's "internal behavior" and thus has potential for playing an important role in the comprehensive treatment of medical disorders in general. As a result, Birk christened biofeedback as a new "behavioral medicine" (p. 2), thus introducing a phrase that has come to mean much more than just biofeedback (cf. Garfield, 1982a).

Applications

Biofeedback also has both specific as well as general applications. In the specific sense, biofeedback is used in the treatment of a range of physiologically based problems for which the control of a particular response or pattern of responses may be useful in managing the disorder (D. Shapiro & Surwit, 1979, p. 49). Some of these areas include cardiovascular dysfunction (Blanchard, 1979), sexual difficulties (Geer, 1979), problems involving the musculoskeletal system (Basmajian & Hatch, 1979), migraine headache (K. P. Price, 1979), and others.

In a broader sense, the biofeedback literature has generated a wealth of data concerning the interaction of different systems, psychological and physiological. As such, biofeedback can be seen as a way of increasing our understanding of human behavior, particularly in terms of its physiological basis.

> In this respect, biofeedback can be viewed as a powerful research tool, not in the sense of necessarily producing large magnitude changes, but rather as a means of gaining experimental manipulation over specific physiological processes so as to explore the nature of their relationships with other such processes and their association with specific environmental and behavioral conditions. It is this aspect of biofeedback that qualifies it as a general research method for studying problems relating biology and behavior. (Schwartz & Beatty, 1977, p. 2)

G. E. Schwartz's Disregulation Model

G. E. Schwartz is perhaps the best known proponent of a systems approach to explaining how biofeedback works. Starting with the assumption that feedback is the central component of all biobehavioral interventions (1978, p. 78), Schwartz has developed a "disregulation" model that involves five stages or components. The first stage includes environmental signals that, in turn, are processed by the central nervous system (Stage 2). The subsequent, somatic response by one or more peripheral organs constitutes Stage 3. Internal feedback loops (Stage 4) carry information from the periphery back to the brain, thus "teaching" the body to respond effectively. Stage 5, biofeedback, augments natural feedback by generating signals that become part of the environmental input (Stage 1). A schematic diagram of the disregulation model is presented in Figure 7 (Compare this diagram with that presented in Figure 6)

Problems can arise at any point in the process. For example, stimuli from the external environment (Stage 1) can be so demanding that the central nervous system is forced to ignore corrective feedback from the peripheral organs. This is what happens when our body tells us to slow down, but we do not because of the pressures at work. Continued

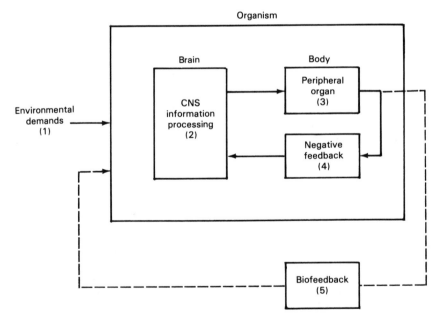

Figure 7. Diagram of the disregulation model. From Psychobiological Foundations of Psychotherapy and Behavior Change," in S. L. Garfield & A. E. Bergin (Eds.), *Handbook of Psychotherapy and Behavior Change* (2nd ed., p. 75) by G. E. Schwartz, 1978, New York: Wiley. Copyright by John Wiley and Sons, 1978. Reprinted by permission.

exposure to stressful environments may lead to the deterioration of the peripheral organ's ability to respond appropriately and thus lead to physical problems, a process similar to that described as the "general adaptation syndrome" by Selye and others (Mason, 1975; Selye, 1956, 1974).

On the other hand, the central nervous system itself (Stage 2) can be predisposed by genetic influence or prior learning to misread or distort external signals and thus cause maladaptive responding in benign or supportive environments. An example of this might be Seligman's (1974, 1975) concept of "learned helplessness." He has hypothesized that previous experience may teach an individual that there is no relationship between one's response and the consequences to that response. As a result, the individual is likely to fail to respond appropriately, even when reinforcers for the adaptive behavior exist.

Problems at the third stage may involve peripheral organs that are hyper- or hyporesponsive to stimuli that are correctly perceived. This is essentially the "weak organ" hypothesis or the concept of "individual response specificity" that appears frequently in the psychosomatic literature (e.g., Lipowski, 1977). Paul Obrist and his associates (Obrist, 1981) have demonstrated that subjects who respond with excessive cardiovascular reactivity in the laboratory are more likely to have hypertensive parents and, it is thought, are more likely to develop high blood pressure themselves than subjects evidencing less reactivity when exposed to the same stimulus conditions. (For a review of this area, see Krantz & Manuck, 1984).

And finally, internal feedback (Stage 4) itself can become "disregulated." This may occur, although Schwartz does not state it in this manner, when systems with different feedback gain find themselves in competition (see Chapter 2). For example, the renin–angiotensin system, a major regulatory component of cardiovascular control, is designed to increase blood pressure by conserving sodium and retaining fluid. Its feedback gain is very high, possibly because of its survival value in maintaining fluid balances and keeping blood pressure from dropping too low. Systems designed to counter increases in blood pressure, on the other hand, display a weaker feedback gain and may be sacrificed as a result. For example, the baroreceptors, which buffer transient increases in blood pressure, adapt over a period of days when blood pressure is elevated by the renin–angiotensin system. This appears to be because the harmful consequences of high blood pressure (e.g., renal damage or stroke) are much less immediate than those associated with low blood pressure (e.g., circulatory collapse).

Biofeedback (Stage 5) is seen as helping resolve problems arising in the other stages by augmenting natural regulation with an *external* source of feedback. It is proposed that the additional information may help achieve physiological stability in two ways. First, it may assist in the diagnosis of organ damage or system dysfunction, thus emphasizing the need for environmental change and other corrective action. This type of intervention is indirect because it manipulates contributory factors rather than affecting the damaged tissue directly. Second, biofeedback may exert its effect by helping the client learn to control his or her physiological responses directly. In this case, biofeedback is seen as attempting to capitalize on the body's natural ability to self-regulate by adding conscious involvement to this ordinarily automatic process.

Mechanisms of Control

Even with the development of conceptual aids such as G. E. Schwartz's disregulation model, no one really knows how or why biofeedback works, for even when biofeedback is successful, it is still very difficult to identify its "active ingredient." For example, Andrasik and his colleagues (Andrasik, Blanchard, Edlund, & Attanasio, 1983) report the successful use of EMG biofeedback with an 11-year-old child in the treatment of tension headache. At the end of a 1-year follow-up there was a 79% reduction in headache intensity and 75% reduction in frequency. This finding suggests clearly that the child's headaches had been controlled using biofeedback. Nevertheless, other investigators working with childhood headache have reported similar results using many different interventions, including thermal biofeedback, autogenic training, dietary management, relaxation training, EMG biofeedback, client-centered therapy, self-hypnosis, and guided imagery (Andrasik, Blanchard, Edlund, & Rosenblum, 1982; Diamond & Franklin, 1975; Houts, 1982; Labbé & Williamson, 1983; Sallade, 1980; Werder & Sargent, 1984). What these diverse procedures have in common is unclear.

This question essentially has two answers. For one, there may be a single mode of action that is shared by the different interventions. On the other hand, there may be different mechanisms for each treatment capable of producing the same result. (Recalling the discussion of systems in Chapter 2, it is noted that a single outcome may result from a number of different causes.) Because there is no simple answer, both perspectives probably contribute to the overall understanding of how we can control our internal selves.

Shared Mechanisms

One of the more obvious mechanisms common to different therapies is a nonspecific (i.e., placebo) effect. Although the nature of their action is uncertain, placebos may work in many ways, such as through the mobilization of hope or the alleviation of fear (A. K. Shapiro & Morris, 1978). Because "nonspecific," in this sense, means "unknown," placebos are too unpredictable to use systematically. Also, in that their effects are usually general rather than specific (e.g., the mobilization of hope), results obtained by their action are usually short-lived because little may be done to change the situation creating the problem in the first place. Thus, whereas biofeedback and other strategies may exert a strong placebo effect, this treatment mechanism by itself tells us little about how these procedures work.

A second mechanism common to most therapies is the mobilization of one's resources. This type of intervention falls under the rubric of "self-control" and involves steps to modify one's environment for behavior change (M. R. Goldfried & Merbaum, 1973; Thoresen & Mahoney, 1974). Biofeedback and related procedures are thought to contribute to self-control by helping identify target responses and situations in which problematic responding occurs (Bakal, 1979, p. 234; G. D. Fuller, 1978; R. S. Lazarus, 1975). This awareness, with the support and often active direction of the therapist, may be translated (often unknowingly) into attempts to alter stimuli (environmental planning) and establish contingencies conducive to change (behavioral programming).

The importance of self-control is highlighted in an excellent study by Holroyd, Andrasik, and Noble (1980) that was designed to control for placebo effects. The authors compared EMG biofeedback (frontalis) with a "credible pseudotherapy." The latter consisted of a pseudomeditation procedure. Subjects were trained to use an actual meditation technique but were instructed not to relax "since relaxation would interfere with proper meditation" (p. 33). Readings of frontalis EMG activity indicated that the biofeedback group exhibited reduced electromyographic activity following treatment, whereas the pseudotherapy group did not. Although both treatments were rated as equally credible, headache activity for only the biofeedback group improved significantly following treatment. However, there was not a relationship between changes in frontalis EMG activity and headache improvement. An earlier study in which EMG feedback from an irrelevant muscle group (forearm flexor) was used as a control condition (Holroyd & Andrasik, 1978) yielded similar results. The authors concluded that

it is less crucial that headache sufferers learn to directly modify EMG activity
than it is that they learn to monitor the insidious onset of headache symptoms and engage in some sort of coping response incompatible with the
further exacerbation of symptoms. (Holroyd et al., 1980, p. 38)

Thus two studies that controlled nicely for nonspecific effects highlight
the role of self-control as the central mechanism for therapeutic change
(cf. M. R. Goldfried, 1980a; Holroyd, 1979).

Mediational Mechanisms

We have considered how a mechanism(s) shared by different
therapies might obtain a common outcome. On the other hand, it is
possible that the same outcome can be achieved in several different
ways (i.e., by several different mechanisms). This is because there is a
domino effect whenever a single variable in a system is manipulated. In
this situation, the effector response is said to "mediate" changes observed in other response systems. Applied to the somatic therapies, this
view suggests that control of the target response may be caused (i.e.,
mediated) in any number of different ways.

The question of mediational control is particularly important when
considering the ability of human beings to exert voluntary control over
responses that were thought to be involuntary. This was illustrated
clearly when M. A. Wenger and Bagchi (1961) obtained polygraph recordings from yogis performing various feats of visceral control. It was
found that their regulation of visceral activity was achieved by manipulating voluntary muscular responses, such as by holding their breath
and increasing muscular tension in the abdomen and thorax, rather than
exerting direct control over the visceral organs themselves.

Another example involves the use of biofeedback training for brain
wave activity. Alpha rhythms are one of four basic patterns of electroencephalographic (EEG) activity ranging in frequency from 8 to 13 Hz
(Blanchard & Epstein, 1978). These rhythms have been associated with a
state of relaxed wakefulness, especially with one's eyes closed. In 1968,
Kamiya wrote an article in *Psychology Today* that attracted widespread
interest. He reported that subjects could be trained to discriminate between alpha and nonalpha activity and that they could learn, with training, to control this response. In that the "alpha state" was reported to
engender feelings of tranquility and calm alertness, it was speculated
that alpha biofeedback might allow subjects to achieve a state similar to
that experienced by the Zen masters of meditation (Nowlis & Kamiya,
1970; B. B. Brown, 1970, 1971).

Questions arose, however, as to how the manipulation of alpha activity was achieved. A series of careful studies suggested that the control of eye movements (particularly with the eyes closed), was responsible for the voluntary generation of alpha rhythms (Mulholland & Peper, 1971; Plotkin, 1976). This explanation (the occulomotor hypothesis) was at odds with the cognitive explanation that held that one could learn to induce a calm, passive state of mind by manipulating brain wave activity directly (Blanchard & Epstein, 1978, p. 131). Although arguments over mediational events have continued unabated (DiCara & Miller, 1968a, 1968b; Katkin & Murray, 1968; H. D. Kimmel, 1967, 1974; S. Miller & Konorski, 1928), it does appear that mediational control does play a significant role in many if not most demonstrations of voluntary control of autonomic responses.

An Example of Mediational Control

One area closely tied to biofeedback for which mediational control is of primary importance is relaxation. The relaxation response has been championed most ably by Benson (1975) who proposes that any number of relaxation-based procedures can achieve the same physiologically beneficial state. These include various forms of meditation as well as biofeedback-assisted relaxation, autogenic training, hypnosis and deep-muscle relaxation (Benson, Beary, & Carol, 1974; Beary & Benson, 1974). Some of the responses said to be affected by the relaxation response include heart rate, electrodermal activity, blood pressure, regional blood flow, and oxygen (O_2) consumption. This new type of "equipotentiality premise" (see Chapter 4) appears to disregard differences between physiological systems or mechanisms by which regulation is said to occur.

Benson identifies four basic components of the relaxation response. The first is a constant stimulus, such as a sound, word, or phrase, that serves to minimize attention to external stimuli. In addition, a passive attitude free of distracting thoughts is considered to be important. Third, a comfortable posture is advocated so that muscular activity is held to a minimum. And finally, the technique should be performed in a quiet environment, free from distracting stimuli.

It can readily be seen that the four components encompass several different mechanisms by which therapeutic benefits might be obtained. For example, there is the obvious potential for a considerable placebo effect. In addition there is a cognitive element that involves attention focusing and keeping the mind free from distractions. However, there is also a somatic component that involves placing the body in a physically quiescent state.

What the body does somatically during relaxation is of considerable interest. For example, it is claimed that meditation can induce a hypometabolic state. In a 1970 article appearing in *Science*, Wallace reported the use of a noncultic meditative technique to decrease O_2 consumption by 20% as compared to the baseline (i.e., resting) condition. Further studies by this same group of investigators (Wallace, Benson, & Wilson, 1971; Beary & Benson, 1974) documented similar reductions of 17% and 13%, respectively. A major methodological problem for these studies, however, concerns the baseline levels against which O_2 consumption during relaxation is compared. If, for example, the baseline condition involves more motoric activity than during meditation, the differences in O_2 consumption can be explained in terms of a reduction of somatic demands entirely (cf. Fenwick *et al.*, 1977; Warrenburg, Pagano, Woods, & Hlastala, 1980).

In the past, we have used a standard meditative procedure (autogenic training) in an attempt to decrease metabolic activity beyond that obtained when the subjects were resting comfortably (Hollandsworth, Gintner, Ellender, & Rectanus, 1984). (Autogenic training is a cognitive technique [G. E. Schwartz, Davidson, & Goleman, 1978] specifically identified by Benson [1975] as capable of inducing a relaxation response.) Although the same controlled, within-subjects, crossover design employed by Beary and Benson (1974) was used, we were unable to demonstrate a significant reduction in O_2 consumption (only 3%).

One explanation for the failure to support the earlier findings is that the relaxation procedure was not effective. However, the subjects reported both during and after the procedure that they were able to achieve levels of relaxation equivalent to those obtained at home during their practice sessions. (Three subjects who failed to report this were dropped from the study.) In addition, the training itself was more extensive than that of Beary and Benson (1974) and included live induction of relaxation during training as well as during the experiment itself. Further, daily training diaries and a postexperimental anonymous check verified that the subjects had practiced the procedure as instructed.

A second explanation for the nonsignificant findings concerns the control condition against which O_2 consumption during relaxation was compared. In the early stages of the study, we employed Beary and Benson's control, which consisted of reading a book. Using this procedure with two pilot subjects, we were able to obtain reductions of 8% and 17% in O_2 consumption during relaxation. However, while observing the subjects during the control periods, we noted much more motor activity than was expected. For example, one of the subjects with eyeglasses had difficulty reading while wearing the face mask used to monitor O_2 consumption. (Beary and Benson used an identical mask in their study.) Consequently, we modified the baseline condition to control for motor responses by projecting emotionally neutral slides on the wall in front of the subject. Subjects determined which slide he or she viewed and the rate at which this occurred by use of a remote-control switch beneath the right hand. This modification reduced the amount of somatic involvement during the resting baseline considerably. It also apparently resulted in a failure to demonstrate significant reductions in O_2 consumption, a finding, incidentally, shared by other investigators (Fenwick *et al.*, 1977; Warrenburg *et al.*, 1980).

Although a failure to find significance is not evidence for the alternative hypothesis, it does seem appropriate to question whether meditation alone (i.e., cognitive control) is capable of inducing the physiologically therapeutic results claimed. What effects that do occur may be the result of placing the body in a quiet, somatically quiescent state. If the latter is true, then any number of "time-out" or other rest-inducing strategies might be employed effectively without recourse to the more complex meditative procedures. Although this conclusion is strongly endorsed by some (e.g., Holmes, 1984) and vigorously contested by others (e.g., Benson, personal communication, March 29, 1985; see Pallak, 1985, for an extended debate on this issue; see also Morrell, in press), the important contribution of mediational (i.e., noncognitive) mechanisms to the regulation of internal states cannot be ignored.

Physiological Limits

The excitement that accompanied biofeedback's early successes appears to have obscured the issue of how these results were obtained. The possibility that many of biofeedback's effects are either indirect or mediational in nature either was not addressed or was discounted. For example, it was argued that the question of how a particular strategy works is less important than whether it works.

> A clinician may not be concerned with obtaining a "pure," unmediated control effect, but only in producing a large, long-lasting effect that will transfer outside the laboratory setting. Thus, for a given patient who must learn to stabilize his [or her] heart rate, if it were found that muscle relaxation and breath control produced the greatest and most rapid stabilization of heart rate, these methods would be utilized. (Gatchel & Price, 1979, p. 10)

In fact, biofeedback is often used with little regard for the multiple pathways by which its effects might occur. Consequently, these techniques have tended to assume a kind of functional autonomy that may actually interfere with treatment by diverting attention from more parsimonious (and less expensive) strategies for achieving equivalent results (cf. King & Montgomery, 1980; Turk, Meichenbaum, & Berman, 1979). If, for example, muscle relaxation and breath control are the most effective methods for gaining control over cardiac arrythmias, these methods should be taught directly. Heart rate feedback might prove a useful adjunct to this training, allowing the patient to judge his or her progress. However, biofeedback *per se* would not be the focus of treatment, and the expectation that the patient was controlling his or her heart rate directly (i.e., cognitively) would be avoided.

A disregard for the mechanisms of action leads to an assumption that almost any response is a likely candidate for biofeedback training. Consequently, there has been a rush to apply the new technology to many systems, including brain waves, skin conductance, and blood pressure, with little appreciation for anatomical and neurological differences between responses. For example, although investigators quickly realized that it was much easier to train subjects to increase heart rate than it was to decrease it, the physiological reasons for this were not examined. This suggests a lack of appreciation for the physiological realities that limit voluntary control of internal events.

Interoceptive Awareness

One such limitation concerns our ability for interoceptive awareness. This limitation is of some importance, for although biofeedback may augment natural feedback loops, it is clear that the new technology cannot replace them. For example, if biofeedback is to be of clinical value, its effects must generalize to situations outside the training setting. This means that subjects must be able, at least to some degree, to detect without the aid of instruments the response being amplified and fed back by the equipment. Further, the subject must be able with training to improve his or her ability to discriminate these naturally occurring signals. It is this "calibration" of the subject's normal, afferent signals with those provided by the equipment that provides a rationale for the use of biofeedback for therapeutic purposes (Brener, 1974).

Monitoring physiological events naturally involves two types of receptors—proprioceptive and visceral. As was discussed in Chapter 3, proprioceptive sensors detect signals arising from the muscles, tendons, and joints and are thus a central part of the musculoskeletal system (i.e., the motoric mode). Visceral sensors, on the other hand, detect signals arising from the soft, interior organs of the body, including the lungs, heart, stomach, and intestines, and are thus an important component of the autonomic nervous system (i.e., the autonomic mode). Together, both types of afferent fibers provide a basis for interoceptive sensation (refer to Figure 6, p. 57).

Exteroceptive sensation, on the other hand, refers to afferent pathways that respond to and convey stimulus information arising from the external environment. These receptors include the special sense organs, such as the nose, eyes, and ears as well as receptors in the skin that detect physical stimuli, such as changes in temperature, pain, or pressure. Biofeedback, as noted before, seeks to augment interoceptive responses by pairing them with signals transmitted via exteroceptive pathways.

The fact that human beings have interoceptive sensors does not mean, however, that they can monitor internal events whenever they desire. As illustrated in the discussion of voluntary-but-unconscious control, there is much that goes on in our bodies of which we are not aware. Internal regulatory systems on many levels enjoy a full complement of sensory, integrative, and motor components, yet they may operate outside our awareness. For example, the kidneys are richly supplied with both afferent and efferent fibers linking each to the brain. There is evidence to suggest, however, that these pathways are designed to initiate compensatory changes in one kidney following a change in function of the contralateral organ (Gottschalk, 1979) rather than to allow individuals to monitor this process consciously (cf. Katkin, 1985).

There are several reasons for the limitations to our internal awareness. First, it is known that a relatively small area of the cortex is devoted to analyzing visceral functions (Chernigovskiy, 1967). In addition, as was mentioned in Chapter 1, signals from the viscera must share afferent pathways with other sensory systems. And finally, afferent pathways from the visceral organs travel to the brain via two different transmission systems that further cloud our awareness.

It will be recalled from Chapter 3 that the dorsal column pathway is relatively fast (35 to 80 meters per second) and sends very discrete signals because of its heavily myelinated fibers. In addition, It has few synapses in the brain stem and sends its signals directly to conscious portions of the cortex. The second system, the spinothalamic pathway, is slower (1 to 30 meters per second) and sends diffuse signals because there is much cross-talk between its unmyelinated fibers. In addition, there are many termination points for this system in the brain stem (the pons and medulla) and midbrain (Guyton, 1981).

The dorsal system transmits messages requiring a high degree of localization and fine gradations of intensity. These signals include not only sensations of touch but viratory sensations, position sensations, and pressure sensations requiring fine degrees of judgment. Many signals arising from exteroceptive and proprioceptive receptors are carried via this pathway. The spinothalamic system, on the other hand, is able to transmit broad-spectrum senses only, such as pain, warmth, cold, crude pressure, and tactile messages as well as sexual, tickle, and itch sensations. These types of signals may arise from visceral receptors and, at times, from the exteroceptive and proprioceptive sensors as well.

Transmission of the special senses, on the other hand, is direct and uncontaminated by inputs from other sources. In addition, large areas of cortex are set aside for detecting and interpreting signals from these sensory organs. Also, unlike the transmission of somatic sensations, there is little cross-talk and few synapses from the point of reception to the primary sensory areas in the brain. All of this means that the special senses are capable of swift communication of high resolution that allows for extremely fine sensory discriminations.

The sensory capabilities of the exteroceptive (i.e., those from the surface of the body) and proprioceptive sensors lie somewhere between those of the visceral and special senses. Both of the former send signals of which we are consciously aware. However, each differs in terms of the fidelity and resolution with which the signals are transmitted. Exteroceptive sensation, such as occurs when picking up an object with one's hand, is capable of fine tactile discriminations. This is because a large area of cerebral cortex is devoted to the task of detecting sensations of touch. Proprioceptive sensation, on the other hand, is capable of sensory discriminations that are much less precise and are more poorly localized.

It can be seen, therefore, that awareness varies greatly across organ systems as well as across sensory modalities. Some sensory systems are well innervated, enjoy direct lines of communication, and have adequate cortical areas in the brain to interpret the incoming information. Others are less well innervated, share their sensory pathways with other systems, and have little if any cortex assigned to the process of reading their input. In addition, different types of signals arising from the same sensory system may be handled differently, depending on the nature of the message being transmitted (i.e., pain versus touch). In short, interoceptive awareness is a matter of degree.

One might conceptualize interoceptive awareness as falling along a continuum with responses of which we are totally unaware, such as the regulation of renal blood flow, at one end and responses of which we are clearly aware, such as vision or hearing, at the other. In between, there is a range of signals and systems capable of varying degrees of awareness. Blood pressure, for example is consciously perceived only rarely, although the afferents and CNS mechanisms charged with its regulation are abundant. On the other hand, exteroceptive sensation from the fingertips is clearly perceived. Sensations originating from the fingertips or lips, in turn, differ markedly in terms of their gradation and localization with exteroceptive sensation arising from the surface of one's back. Visceral pain, on the other hand, is a clearly conscious phenomenon, although it is poorly localized. Signals from the muscles, joints, and tendons fall somewhere in the middle of this continuum.

Voluntary Control

The implications of this in terms of voluntary control of internal organs using biofeedback are obvious. Physiological systems capable of higher levels of interoceptive sensation should lend themselves most readily to biofeedback training. Those for which natural feedback is more difficult to obtain should prove resistant to interventions based on biofeedback. Reviews of the literature on biofeedback suggest that this is the case (Blanchard & Epstein, 1979; Gatchel & Price, 1979; Shapiro & Surwit, 1979). For example, EMG biofeedback training of specific muscle groups, the prototypic biofeedback model, continues after 20 years to yield useful results, such as with muscle reeducation in rehabilitation settings (Basmajian & Hatch, 1979). On the other hand, the modification of visceral responses, such as blood pressure, using biofeedback has met with much less success (Blanchard, 1979; Carroll, 1977). In short, the idea of a sensory gradient explains why "not all physiological systems are equally responsive to biofeedback intervention" (G. E. Schwartz & Beatty, 1977, p. 3).

To put it in other words, just as awareness may fall along a gradient, our ability to exert voluntary control over our body's physiological processes also appears to vary in degree. At one end of the continuum are responses that we are able to direct voluntarily and that are characterized by flexible adaptability. On the other end of the continuum are responses that are reflexive in nature and essentially programmed or fixed in their pattern of action (see Chapter 4).

Described in terms of the triple modes, this continuum moves from the cognitive to the motoric and then to the autonomic mode with the greatest flexibility and volition on the cognitive end. More specifically, messages that initiate a voluntary (i.e., cognitive) act are transmitted from the brain to the appropriate effector system(s). Some effectors are controlled directly, as in the case of the musculoskeletal system. This is because, as discussed earlier, adequate or even superior interoceptive pathways exist, and large portions of the cerebral cortex are assigned to the process of directing responses concerned with locomotion in one's environment.

The ability of the cognitive mode to impose control over the autonomic system is less clear for similar reasons. Again, the afferent fibers from the viscera are less abundant and evidence lower resolution, whereas, in addition, relatively small portions of the cortex are assigned to the task of interpreting these signals or controlling these organs. As a result, much of the cognitive control of autonomic responses appears to be mediated by the motor system. This is because there are numerous local regulatory systems at the segmental and local level that tie autonomic responses to motoric demands (Astrand & Rodahl, 1970). In other words, the autonomic nervous system is primarily in the service of motor behavior, which in turn is directed to a large degree by responses originating from the cognitive mode (Lang, Levin, Miller, & Kozak, 1983).

Not all visceral activity is tied directly to motor responses, however. It is believed that there are some efferent pathways from the higher regions of the brain that would enable a degree of cognitive control over autonomic responses, such as in the fight–flight response when collateral signals are sent to the visceral organs at the same time the motor system is activated (Guyton, 1981). However, these commands affect visceral function only for short periods of time with durable changes in autonomic activity occurring as a result of the ongoing requirements of the musculoskeletal system.

In addition, this hierarchy is not absolute. There are counterinfluences originating from the systems that are being controlled. For example, the autonomic system determines what the motor system can perform. A weakened cardiovascular system or depleted energy stores will determine to what degree the musculoskeletal system will be able to carry out commands originating in the cortex. Or, conversely, enhanced autonomic responding may facilitate the performance of some motor tasks (Oxendine, 1970). This influence reaches even to the cognitive mode when autonomic influences increase alertness and help focus attention (Duffy, 1972; Landers, 1979). On the other hand, disregulation of the autonomic nervous system disrupts cognitive activity, such as occurs when pain interferes with one's concentration.

The motoric mode also determines to some extent what the cognitive mode is capable of directing. The best intentions for performance can be inhibited by insufficient motor skills. Patterns of rapid motor responses appear to be established within the motor system itself and probably depend on a complex circuitry involving the primary motor cortex, the motor association cortex, the basal ganglia, and the cerebellum (Guyton, 1981, p. 668; also see Chapter 3). If these responses have to be controlled consciously, they will be performed much more slowly. Repeated performance allows for the integration of patterns within the motor system, which is why the practice component of social skills training is so important (cf. Hollandsworth & Sandifer, 1979). Although the cognitive mode may play an important role in organizing behavior in the early stages of learning (Meichenbaum, 1977a), the absence of established patterns of skilled motor performance will severely limit what a person can do, regardless of his or her best intentions.

Clinical Implications

Given this understanding of the limits to voluntary control, the clinician is interested essentially in two things. First, what can be controlled voluntarily that is not being controlled? Second, what is preventing volitional control from occurring? The former concerns the client's "instrumental" responses that are important for modifying the environment, internal or external. The latter takes into account restraints imposed by the client's state of health and behavioral repertoire as well as the realities of his or her biological makeup.

A clinical example of this can be found in a single-case study of a young man with extreme anxiety and deficient verbal skills in the job-interview setting (Hollandsworth, Glazeski, & Dressel, 1978). The treatment goal was to provide instrumental skills while counteracting the disruptive influence of anxiety at the same time. Consequently, one objective was to provide the client with the ability to answer questions in a concise and focused manner. An important part of this process was providing him with a cognitive, "stop-think-speak" strategy. This illustrates attending to the more flexible, voluntary end of the continuum. On the other hand, the more reflexive, programmed end was dealt with through the use of models, shaping, and practice through which his anxiety over the interview process was desensitized. Thus, both types of control over the client's behavior—voluntary and permissive—were taken into account and planned for systematically.

Summary

The chapter began with the assertion that biofeedback had expanded the possibilities for voluntary control of our behavior while reminding us of our limitations at the same time. The reasons why this might be true were discussed with particular attention to the limitations imposed by the automaticity of physiological regulation. Although mediational control and self-management skills may extend the ability of human beings to regulate bodily functions, it was concluded that the clinician must consider not only what he or she can encourage the client to try but also what must be remedied in order for these efforts to be successful. The interaction of person, behavior, and environment provides a basis for understanding why we do what we do. This approach will be used in an attempt to deal with one of the most difficult of all psychological constructs—emotion—in the next chapter.

Recommended Reading

Blanchard, E. B., & Epstein, L. H. (1978). *A biofeedback primer*. Reading, MA: Addison-Wesley.

There is no shortage of books on biofeedback, but few are as even-handed as this review. Although dated in terms of the literature, it remains one of the more responsible introductions to the area. Its empirical orientation has insured that the conclusions and recommendations of 1978 have a currency today that many other pronouncements of that time do not share.

CHAPTER 7

Emotion

It would seem surprising that something as familiar as human emotion is such a difficult construct to define. We experience it almost every day; it is as common to our lives as bread and butter. Yet, deciding just what it is, why we feel it, and how one deals with it are issues still far from being resolved.

The American College Dictionary defines emotion as "an affective state of consciousness in which joy, sorrow, fear, hate, or the like is experienced (distinguished from cognitive and volitional states of consciousness)" (1958, p. 393). The term *affective* does not help much because its definition ("emotional," p. 21) reveals it to be a synonym. Emotion, therefore, is defined as something consciously experienced, somehow different from cognition, and involuntary.

Historically, what we think of as emotion today was called "passion." This term emphasizes the involuntary aspect of emotion and distinguishes it from purposeful actions. "An action is something a person does deliberately. A passion, in the generic sense of the term, is something a person suffers" (Averill, 1982, p. 13). As such, many persons of different backgrounds have shown an interest in emotion, particularly painters, writers, and actors. For example, Darwin (1872/1979), in his classic work entitled *The Expression of Emotions in Man and Animals,* reviewed a number of treatises on emotion dating back to the 17th century, most of which approached the subject from an artistic (i.e., expressive) point of view.

The range of emotions studied over the years is extensive and includes anger, fear, grief, jealousy, love, envy, hope, joy, and many more. Averill (1975) has listed over 500 terms in the English language that relate more or less directly to emotional states. Generally, these emotions can be classified into three categories—impulsive emotions such as grief, joy, and hope; conflictive emotions such as anger; and transcendental emotions that include disorganized anxiety states and mystical experiences (Averill, 1982).

Traditionally, psychological formulations of emotion have thought of it as a unique process resulting in "a distinct class of behavior" (Bindra, 1970, p. 14). Thus, emotion may be conceptualized as the "feeling" of bodily changes (W. James, 1884), a set of visceral reactions (M. A. Wenger, 1950), the thalamic release of cortical inhibition (Cannon, 1927), an "emotional attitude" resulting in "emotional expression" (Arnold, 1950), increased activity of the reticular activating system (RAS; Lindsley, 1951), or neurological disturbances in the cerebrum (Hebb, 1949). This approach to emotion has been criticized, however, because it is doubtful that a single process can account for the wide variety of affective states. In addition, it is difficult to think of emotional responses that are truly independent from other behaviors (cf. Duffy, 1941, 1948).

A second approach to emotion conceptualizes it as an intervening variable, a drive state (McDougall, 1908). From this perspective, emotion is seen as serving to goad organisms into action. J. S. Brown and Farber (1951) suggest that emotion can be used in this manner within the framework of Hull's (1943) drive theory. The problem with this approach, however, is that emotion does not require intentionality. Unlike hunger or thirst, emotion often may not have a specific goal (Averill, 1982). For example, one can be angry without being angry *at* anyone or anything. Further, it is important to distinguish between emotion as a description rather than an explanation of behavior. Skinner (1953) has argued:

> The names of the so-called emotions serve to classify behavior with respect to various circumstances which affect its probability. The safest practice is to hold to the adjectival form. Just as the hungry organism can be accounted for without too much difficulty, although "hunger" is another matter, so by describing behavior as fearful, affectionate, timid, and so on, we are not led to look for *things* called emotions. (p. 162)

For various reasons both the unique process and intervening variable approaches to emotion appear to have been supplanted more recently by a perspective that views emotion as an emergent pattern of existing parts (Averill, 1983; Bindra, 1970; Izard, 1977; Reisenzein, 1983). This approach emphasizes the multidimensional nature of emotion and views it as an "organic mix of action impulses and bodily expressions, diverse positive or dysphoric (subjective) cognitive-affective states, and physiological disturbances" (R. S. Lazarus, 1984, p. 125).

The Triple Modes of Emotion

The usefulness of describing emotions in terms of the triple modes of responding presented in Chapter 5 is apparent. The subjective experience of emotion falls under the cognitive mode, whereas the physiological arousal component refers to the autonomic mode. In terms of the motoric mode, it appears there are two components. One, instrumental behavior, encompasses voluntary responses of the musculoskeletal system. The other, expressive reactions, appears to reflect the more reflexive (i.e., programmed) aspect of the motoric mode.

The fit between the triple modes and emotion will come as no surprise because the triple modes grew out of the study of a particular type of emotion—fear. The early studies of fear, in turn, led to its application to emotions more generally.

> In human subjects, emotional behavior includes responses in three expressive systems: verbal, gross motor, and physiological (autonomic, cortical, neuromuscular). The responses of no single system seem to define or encompass an "emotion" completely. Verbal statements of hostility are obtained from subjects who show no tendency to overt attack. Individuals may report no fear of objects they have systematically avoided for a lifetime. Subjects in rage show elevated blood pressure, but the same reading can be caused by kidney failure or exercise. The clinical examples are legion, and the laboratory is yielding similar evidence of low correlations between systems, even when the subject population and the emotional stimuli are quite homogenous. (Lang, Rice, & Sternbach, 1972, pp. 624–625)

In spite of the effort to identify stable patterns of physiological responses characteristic of different emotional states such as anger and fear (Ax, 1953; Lacey, 1967), "the overall impression from a review of the literature is that the systems do not covary, and especially not in clinically significant emotions" (Hugdahl, 1981, p. 76). Hodgson and Rachman (1974) have suggested several reasons for this. For one, the intensity of the emotional arousal may be an important factor. At the extremes (e.g., terror or serenity), a high degree of synchrony across systems can be expected. Yet clinicians seldom see clients who operate at the extremes. (Even the most fearful client is not terrified all of the time.) In addition, the demand characteristics of the situation may play a role, so that a calm demeanor may belie internal turmoil. Also, the type of emotion being assessed is likely to make a difference. For example, verbal reports of subjective states can be expected to be more sensitive to demand characteristics than autonomic reactivity. And finally, different components of the same mode may respond differently to the same stimulus. Thus, a measure of skin-conductance "often displays wayward tendencies" when compared to heart rate, suggesting "the influence of factors other than fear" (Hodgson & Rachman, 1974, p. 323). That is one reason why electrodermal measures have been used so consistently as the best predictor of deception in lie detection (Bradley & Janisse, 1981; Dawson, 1980; Podlesny & Raskin, 1977, 1978; Waid, Orne, Cook, & Orne, 1978).

Levels of Analysis

The variation of responses both across and within modes emphasizes the complexity of emotion. To deal with this complexity, Averill (1982) proposes that one must consider three levels of analysis—biological, psychological, and sociocultural. Each refers to a subset of systems affecting emotional responses. The biological level, for example, includes physiological principles that have their origins in the evolution of the species and whose basis is genetic. Principles at the psychological level, on the other hand, are the product of individual experience or learning, whereas the sociocultural level involves institutional principles whose basis is in the history of the society. Averill argues that taking all three levels into account is necessary for understanding emotion completely.

Investigators of emotion have frequently chosen to work primarily on one level at a time, often neglecting the others, just as health-care providers often focus on one of the three modes while ignoring the other two. For example, at various times, the study of emotion has emphasized either its physiologic (Dewey, 1896; W. James, 1890), behavioral (Tolman, 1923; Watson, 1924), or cognitive (Arnold, 1960; R. S. Lazarus, 1966; Schachter, 1966) basis.

The Biological (Physiological/Autonomic) Level

Darwin (1872/1979) was among the first to study emotion systematically. His interest in emotions was biological, for he believed they helped establish the evolutionary link between human beings and lower organisms. In fact, his study of emotion was initially planned as part of the broader work, *On the Origin of Species*, which appeared in 1859. However, his study of emotions, which involved the collection of data from around the world, grew too big to be included in the original book and was thus published some years later in 1872.

Drawing on similarities in the expression of emotions across cultures and across species, Darwin proposed that emotions have a basis in evolution. Astonishingly, his thoughts as to how emotions come to be associated with specific stimuli, such as people or things, anticipated Pavlov and classical conditioning by 30 years.

> From the foregoing remarks it seems probable that some actions, which at first performed consciously, have become through habit and association converted into reflex actions, and are now so firmly fixed and inherited, that they are performed even when not of the least use, as often as the same causes arise, which originally excited them in us through the volition. (Darwin, 1872/1979, p. 39)

The idea that many emotions, such as fear, are evolutionary "remnants" is still held today (e.g., Rachman, 1978) and gains indirect support from a number of studies that suggest that many forms of "emotional" behavior in laboratory animals are inherited (Bruell, 1970). MacLean's concept of a triune brain (1970), in which the limbic system plays a major role in affective responses, provides another biological model of emotion. A similar view is shared by Kety, who expresses it this way.

> It is thus compatible with the anatomical, physiological, pharmacological, and behavioral evidence to suggest the existence of an important neural system, parallel and complementary to the sensorimotor systems, but more sluggish, coarse, and diffuse, and closer to the primitive parts of the brain; one which evaluates experience and the outcome of action in terms of built-in or acquired survival value, which prompts vigilance, determines attention, and integrates adaptive, vegetative, and endocrine behavior, and which reinforces learning and colors recall. (1970, p. 69)

Although more cognitively oriented psychologists have criticized the approach as "neuroanatomical reductionism" (R. S. Lazarus, 1984) and have pointed to the futility of localizing emotion in any particular area of the brain (Sperry, 1982), other investigators continue to find the idea of the limbic system as an "emotional brain" a useful if not infallible heuristic aid (Izard, 1984; Konorski, 1967).

The James Theory. Viewing emotion on the biological level led to the first, explicit psychological theory of affective behavior. William James (1884) proposed that "reflex currents" initiate visceral reactions and overt muscular activity that, in turn, are interpreted by the cortex as the experience of emotion (Bindra, 1970). In other words, physiological reactions precede and, in fact, cause the experience of emotion.

The most telling criticisms of James's hypothesis came from the eminent physiologist Walter Cannon (1915) who felt that physiological activity is too diffuse to allow for the identification of different emotions. His studies led him to believe that there are only two broad patterns of autonomic discharge—one coordinated by the sympathetic and the other the parasympathetic branch of the autonomic nervous system (ANS). Cannon questioned whether ANS activity is fast enough or discrete enough to account for the range of experiences considered "emotional." Further, he noted that surgical separation of the ANS from the central nervous system does not alter emotional behavior and that the artificial induction of autonomic activity results in an "as-if" feeling dissimilar from an actual emotional state.

Cannon's criticisms are compelling. In the previous chapter, we considered the limitations to interoceptive awareness at length. In addition, one must take into account the diffuse nature of the reticular activating system (RAS) that plays a central role in mediating arousal. Lindsley (1970) notes that activation of the RAS affects all three modes. Consequently, an individual may experience worrisome thoughts and subjective distress cognitively; facial reactions, tension, and tremors motorically; and weeping, sweating, and other visceral activities autonomically at the same time. This means that many peripheral response systems are shared across emotions, making it difficult to tie a specific autonomic pattern to a specific emotion.

The Psychological (Cognitive) Level

One's personal experience and past learning history has particular relevance to those theories of emotion that emphasize the role of individual perception and cognitive labeling. These theories seek to explain emotion in terms of an interaction between physiologic (i.e., autonomic) and cognitive factors. Arousal *per se*, from this perspective, does not determine emotion (as James suggested) but contributes to that state only if it is perceived and labeled as "emotional."

Schachter's Theory. Perhaps the best known proponent of this approach is Schachter (1964, 1971). Agreeing with Cannon, Schachter views physiological arousal as emotionally nonspecific. Arousal provides an affective tone for an emotional experience. The meaning an individual attaches to this state determines the type of emotion experienced. This type of appraisal takes into account one's arousal as well as the situation in which it occurs. Thus, autonomic activation, according to Schachter's theory, determines intensity, whereas cognitive factors determine the content of an emotion.

Schachter sought to demonstrate this in his classic study with Singer in 1962. It will be remembered that the investigators administered a placebo (a subcutaneous injection of saline solution) to some subjects and epinephrine (a saline solution of epinephrine bitartrate) to others. The situational context was manipulated to provide an angry (i.e., insulting, demeaning) or euphoric (i.e., playful, silly) environment. It was found that the autonomically active agent (epinephrine) was necessary for an emotional reaction to occur, but that the situational context determined which emotion was experienced.

An interesting example of Schachter's theory is known as "medical student disease" (Mechanic, 1974), This syndrome, which is estimated to occur in 70% of all medical students, involves experiencing a number of psychological and physiological complaints during medical school. The arousal component is said to arise from the realistic stresses of medical training. The cognitive component results from the material covered in lectures and medical texts.

Although Schachter's theory has been favored for a number of years, it is not without its critics. One problem has been replicating Schachter and Singer's (1962) classic study (Marshall & Zimbardo, 1979; Maslach, 1979). Another criticism is that Schachter's theory is too cognitive (e.g., Zillman, 1978). Reisenzein (1983) refers to Schachter's proposal as actually a "theory of subjective feeling" (p. 243) and faults it for failing to specify the nature of the relationship between the feeling and the resultant behavior. In addition, Reisenzein concluded that although feedback of autonomic activity can have an intensifying effect on an emotional state, there is no evidence that arousal *per se* is a necessary component. All of this is to say that Schachter's theory by itself seems insufficient to explain emotion and that factors other than cognitive appraisal must be taken into consideration (Averill, 1983).

The Sociocultural (Motoric) Level

Up to this point, we have looked at a possible biological basis to emotion, the potential cognitive contribution to this process, and the interaction between the two. The resultant model, however, is still incomplete, for emotions do not occur in isolation; they are not private events in spite of our best efforts to make them so. It can be argued that there is no such thing as an "authentic emotion" apart from the social norms and environmental contingencies that affect its expression (Averill, 1983).

The social contribution to affective behavior is well established in the experimental literature (e.g., Harlow & Harlow, 1970). Social psychologists have long been interested in emotion, often using anger and aggressive behavior as prototypic examples of the construct (e.g., Averill, 1982) and believe that emotion can be understood completely only in terms of its interaction with the environment (R. S. Lazarus, 1984).

It is very difficult to identify a specific emotion without knowledge of the context in which it occurs (Rachman, 1978). For example, Hugdahl (1981) has pointed out that a triple modes approach to emotion can lead to circular reasoning unless the situational cues are included in its definition. Because affective behavior varies across individuals as well as within individuals across situations (i.e., desynchrony), one can not define emotion in terms of a predictable pattern of responses. Therefore, the "emotionality" of one's response cannot be verified independently of the behavior itself or without inferring some unobservable, internal state. One way out of this dilemma is to analyze the situation in which the behavior occurs. For example, if the situation is rated by observers as having a high potential for inducing anger, one is more confident in stating that a particular response is an "angry" one. An example of this approach to defining affective states is found in the social skills literature when applied to differentiating assertive from aggressive responses (Hollandsworth, 1977, 1985b).

The social context is also seen as helping explain the lack of correspondence across modes. Some environments, for example, may favor the expression of emotions motorically, whereas others may punish this type of response (Averill, 1982). The expression of the motoric component of emotion will thus vary, depending on the situation. Hodgson and Rachman (1974) argue that a situation with high demand characteristics will contribute to desynchrony, such as when a fight or flight response is inhibited in the face of high levels of autonomic arousal and subjective distress. When this occurs, the consequences of an emotional state may have psychosomatic relevance, such as in the case of John Hunter presented in Chapter 1. Low levels of demand, however, allow for a greater synchrony between modes because each is free to follow its natural path.

The Zajonc–Lazarus Debate

In 1980, Zajonc offered a provocative view of emotion that differs sharply with the cognitive emphasis of Schachter's theory yet does not depend on the problem of interoceptive awareness inherent to James's position. Zajonc proposes that affect and cognition are relatively independent systems. Further, he argues that "affective reactions can occur without extensive perceptual and cognitive encoding, are made with greater confidence than cognitive judgments, and can be made sooner" (p. 151). Emotion and cognition, from this perspective, constitute two independent ways of processing information.

His view challenges the contemporary assumption that affect is "postcognitive" (i.e., objects must be "cognized" before they can be evaluated). In support of his position, Zajonc reviews an extensive literature that suggests that emotions are primary, basic, inescapable, irrevocable, often nonrational, and difficult to verbalize. In other words, emotion is characterized by numerous features uncharacteristic of cognition, at least of cognition in terms of its conscious, rational sense.

Agreeing with those who study emotion from a biological perspective, Zajonc feels that the separation between affect and cognition has a physiological basis. Citing the limbic system as a possible anatomical site for this process, Zajonc proposes that affect (emotion) evolved in the basic areas of the brain before we developed language and our present form of thinking. The instantaneous, reflexive nature of affective judgments is seen in contrast to a more deliberate, logical evaluation characteristic of cognitive information processing. This type of responding is seen as having a survival value in an evolutionary sense. With the development of higher structures, he suggests that the affective systems retained their autonomy, relinquishing exclusive control over behavior "slowly and grudgingly" (p. 170).

In summarizing his position, Zajonc makes the following observation:

> People do not get married or divorced, commit murder or suicide, or lay down their lives for freedom upon a detailed cognitive analysis of the pros and cons of their actions. If we stop to consider just how much variance in the course of our lives is controlled by cognitive processes and how much by affect, and how much the one and the other influence the important outcomes of our lives, we cannot but agree that affective phenomena deserve far more attention than they have received from cognitive psychologists and a closer cognitive scrutiny from social psychologists. (p. 172)

In a reasoned and detailed reply, Richard Lazarus (1982) argues that cognitive appraisal, "the way one interprets one's plight at any given moment" (p. 1019), is a prerequisite for any emotional response. Lazarus's view of cognition is similar to Schachter's and is characterized by the *subjective representation* of the world (Baldwin, 1969). Subjective representation involves evaluation, values, expectancies, and causal beliefs about the events perceived (Reisenzein, 1983). This view of cognition proposes

> that meanings for decision and action are built up from essentially meaningless stimulus display elements or bits and that systematic scanning of this display generates information. Thus, human cognition, like the operations of a computer, proceeds by serially receiving, registering, encoding, storing for short- or long-run, and retrieving meaningless bits—a transformation to meaning that is called "information processing." (R. S. Lazarus, 1982, p. 1020)

Lazarus argues that Zajonc is unnecessarily restrictive in his definition of cognition. Rather than being limited to reflective, rational processes of which we are aware, present-day cognitive psychology includes those processes that often proceed without awareness. Lazarus, however, does not assert the complete primacy of cognition. He acknowledges, for example, that human beings may be "instinctually" wired (cf. Hebb, 1946) to react to certain fears, such as of spiders, snakes, or strangeness, a concept in keeping with the preparedness hypothesis presented in Chapter 4. Further, although cognition is seen as a precondition for emotion, that does not imply that emotions, once elicited, do not affect cognitions. Nevertheless, Lazarus insists that cognition is a prerequisite for emotion, even when the emotional response is instantaneous and nonreflective (e.g., the "hot cognition" of Arnold [1960] and others.[1]) Lazarus (1982) extends the concept of cognitive appraisal to all mammals and includes "the types of process described by ethologists in which a fairly rigid, built-in response to stimulus arrays differentiates danger from no-danger" (p. 1023).

Zajonc (1984) countered by noting that Lazarus presents a "broadened definition of cognitive appraisal to include even the most primitive forms of sensory excitation, thus obliterating all distinction between cognition, sensation, and perception" (p. 117). For Zajonc, the use of the term *cognition* implies some form of transformation of past or present sensory input. For Zajonc, cognition requires some form of "mental work." Lazarus (1984), however, defends the broader meaning of cognition and questions the value of proposing two more or less independent subsystems when a cognitive theory of emotion provides a more parsimonious explanation of the construct.

What is Cognition?

Clearly, the basic issue is how one defines cognition. At the heart of the matter is whether one defines it in terms of a conscious, mediating event or an unconscious, automatic coupling of sensation to output. Thus, the problem is one of deciding what to include and what not to include. As S. E. Taylor (1983) put it:

> Indeed, cognitions are both the easiest and the hardest things to study empirically. They are easy because there are so many of them, and they are hard because it is so difficult to know which ones are important and when. (p. 1167)

---

[1]Interestingly enough, Arnold (1970) suggests that appraisal, upon which cognition depends, is integrated in the limbic cortex.

To start, one can question the value of equating cognition with all forms of information processing as some have done (e.g., Murray & Jacobson, 1978). As noted in several places earlier, information is processed at many levels throughout the body with only some of this activity construed reasonably as being "cognitive" in nature.

The notion that there are levels or types of information processing is not new (Erdelyi, 1974). Piaget, for example, wrote of three "types of knowledge" (Furth, 1969), which include innate know-how, the prototype of which is instinct, environmental data from the physical world, and logico-mathematical operations (i.e., reason). Cognition, therefore, can be viewed as encompassing several components.

One of cognition's major components involves physiological arousal that provides for the orienting response and a background level of alertness necessary before appraisal can occur (Mackworth, 1969). Directed primarily by the RAS, arousal depends on the current state of the organism, including factors such as fatigue, circadian rhythms, and medication as well as individual differences in terms of one's biological makeup. Further, the nature of the orienting response is both non-specific and specific. The limbic system and basal areas are responsible for the general background level of alertness, whereas the thalamic-neocortical feedback loops (see Chapter 3) create the attention-focusing aspects of arousal.

Once the organism is sufficiently alert to make an appraisal, information can be processed. There is evidence that even at this point there is more than one level of information processing. More specifically, it has been proposed that the initial stage in this process is "preconscious" (Dixon, 1971, 1981). At this level, environmental information is perceived, integrated, and evaluated outside awareness. This process has been described in several ways, such as "automatic processing" (E. R. Smith & Miller, 1978), "automatic encoding" (Hasher & Zacks, 1984), or "automatic detection" (Schneider & Shiffrin, 1977). Shevrin and Dickman (1980) likened the process to the filtering of signals in terms of basic (i.e., intensity and frequency) as well as more complex (i.e., importance) properties.

This stage of information-processing is automatic (Shevrin & Dickman, 1980), as demonstrated by its failure to be influenced by several variables, such as training, individual ability, and motivation, which are known to affect more conscious cognitive processing (Glass, Holyoak, & Santa, 1979; Kausler, 1982). It is suspected that many of these unconscious decision-making routines are innate (i.e., programmed) so that many unwanted stimuli are "tuned out," leaving the conscious brain free to operate on more complex tasks. One might draw the analogy to "front-end processors" for large computers that deal with a variety of input before sending it along in modified and condensed form to the central core for processing.

As might be expected, this type of information processing is different from what we usually consider cognition. Broadbent (1977) characterizes this stage as a passive process that analyzes input globally and compares it to a second stage that is more active and detailed in its search for information. The latter stage is more similar to the usual meaning of cognition. Schneider and Shiffrin (1977) propose a similar view that involves both "automatic detection" and "controlled search." The former is a learned sequence of elements stored in long-term memory that is prompted by appropriate inputs and proceeds automatically once invoked. This type of processing does not stress the capacity of the information-processing systems because it is basically a programmed activity. The controlled search component, however, involves the temporary activation of parts of the brain (such as the prefrontal area), requires conscious control, and displays a limited capacity for processing information (G. A. Miller, 1956; E. R. Smith & Miller, 1978).

Hasher & Zacks (1984) also propose that human beings are designed for the automatic encoding of certain basic types of data originating in the environment. It is argued that the automaticity of this process is needed given the limits of an individual's momentary capacity for cognitive activity (e.g., Kahnerman, 1973). Evidence for the automatic, preconscious processing of information is supported by studies that demonstrate the ability of humans to detect subliminal stimuli (verified electroencephalographically), which can be shown to alter verbal responses elicited later under conditions of free association (Shevrin & Fritzler, 1968; Shevrin, Smith & Fritzler, 1971).

In summary, there is considerable evidence that human beings are capable of preconscious (Dixon, 1981) as well as conscious processing. Averill calls the two types first-order monitoring (Harré & Secord, 1972) and second-order monitoring. Phenomenological psychologists refer to the former as a "prereflective" experience. This type of cognition is differentiated from second-order monitoring in which awareness reflects back upon itself and by which we impose meaning on the original experience.[2]

It can be argued that emotion can be elicited by a preconscious (and thus "noncognitive," as Zajonc defines it) process. This is the "short

---

[2]The discussion of preconscious and conscious processing will remind the reader of psychoanalytic explanations of different psychic states. Primary process thinking, for example, would seem to share several characteristics with preconscious processing.

circuiting" of conscious cognition by linking sensation to affective output directly (Zajonc, 1984, p. 122). However, it also can be argued that the actual experience of emotion involves reflective (i.e., postaffective) cognition. Smythies (1970) describes the process as involving an interaction between the neocortex, which recognizes stimuli, and the lower areas of the brain (particularly the primitive cortex of the limbic system), which attaches significance to the events perceived. Appraisal, in this sense, involves both systems.

Thus, Lazarus and Zajonc may both be right. Emotion may be *elicited* via a preconscious process but *experienced* consciously. This would explain the "involuntary" aspect of emotion as well as its more subjective (i.e., conscious) nature. The issue of whether both types of information processing should be considered as "cognitive" becomes more than a semantic game when one considers the clinical implications.

Clinical Implications

Zajonc's assertion concerning the primacy of affect has a number of clinical implications. Rachman (1981) has noted, for example, that viewing the affective and cognitive systems as partially independent supports a triple modes approach to matching treatment with type of response. In other words, one must target the disordered system specifically for optimum results. This possibility explains, according to Rachman, why most emotions are seen as "irrational," and thus predicts the relative ineffectiveness of rational psychotherapy in treating these disorders. He argues that interventions, such as exposure-based procedures for fears and phobias, which deal with affective responses directly (as opposed to dealing with the cognitions that supposedly mediate emotions) are preferred for both theoretical and empirical reasons. From this perspective, formulations such as Seligman's notion of prepared phobias (see Chapter 4) is supported, whereas theories based on a postcognitive understanding of emotion are not.

Given the widespread popularity of cognitively based interventions, Zajonc's position has caused quite a stir. It will be remembered that the cognitive therapies assume that (a) human behavior is mediated by cognition (e.g., appraisal) and that (b) emotional disorders are therefore essentially a consequence of cognitive deficiencies (Marzillier, 1980). These interventions seek to alter cognitions using techniques designed to restore rationality (e.g., Ellis, 1962), improve thinking skills (e.g., Beck, 1976), increase problem-solving ability (D'Zurilla & Goldfried, 1971), or enhance self-instructional capabilities (e.g., Meichenbaum, 1977a). The common denominator of the "cognitive-behavioral" interventions is emphasis on verbal procedures directed at modifying self-statements (Dush, Hirt, & Schroeder, 1983). Although performance-based homework assignments are often used in conjunction with these strategies, the cognitive therapies generally focus on those aspects of human information processing that are both *conscious* and *rational.*

Many cognitive therapists are quick to argue that this is not the case, that cognitive interventions are very much concerned with processes that are both unconscious and irrational (i.e., intuitive). Nevertheless, although cognition is defined in the broadest possible sense theoretically (cf. Kleinginna & Kleinginna, 1985), its application clinically has assumed a more narrow meaning (i.e., verbal behavior). This is because, as Seligman observes:

> The techniques of cognitive therapy are only loosely deduced from cognitive "theory," and part of the reason for this has to do with the lack of definition of the terms of cognitive therapy and the lack of underpinnings in experimentation. (1981, p. 136)

The question as to what does and what does not constitute a cognitive treatment is an important issue as illustrated by what happened when Emmelkamp and his associates (Emmelkamp, Kuipers, & Eggeraat, 1978) compared a cognitive-restructuring procedure with *in vivo* exposure in the treatment of 21 hospitalized agoraphobics. The cognitive intervention was chosen because

> reactions of anxiety can be aroused by the erroneous interpretation that is attached to a certain situation. Hence the modification of the label that is applied to the situation can be effective in altering the emotional reaction and the avoidance behavior of phobics. (p. 33)

The cognitive treatment package, which included relabeling (Goldfried & Goldfried, 1975), rational-emotive training (Ellis, 1962; Young, 1974), and self-instructional training (Meichenbaum, 1975), was contrasted with the more traditional intervention of prolonged exposure *in vivo* (Emmelkamp & Wessels, 1975; Hafner & Marks, 1976; Hand, Lamontagne, & Marks, 1974). The latter involved taking a short walk to the center of town, at first with the therapist but later with fellow patients or alone. Also brief group discussions after exposure were a part of this intervention.

The results were clear. On all measures of avoidance behavior in problematic situations, the prolonged exposure treatment was superior to cognitive restructuring. In discussing the outcome, Emmelkamp *et al.* (1978) noted that their results were different from other findings in the literature and attempted to resolve those differences in this manner.

> Unlike the present study, all the other studies on this subject were analogue studies: the effects of treatment in analogue studies might be more strongly

influenced than in clinical trials by factors such as demand characteristics (Borkovec, 1973) and expectancy of therapeutic gain (Emmelkamp, 1975). Besides, it seems probable that the level of intelligence of our (mostly lower-class or middle-class) clients will on the average have been lower than that of the subjects in the analogue studies, who were students in almost all cases. Cognitive restructuring might well be more effective with intelligent students used to thinking rationally than with a clinical population. The degree of physiological arousal in anxiety engendering situations too might differ considerably for agoraphobics and for subjects in analogue studies: the latter probably react with a much slighter degree of arousal than the former (Lader, 1967). It is quite possible that cognitive restructuring constitutes an effective form of treatment for low physiological reactors (such as the subjects of analogue studies) while such treatment will be effective for high physiological reactors (such as agoraphobics) only after the autonomic component has been reduced. (p. 39)

This explanation clearly endorses a triple modes view of differential treatment effects. Nevertheless, Ellis (1979) argued in response to this interpretation that the exposure treatment itself involved cognitive modification. Although acknowledging that *in vivo* exposure is useful or even necessary for disorders of this type, he maintained that the central mechanism for the change that occurred was cognitive in nature.

An argument such as this has no resolution because cognition, broadly defined, can be implicated as the causal link for almost any response (e.g., Ellis, 1985). Nevertheless, the cognitively based therapies tend to rely most heavily on the verbal modification of one's thinking (cf. Bornstein, 1985). Performance-based strategies, on the other hand, are often accomplished with little verbal direction and a minimal attempt to manipulate the client's cognitions directly. The success of the latter has resulted in what is termed a "therapeutic paradox" (Rachman, 1981) that Bandura (1977) explains as follows:

> On one hand, explanations of change processes are becoming more cognitive. On the other hand, it is performance based treatments that are proving most powerful in effecting psychological changes. Regardless of the method involved, the treatments implemented through actual performance achieve results consistently superior to those in which fears are eliminated to cognitive representations of threats. . . . The apparent divergence of theory and practice is reconciled by recognizing that change is mediated through cognitive processes, but that cognitive events are induced and altered most readily by experiences of mastery arising from successful performance. (pp. 78–79)

Bandura is not the only one to suggest that performance is one of the most effective means of affecting cognitions (e.g., M. R. Goldfried, 1980b; Meichenbaum & Jaremko, 1983; G. E. Schwartz, 1982b). Because performance inevitably involves the processing of information, particularly if one includes the numerous preconscious and physiological processes discussed earlier (see Chapter 1; also Watts, 1983), it is not surprising that behavior is able to modify cognitions just as cognitions influence behavior. However, for many disorders such as fears and phobias the process does not proceed equally in both directions, and performance, not cognition, may be the crucial element for therapeutic change across treatments, including the more cognitive ones (Barlow, Hayes, & Nelson, 1984). This possibility was not lost on Freud (1919/1953) who observed that psychoanalysis for agoraphobics is not sufficient in itself and that the therapist must also induce his or her patients "to go about alone and to struggle with their anxiety while they make the attempt" (p. 400).

It would appear, therefore, that distinguishing between verbally oriented and performance-based interventions is of some importance. Consequently, insisting on defining cognition is the broadest sense is of little practical value, for a definition that is all-inclusive fails to discriminate between those treatment strategies that focus primarily on cognitions and those that emphasize behavior.

Emotion as a System

It should be apparent by now that "an emotion is not just the sum of its parts" (Averill, 1982, p. 19). As with the product of any system, emotions are complex, "polythetic" syndromes of which no subset is either necessary or sufficient for a complete understanding or explanation of the phenomenon.

More specifically, emotions can be thought of as consisting of a variety of semiautonomous response elements for which there is no single, core component. Any particular element may be a component of one or more emotional states. Also, although the overall organization of these states may have an adaptive significance biologically and thus share some common features, the particular configuration at any given time will be determined by the context in which it occurs. In other words, emotions are not preprogrammed within the CNS but represent the complex product of an interaction of neurological, psychological, and sociocultural factors.

This "social-constructionist" view of emotions (Averill, 1982, pp. 41–52) is an application of Delgado's "theory of fragmental representation of behavior" that was initially discussed in Chapter 1 (Delgado, 1967, 1970; Delgado & Mir, 1969). It will be remembered that this theory postulates that certain areas of the brain are responsible for organizing fragments of behavior, such as autonomic responses, vocalization, facial expression, and motor activity both tonic and phasic. Other neural structures are charged with organizing these fragments into more complex patterns of responses. Some of these fragments are shared among patterns, such as in the case of fight–flight responses, whereas other fragments may be specific to a particular pattern, such as in facial displays (Rinn, 1984) and nonverbal features of speech (i.e., pitch, loudness, and rate; Frick, 1985). The complex interaction of fragments is described by Averill (1982).

> The elements of a biological system are encoded within the nervous system and can be elicited as behavioral "fragments" by electrical stimulation of the brain. These fragments are hierarchically and heterarchically organized; there is, however, no core neural structure that binds them together as thread binds together the beads of a necklace. Rather, the fragments are more like the interlocking pieces of a puzzle. But unlike the pieces of an ordinary puzzle, behavioral fragments are dynamic structures the "shape" of which is constantly changing as a function of social (symbolic) as well as biological (genetic) factors. (p. 51)

Often the puzzle involves an interaction of innate (i.e., programmed) and acquired (i.e., instrumental) responses. Thus, facial expression is a highly programmed component of the motoric mode. This fragment can be contrasted to the motoric aspects of emotion that are acquired, more flexible and adaptive, and often are under the control of external contingencies (Averill, 1982). The cognitive contribution, on the other hand, may consist of reflective as well as reflexive components, the former providing the element of subjective experience with the latter furnishing highly automated sequences of information processing discussed earlier. Each of these "fragments" is important for emotion. However, their relative importance varies, depending on the environmental context, the individual, and the type of emotion experienced. For example, Rachman (1978) has argued that acquired factors predominate in fear responses, whereas happiness may be more innately expressed (cf. Ekman, Friesen, & Ellsworth, 1972).

Tying this thinking to the triple modes, one can see that each mode exhibits characteristics of both types of responses. For example, it has just been argued that cognition (i.e., information processing) can be preconscious, automatic, and stereotyped as well as conscious, voluntary, and flexible. Motor responses can also be programmed, as in the case of highly overlearned habit patterns, or entirely malleable in novel situations calling for adaptive responding. And even autonomic responses, which exhibit the clearest evidence for preprogrammed activity, evidence some capacity for voluntary modification via biofeedback and related techniques.

Emotion, therefore, can be viewed as a reciprocally determined product of multiple factors. The relative importance of each depends on numerous variables, such as the physiological makeup of the person, his or her past learning history and personal experience, and the context in which the emotional response occurs. This concept corresponds closely to Bandura's concept of reciprocal determinism (Bandura, 1974, 1977). From this perspective, there is an interaction between the person, his or her behavior, and the environment. As Bandura (1977) notes, it is probably fruitless to try to determine which of these factors is most important.

> The efforts to gauge the relative importance of these factors have not been especially informative because one can obtain almost any pattern of results depending upon the types of persons, behavior, and situations selected. For example, in deciding which movie to attend from many alternatives in a large city there are few constraints on the individual so that personal preferences emerge as the predominant determinants. In contrast, if people are immersed in a deep pool of water their behavior will be remarkably similar however uniquely varied they might be in their cognitive and behavioral make-up. (p. 194)

In short, understanding and treating emotional problems requires flexibility and attention to the uniqueness of the individual and his or her environment. The way one goes about this will be the topic of the next section of the book that attempts to apply what we have discussed so far to the treatment of anxiety and depression.

Recommended Readings

Averill, J. R. (1982). *Anger and aggression: An essay on emotion.* New York: Springer-Verlag.

This is one of the best views of emotion from the "social constructionist" perspective. Although not written for a general audience, this work will be of interest to anyone desiring a closer look at emotion, particularly as it relates to the expression of anger and aggressive behavior.

Bandura, A. (1973). *Aggression: A social learning analysis.* Englewood Cliffs, NJ: Prentice-Hall.

Bandura's classic work on aggression provides an alternative to the view of emotion as an internal force. His analysis is particularly valuable in that it leads to a set of predictions that are exactly opposite to those postulated from a psychodynamic perspective. Consequently, basic questions concerning the nature of emotional behavior can be tested directly—a happy, if unusual, situation for psychology.

PART **III**

Clinical Applications

It is hoped that by this point the utility of a triple modes approach has been documented sufficiently to justify its use. In addition, the flexible, interactive, and dynamic contributions of multiple factors in the prediction of behavior can be appreciated. As was seen in Part II, these factors include a range of variables, some of which are essentially reflexive and proceed in a programmed manner, whereas others are under voluntary control allowing for greater flexibility in responding.

Tying this thinking to the triple modes, one can see that each mode exhibits characteristics of both types of responses. For example, it has been argued that cognition (i.e., information processing) can be preconscious, automatic, and stereotyped as well as conscious, voluntary, and flexible. Motor responses can also be programmed, as in the case of highly overlearned habit patterns, or entirely malleable in novel situations calling for adaptive responding. And even autonomic responses, which exhibit the clearest evidence for preprogrammed activity, evidence some capacity for voluntary modification via biofeedback and related techniques.

All of this is to say that many of the traditional distinctions may be arbitrary. Just as the mind–body dichotomy has fallen, so has the distinction between innate and acquired aspects of behavior. The multidimensional and multidetermined nature of human activity, including those disorders that we as behavior therapists seek to treat, calls for an abandonment of single cause–effect explanations and inflexible treatment models (cf. Delprato & McGlynn, 1984), a point that will be illustrated in Part III.

CHAPTER **8**

Anxiety

It has been estimated that 30 to 40% of the general population are bothered by anxiety (Barlow *et al.*, 1984), with nonphobic anxiety disorders accounting for 15% of all outpatient problems (Lader, 1978; Reed, 1973). A survey of more than a half-million patients seen by family practitioners found that anxiety ranked fifth behind the preventive examination, hypertension, lacerations or trauma, and sore throat as the most common diagnosis (Marsland, Wood, & Mayo, 1976). Clearly, among the emotional disorders, anxiety is one of the most common.

Diagnosis

The *Diagnostic and Statistical Manual of Mental Disorders* (DSM-III) classifies anxiety according to three general categories that include phobic disorders, anxiety states, and the posttraumatic stress disorder. A fourth anxiety-related classification is adjustment disorder with anxious mood.

The phobic disorders include three types of fears—agoraphobia with and without panic attacks, simple phobias, and social phobia. *Agoraphobia* is a marked fear of being alone or of being in places from which escape might prove difficult or in which help is unavailable, such as in crowds, tunnels, or on bridges. As with most anxiety disorders, agoraphobia leads to avoidance behavior that interferes with the individual's normal activities. In addition, panic attacks are common (Thyer, Nesse, Cameron, & Curtis, 1985). In fact, a survey of clients referred to a phobia and anxiety disorders clinic did not find a single agoraphobic who did not also experience panic attacks (Di Nardo, O'Brien, Barlow, Waddell,

& Blanchard, 1983). Its chronic, pervasive nature has lead agoraphobia to be characterized as a "fear of fear" (Mavissakalian & Barlow, 1981, p. 5).

A *simple phobia* is tied to a specific stimulus, such as an object, person, or place. However, simple phobias do not include the fear of being alone or in public places (agoraphobia) or of humiliation and embarrassment (social phobia). As with all phobias, the individual who experiences it recognizes that the fear is excessive or unreasonable. This is also true of *social phobias* that occur in situations in which the person is exposed to the possible scrutiny by others or fears that he or she may act so as to suffer embarrassment or humiliation.

Anxiety states, the second category, encompass three problem areas as well—panic disorder, generalized anxiety disorder, and obsessive-compulsive disorder. A diagnosis of the first, *panic disorder*, requires at least three panic attacks within a 3-week period that are not precipitated by physical exertion or a life-threatening situation. Further, these attacks do not occur as part of a phobic response. Panic attacks vary in symptomatology from individual to individual. Consequently, for an attack to be diagnosed a person must experience 4 of 12 possible symptoms, including dyspnea ("air hunger"), palpitation (rapid beating of the heart), chest pain or discomfort, choking or smothering sensations, dizziness or vertigo, feelings of unreality, paresthesia (tingling in the hands and feet), hot or cold flashes, sweating, faintness, trembling or shaking, and a fear of dying, going crazy, or doing something uncontrollable.

The hallmark of a *generalized anxiety disorder* (GAD) is persistent, pervasive anxiety manifested in at least three of four ways—motor tension (e.g., shakiness, jitteriness, inability to relax, muscle aches, etc.), autonomic hyperactivity (e.g., sweating, heart pounding or racing, dry mouth, light-headedness, etc.), apprehensive expectation (e.g., worry, fear, rumination, etc.) or vigilance and scanning (e.g., hyperattentiveness resulting in distractibility, difficulty in concentration, insomnia, feeling "on edge," irritability, or impatience). To distinguish this disorder from anxiety-based problems occurring during childhood or adolescence, these symptoms must be continuous for at least 1 month in an individual 18 years of age or older.

Obsessive-compulsive disorder, as the name indicates, involves either recurrent, persistent ideas, thoughts, images or impulses (obsessions), or repetitive, stereotyped yet seemingly purposeful behaviors (compulsions), or both. Neither are voluntary and cannot be controlled rationally. It is possible that obsessive-compulsive individuals suffer from a biologically based state of chronic overarousal (Turner, Beidel, &

Nathan, 1985). Whatever the case, the obsessive thoughts invade consciousness and are experienced as repugnant, and the individual's attempts to suppress or ignore them are unsuccessful. Compulsions are also irrational, for they are not seen as an end in themselves but as a means for preventing some future event or situation from happening. To warrant being classified as a DSM-III disorder, the obsessions or compulsions must be a significant source of personal distress and interfere with the individual's social or role functioning.

The third category, *posttraumatic stress disorder* (PTSD), stands by itself and is a recent addition to the diagnostic literature. What differentiates PTSD from the other anxiety disorders is the existence of a traumatic situation that would evoke a significant response in almost anyone. For individuals suffering from PTSD, the original trauma is reexperienced in the form of dreams, intrusive recollections, or sudden actions or feelings as if the event was reoccurring. These experiences result in a numbing of responsiveness to or reduced involvement in the external world. In addition, the individual must display at least two of the following six symptoms; hyperalertness or exaggerated startle response, sleep disturbances, guilt about surviving, memory impairment or trouble concentrating, avoidance of activities that might trigger a recollection of the past event, or intensification of symptoms when exposed to events that symbolize or resemble the initiating circumstance.

Like PTSD, *adjustment disorder* is a reaction to an identifiable psychosocial stressor. The response is seen as maladaptive in that it impairs social or occupational functioning and because the symptoms are in excess of what would be considered normal. Unlike the other anxiety disorders discussed earlier, it is assumed that if and when the stressor is removed or modified, the disturbance will remit. Of the several types of adjustment disorders (e.g., with depressed mood, with disturbance in conduct, etc.), the diagnosis "with anxious mood" denotes the presence of symptoms such as nervousness, worry, and jitteriness.

Whereas adjustment disorders are common, agoraphobia is most frequently diagnosed for clients referred to specialized treatment settings, such as a phobia and anxiety clinic, and represents as much as one-third of that population (Di Nardo *et al.*, 1983). Social phobias and panic disorders are also common with each accounting for as much as 13% of the client population in this type of setting. GAD is slightly less common (10%), with obsessive-compulsive disorders and simple phobias even less frequent (5 and 3%, respectively). The incidence of PTSD depends on the type of clinic, with this diagnosis encountered most frequently in facilities working with war veterans (Keane, Fairbank, Caddell, Zimering, & Bender, 1985).

Medical Conditions Presenting with Anxiety Symptoms

The central role of the autonomic nervous system (ANS) in anxiety disorders means that a number of medical conditions and physiological states can result in symptoms that mimic anxiety, especially panic attacks. Table 4 (Jacob & Rapport, 1984) lists some of these conditions according to symptom.

There are two ways in which a medical condition can result in anxietylike symptoms. First, some medical disorders affect the autonomic nervous system (ANS) directly. One example would be pheochromocytoma which is a tumor on the adrenal gland. The tumor causes the exaggerated production and release of norepinephrine (NE). The generalized effect of this powerful neurotransmitter is felt throughout the body and can be reversed only by the surgical removal of the tumor itself.

A second way in which medical disorders can produce anxietylike symptoms is through their indirect effects. It will be remembered that the ANS, particularly the sympathetic branch, is the emergency system of the body. Thus, in time of danger or physiological crisis, the sympathetic branch responds quickly and emphatically. For example, if blood pressure drops too low by reason of hemorrhage, dehydration, or cardiac insufficiency, the adrenal glands release catecholamines (mainly NE) into the blood to constrict the vessels throughout the body, quicken heart rate, and thus restore blood pressure (an example of negative feedback). The all-or-nothing nature of the response, however, means that its autonomic effects are not limited to the cardiovascular system. Consequently, many anxiety-like symptoms will appear as well.

Vestibular Abnormalities. A good example of an indirect effect is found in vestibular abnormalities. The vestibular apparatus is part of the ear and detects sensations concerned with the maintenance of equilibrium. Abnormalities of the apparatus result in dizziness. Of the four types of dizziness—rotational dizziness, loss of balance, feeling faint, and "light-headedness" (Drachman & Hart, 1972)—the first two are more likely due to problems with the vestibular apparatus. (The latter two are usually of cardiovascular or vagal origin.) Many cases of dizziness thought to be psychogenic have been found to be due to vestibular problems. For example, Drachman and Hart (1972) noted that of 125 cases referred for dizziness, 38% were due to vestibular problems with another 23% resulting from hyperventilation (to be discussed shortly). More startling is the report of Jacob, Moller, Turner, and Wall (1983) who administered a battery of vestibular and audiological tests to a group of 8 patients with panic disorder and 13 agoraphobics with panic

Table 4. *Differential Diagnosis of Panic Disorder*

Main symptoms	Condition suspected	Differentiating symptoms	Confirming test
Tremor, sweating, pallor, dizziness	Reactive hypoglycemia	Symptoms 2 to 4 hrs after meal	5-hr glucose-tolerance tests
	Insulin-secreting tumors		Fasting blood-glucose and blood-insulin levels
Palpitations	Paroxysmal atrial tachycardia, ventricular extrasystoles	Sudden onset of rapid heart rate	24-hr electrocardiographic monitoring, event recording
	Mitral-valve prolapse	Systolic click or late systolic murmur	Echocardiogram
Weakness	Multiple sclerosis	Age < 40, fluctuating symptoms	Neurologic examination
	Transient ischemic attacks	Age > 40, paralysis	
Dyspnea, hyperventilation	Congestive heart failure	Rapid shallow breathing	Chest X-ray, EKG
	Pneumonia, pleuritis	Fever	Chest X-ray
	Asthma	Wheezing on expiration	Pulmonary function tests
	Chronic obstructive pulmonary disease	Precipitated by smoking	
	Alcohol withdrawal	History of alcohol use	

(continued)

Table 4. (Continued)

Main symptoms	Condition suspected	Differentiating symptoms	Confirming test
Dizziness	Orthostatic hypotension, anemia	Worse upon arising and exercise	Blood pressure and pulse, standing vs. sitting or lying down, blood count
	Benign positional vertigo	Triggered by rotation of head, jogging, stooping	Barany maneuver, otoneurological examination
Chest pain	Angina pectoris	Precipitated by physical exercise, emotions, or heavy meals	EKG, exercise EKG
	Myocardial infarction	Prolonged severe pain	EKG, cardiac enzymes
	Costal chondritis	Tender spots in costochondral junctions	Normal cardiac evaluation
	Pleuritis, pneumonia	Fever	Chest X-ray
Feelings of unreality	Temporal lobe epilepsy	Micropsia, macropsia, perceptual distortions, hallucinations	EEG with nasopharyngeal leads

		History of use	
	Hallucinogen abuse		
Hot and cold flashes	Carcinoid syndrome		5-HIAA in 24-hr urine
	Menopause	Female, appropriate age	
Miscellaneous	Hyperthyroidism	Rapid heart rate, warm sweaty hands	Thyroid function test
	Hypothyroidism	Voice changes	
	Hyperparathyroidism	Varied psychiatric symptoms	Blood calcium levels
	Hypoparathyroidism	Tetany, increased sensitivity to hyperventilation	
	Pheochromocytoma	High blood pressure	Catecholamines in 24-hr urine
	Acute intermittent porphyria	History of barbiturate intake	Urine porphobilinogen during attack

Note. From "Panic Disorder: Medical and Psychological Parameters" by R. G. Jacob and M. D. Rapport in *Behavioral Theories and Treatment of Anxiety* edited by S. M. Turner. Copyright 1984 by Plenum Publishing Corporation. Reprinted by permission.

attacks. The investigators found evidence of vestibular dysfunction in 14 of the 21 cases (including 6 of the 8 [75%] panic disorder patients). This disorder appears to play an important role in initiating the "panic cycle," and because symptoms can be provoked by simple maneuvers such as those involved when driving a car or jogging, the importance of checking patients with a history of panic attacks for vestibular problems is evident.

Hypoglycemia. Although vestibular problems probably have not received enough attention, hypoglycemia (low blood sugar) has likely received too much. Some investigators estimate that this relatively uncommon disorder is overdiagnosed at least five times or more (Ford, Bray, & Swerdloff, 1976; Permutt, 1980; Yager & Young, 1974). Hypoglycemia involves the excessively high secretion of insulin after a meal resulting in the rapid decline of blood sugar. In response, the ANS initiates a compensatory secretion of NE that causes an anxietylike state.

Hypoglycemia is not a primary disorder. Like many medical problems, it is the result of some other medical dysfunction, such as adult-onset diabetes in the early stages and liver disease. Hypoglycemia can also occur as a response to gastric surgery, carbohydrate restriction, or alcohol ingestion (Jacob & Rapport, 1984).

Mitral-Valve Prolapse. Another example of a compensatory response by the ANS in response to a physiological abnormality is a cardiac condition known as mitral-valve prolapse (MVP). (Prolapse means the movement of an organ or anatomical structure from its original position.) The mitral valve connects the left atrium with the left ventricle and prevents the flow of blood back into the atrium when the left ventricle contracts. In some cases, the mitral valve becomes so weakened that during the latter part of cardiac systole it balloons back into the atrium allowing blood to regurgitate, thus compromising the heart's ability to pump blood (Harvey, Johns, Owens, & Ross, 1972). When this occurs, the individual may experience palpitations, stabbing chest pain, and a general "nervousness." These symptoms are often sufficient to meet the diagnostic criteria for an anxiety disorder (Pariser, Pinta, & Jones, 1978).

In a normal population, the incidence of MVP may be as high as 10% in healthy females (Markiewicz, Stoner, London, Hunt, & Popp, 1976) and 7% in healthy males (Darsee, Mikolich, Nicoloff, & Lesser, 1979). Kantor, Zitrin, and Zeldis (1980) evaluated 25 agoraphobic women with panic episodes selected specifically because heart palpitations were prominent. This group was compared to 23 age-matched female hospital employees. It was found that 8 of the agoraphobic patients (32%) yielded electrocardiograms diagnostic of MVP as compared to 2 of the controls (9%). In another study the same base rates were observed—

8 of 21 (38%) patients diagnosed as anxiety neurotics versus 2 of 20 (10%) controls (Venkatesh et al., 1980). In short, the possibility that cardiac abnormalities of this type may contribute to the diagnosis of a panic disorder needs to be considered.

Hyperventilation Syndrome. Of the three medical conditions discussed so far, all have involved the presence of an identifiable, pathophysiological condition resulting in anxiety-like symptoms. In contrast, the hyperventilation syndrome is not the product of a diseased or abnormal state. Rather, it is an example of normal physiological regulation caught in a positive feedback loop (Ley, 1985).

Hyperventilation is pulmonary respiration in excess of what is needed to satisfy the body's requirements for blood oxygenation and carbon dioxide elimination. As a result, an excess of carbon dioxide (CO_2) is eliminated from the lungs. Because the serum CO_2 level is an important factor for maintaining the acid-base balance of the body, the excessive elimination of CO_2 shifts the body's pH in the alkaline direction. Alkalosis, in turn, has the direct effect of making both the peripheral and central nervous systems *hyperexcitable.* In addition, hyperventilation causes oxygen to become bound more tightly to the hemoglobin in the red blood cells resulting in the vasoconstriction of blood vessels (via autoregulation) throughout the body, including the brain and coronary arteries. The resultant symptoms include dizziness, giddiness, and an inability to concentrate.

Although hyperventilation syndrome and panic attack are not synonymous (the former lacks the high levels of sympathetic discharge characteristic of the latter), the two are often linked (Rapee, 1985). For example, if one hyperventilates unintentionally when excited, the resultant physiological state can induce anxiety-like symptoms. If the individual attributes the symptoms to fear, he or she may become even more anxious and hyperventilate further. The result is a predictable but unwanted synergistic effect. Consequently, clients for whom this may be a problem need to be informed of the physiological realities of the hyperventilation syndrome and be provided with somatic strategies for controlling these episodes when they occur. Some of these techniques include breathing into a small plastic bag or relaxation techniques (Emmelkamp & Emmelkamp-Benner, 1983).

Caffeinism. None of the conditions discussed so far are as common as caffeinism. Caffeine is the most widely used nonmedical central nervous system (CNS) stimulant in the world (Brecher, 1972). Caffeine is found in varying amounts in coffee, tea, cocoa, soft drinks, and several nonprescription drugs. Caffeinism is defined as the intake of more than 500 to 600 mg per day (Greden, 1974), which is equivalent to six to seven brewed cups of coffee. Symptoms of caffeinism include jitteriness, agitation, light headedness, tachypnea (rapid breathing), muscle twitching, and gastric distress (Greden, 1979). Caffeinism is also associated with insomnia (Karacan *et al.*, 1977) and often results in symptoms that may be impossible to differentiate from anxiety neurosis or situational anxiety (Greden, 1974, 1979).

Caffeine's physiological effects are numerous. For one, caffeine acts directly on the adrenal medulla to increase the secretion of NE and epinephrine into the blood (Bellet, Roman, DeCastro, Kim, & Keushbaum, 1969; Levi, 1967). In addition, caffeine stimulates the respiratory and vasomotor centers in the medulla thus increasing respiratory rate, oxygen consumption, and CO_2 elimination (Ritchie, 1975). Caffeine also exerts a stimulatory effect on all portions of the cortex as well as generally increasing the metabolic rate at the cellular level throughout the body (Julien, 1981).

There are a number of individual differences that affect a person's response to caffeine (Sawyer, Julia, & Turin, 1982). Some of these include age, mental state, and degree of physical fitness. Although the effect of chronic caffeinism is unknown, it is clear that caffeine withdrawal involves both salubrious as well as unpleasant effects. On the favorable side, blood pressure, heart rate, and gastrointestinal complaints decrease (Edelstein, Keaton-Brasted, & Burg, 1983). On the other hand, headaches may increase dramatically during the withdrawal phase. Thus, almost any problem that presents with symptoms of anxiety might benefit from an inquiry into the client's pattern of caffeine consumption.

Functional Diagnosis[1]

Although the DSM-III is seen as a considerable improvement over the DSM-II, a differential diagnosis on this level leaves much to be desired. Although classifications of this type may tell us much about how one individual is like another, they provide little information about what makes that person different from everyone else. In terms of designing a treatment plan suited to individual needs, a finer level of analysis is needed. There are several ways of going about this, some of which will be discussed in the final chapter. However, the triple modes approach is a good place to start.

---

[1]No attempt will be made to review the assessment and treatment of anxiety in detail here. Readers interested in the application of behavioral procedures to anxiety-based problems are referred to Turner's (1984a) excellent collection of readings in the area.

Triple Modes of Anxiety

The triple modes of responding has been applied to anxiety-based problems for a number of years (Deffenbacher & Suinn, 1982). The autonomic mode, for example, includes heightened arousal and anxiety-related psychophysiological symptoms, such as sleep difficulty, fatigue, diarrhea or dermatological disorders. The motoric mode includes muscular tension and disruptions in motor performance. The cognitive mode encompasses disruption in attention and concentration as well as impaired cognitive functioning. (An example of the latter is test anxiety that will serve as a clinical example at the end of this chapter). In addition, the cognitive mode involves worrisome thoughts and self-reports of subjective distress.

No single mode is sufficient in and of itself to determine the presence of anxiety. For example, although it is difficult to think of anxiety without considering its autonomic component, excessive sympathetic discharge by itself is not indicative of anxiety because the same sort of response can occur in other ways, such as during vigorous physical exertion (Hollandsworth & Jones, 1979). To define anxiety, one must include subjective experience and impaired performance or avoidance responses as well (Wolfe, 1984). In short, anxiety, like any other emotion, is the complex product of multiple variables finding expression in numerous ways. Optimally, treatment is based on an analysis of the relative contributions of each of the three modes (Himadi, Boice, & Barlow, 1985).

Treatment Strategies

Treatment of the anxiety disorders from a triple modes perspective has met with a large degree of success. The efficacy of some treatment by disorder combinations, such as those linking phobic and obsessive-compulsive disorders with controlled exposure, is well established (Turner, 1984b). For other problem areas, such as panic states and GAD, the picture is less clear.

The behavioral interventions for anxiety disorders fall primarily into two categories. One approach involves various exposure techniques, both *in vivo* and imaginal, and is based on the principles of respondent conditioning. These conditioning treatments are thought to be particularly appropriate for disorders with strong involvement of the autonomic mode. A second approach is based on principles of social learning theory and thus emphasizes the acquisition of behavioral skills and coping strategies as well as the vicarious extinction of distress. These techniques would seem more appropriate for disorders involving dysfunctions of the motoric and cognitive modes.

Conditioning Approaches. The conditioning (i.e., exposure) treatments have been most successful with phobias (O'Brien & Barlow, 1984; Sturgis & Scott, 1984), obsessive-compulsive disorders (Turner & Michelson, 1984), and PTSD (Keane, Zimering, & Caddell, 1985). A common theme throughout is the strong autonomic component often evidenced by panic attacks. A possible exception to this rule is the panic disorder itself for which the exposure treatments have been only moderately successful. Jacob and Turner (1984) suggest that one reason for this is the frequent inclusion under this diagnostic label of conditions with a medical basis.

The success of the exposure treatments raises the obvious question of why these disorders do not extinguish naturally. There are several possible answers to this question. One explanation that has weathered the critical storm better than most is the "two-factor theory" introduced by O. H. Mowrer (1947). Two-factor theory proposes that one may be conditioned in a classical sense initially and then avoid the situation later, thus preventing extinction from occurring. Variations of this basic theme can be found in Eysenck's (1979, 1982) incubation theory and Solomon and Wynne's (1954) "conservation of anxiety" hypothesis. Nevertheless, the basic idea in each of these explanations is that "the patient's symptoms (avoidance responses) terminate the conditioned fear cues before sufficient exposure to these cues can occur to produce a substantial extinction effect" (Levis & Malloy, 1982, p. 88).

An explanatory entity such as the two-factor theory is simply unable to deal with the wide range of problems that involve anxiety (Delprato & McGlynn, 1984, p. 35). Rachman (1977), for example, has noted that the theory does not explain why more clients have unreasonable fears of snakes and spiders than of dentists, although the opportunity for conditioning lies much more clearly with the latter. Also, he notes that the learning histories of many phobic clients do not provide evidence of a conditioning experience. Further, there are many situations in which fear that should have been conditioned was not. For example, during the air raids on London in World War II, people did not become conditioned to fear the sound of planes, sirens, and the like. Also, Rachman suggests that the ability to reduce some fears vicariously means that they can be acquired in a similar manner. In short, "at its best the conditioning theory can provide a partial explanation for the genesis of some fears" (1977, p. 383). •

As an alternative, Rachman proposes that fears can be acquired in multiple ways. One such pathway is, in fact, conditioning in the classical sense. Another avenue is vicarious in nature, whereas a third involves the provision of information and/or instruction, as when a child is directed to fear sexual intimacy by a parent. The classically conditioned fears are seen as biologically oriented and involve a strong innate (i.e. programmed) component. These are best treated by exposure-based interventions, as discussed earlier. Many social fears, on the other hand, may be acquired vicariously and thus approached most effectively using models and graduated practice. Misinformation, in turn, might be handled best by correcting misperceptions and misunderstandings. Although clinical investigations of this hypothesis have generated conflicting results (e.g., Ost, Jerremalm, & Jansson, 1985; Ost, Jerremalm, & Johansson, 1981; Ost, Johansson, & Jerremalm, 1982), its usefulness as a heuristic device in tailoring individual treatments warrants further study.

Social Learning Approaches. Although anxiety can become conditioned to neutral stimuli and thus be inappropriate or maladaptive, it also can be a reasonable reaction in situations for which the individual lacks the necessary skills (Paul & Bernstein, 1976). This type of response is termed *reactive anxiety*. Although understandable given the circumstances, the response can still be a cause of concern and thus a legitimate target for intervention.

The social phobias, for example, often involve more than the conditioning of anxiety in a particular setting. Trower and Turland (1984) note that social phobia (which may not be a phobia in the true sense of the word) consists of two components—an appraisal and a coping response. The former often involves self-defeating expectations and maladaptive self-statements. The latter is concerned more with interpersonal behaviors. A treatment approach that focuses on the acquisition of skills, both cognitive and motoric, would seem in order. Usually this involves procedures developed from social learning theory, such as modeling and practice with focused feedback, in conjunction with self-instructional and cognitive restructuring strategies (Kelly, 1982).

A comprehensive social learning approach also may be particularly useful for those disorders, such as GAD, that are more heterogeneous than phobic reactions. It is generally acknowledged, for example, that GAD is a residual diagnosis for clients failing to fit any of the more clearly defined codes (Di Nardo *et al.*, 1983). Consequently, successful treatments for this disorder are normally multidetermined and thus require more than controlled exposure. For example, Barlow and his associates (1984) used a treatment that included both cue-controlled and biofeedback-assisted relaxation, stress-inoculation training (Meichenbaum & Turk, 1973), and cognitive therapy for anxiety disorders (Beck &

Emery, 1979) to achieve a successful outcome for a group of GAD patients.

Given the complexity of anxiety-based problems, treatments tailored to fit individual needs are necessary. For example, the individual suffering from a simple phobia may also have deficient social skills and maladaptive cognitions. Consequently, alleviating autonomic reactivity in this case will not guarantee that appropriate and effective behavior will follow. In fact, it can be argued that dysfunctions in one mode make problems in another mode more likely due to interrupted development or impaired learning. A functional analysis can provide the basis for a comprehensive and flexible treatment program designed to meet these individual needs.

An Example: Test Anxiety

The complexity of clinical problems means that often the most obvious explanation is not necessarily the best. An example of this can be found in the test anxiety literature. Originally, test anxiety was conceptualized as an anxiety state that blocked appropriate responding in the examination setting (Mandler & Sarason, 1952). Because the situational context (i.e., tests) is clearly defined and because the autonomic response (i.e., stomach discomfort, palpitations or perspiration) is well established, test anxiety was viewed pretty much as a stimulus-specific fear and treated using systematic desensitization. Although it is possible to document improvement on self-report measures using this approach, more than two-thirds of the studies were unable to provide evidence of improvement in actual performance on tests or examinations (Denny, 1978; Finger & Galassi, 1977).

The problem with applying desensitization to test anxiety is that it fails to take into account a number of variables that can cause anxiety in testing situations, such as being unprepared or having inadequate test-taking skills. In response to Meichenbaum's (1977b) call for a moratorium on outcome research in this area until more of these variables could be identified, we initiated a series of studies that attempted to determine what distinguished students reporting high versus low test anxiety (Hollandsworth, Glazeski, Kirkland, Jones, & Van Norman, 1979; Kirkland & Hollandsworth, 1979).

One of our primary concerns was determining the relative contribution of autonomic arousal to impaired test performance. To determine this, we monitored heart rate, respiratory rate, and the skin conductance responses of three high test-anxious and three low test-anxious subjects during the administration of a test of intellectual aptitude (Otis-Lennon).

It was found that both groups of subjects evidenced similar levels of arousal (as measured by these indexes) during the test. It was discovered at debriefing, however, that the differences between the two groups was more in terms of how they responded to the arousal. The low test-anxious subjects, who also performed significantly better on the examination, reported getting "psyched-up" for tests, actually using the arousal to facilitate their problem solving. The high test-anxious subjects, on the other hand, reported being distracted by these sensations and diverting attention from the test in an effort to reduce their reactivity. Other studies appearing about the same time confirmed the equivalency of autonomic responding for both high and low test-anxious subjects (Glazeski, Hollandsworth, & Jones, in press [first presented in 1978]; Holroyd, Westbrook, Wolf, & Badhorn, 1978) and supported the assertion that arousal may distract some students but actually facilitate test taking for others (Deffenbacher, 1978).

The implications of these findings are obvious—one should focus more on how arousal is used than on its reduction. Because desensitization is designed to reduce anxiety, a potentially important aid to test taking may be neutralized. Although this procedure may be helpful to some students for whom the test-taking situation has become a conditioned aversive stimulus, the treatment fails to deal with the problem of cognitive distraction and ineffective test-taking techniques. In fact, the occasional performance successes desensitization did enjoy may have been due more to its attention-focusing properties than its ability to reduce anxiety (e.g., Counts, Hollandsworth, & Alcorn, 1978).

As a result of these investigations, we came to view test anxiety more as ineffective test taking than a problem of excessive arousal. Building on the earlier work of Wine (1971) and Meichenbaum (1972), a treatment program was developed that deemphasized the autonomic component and focused on self-instructional skills and information-processing strategies instead. This approach was then compared with two interventions (cue-controlled relaxation and meditation) based on the earlier, arousal-reduction view of test anxiety (Kirkland & Hollandsworth, 1980).

The results were clear. The cognitively oriented, skills-acquisition approach resulted in significantly improved performance on a pre-post anagram task as compared to the other two treatment groups and a control condition that practiced solving anagrams only. More specifically, the skills-acquisition program solved 55% more anagrams at posttesting than the cue-controlled condition, 143% more than the meditation group, and 180% more than the practice-only control. Perhaps most importantly, the skills group also obtained a significantly higher grade point average at the end of the semester than the other groups.

In spite of the promise of these findings, these studies do not suggest that a skills-acquisition approach is the treatment of choice for all test-anxious individuals. Although it may be effective for many, we did not look at the possibility that some individuals have, in fact, become conditioned to test-taking situations. Nor did the studies investigate the role of study skills and other preparatory behaviors that are also thought to contribute to academic performance.

What the studies do emphasize is that interventions need to be functionally related to the disorder rather than chosen on the assumption that a particular disorder has a single cause. Further, just because a treatment has worked for other clients or for similar problems, there is no guarantee that it is the treatment of choice of the client sitting in front of you at that moment. One therefore approaches clinical problems with multiple working hypotheses and flexible treatment protocols. Although the research literature and clinical experience are invaluable resources, each client presents a unique challenge, and unique challenges require unique solutions.

Recommended Reading

Turner, S. M. (Ed.). (1984a). *Behavioral theories and treatment of anxiety.* New York: Plenum Press.

This recent collection of readings is a valuable reference for anyone interested in anxiety-based disorders. The chapters are written by some of the most able contributors in their respective areas and are of uniformly high quality. Organized according to the DSM-III diagnostic classification system, this work is as useful to the practitioner as it is for the researcher. This book's influence on the present chapter can be noted throughout.

CHAPTER 9

Depression

Like anxiety, depression is defined in terms of its symptoms rather than its cause. *Depression* is "a label for a feeling or affective state of dysphoria" (Craighead, 1981, p. 76). Symptoms that occur in at least 75% of individuals diagnosed as depressed include feelings of inadequacy and helplessness, indecisiveness, crying spells, loss of interest and enjoyment, fatigability, sleep disturbance, pessimism, dejected mood, and self-devaluation (Beck, 1973). Agreement, however, as to what constitutes a depressive state is often difficult to achieve in that these symptoms are neither unique to depression nor universally ascribed to that condition (Glazer, Clarkin, & Hunt, 1981; Harrow, Colbert, Detre, & Bakeman, 1966; Levitt, Lubin, & Brooks, 1983).

Part of the problem in defining depression is its vagueness. Unlike the anxiety disorders that "wax and wane as a function of circumstances and consequences" (Glazer *et al.*, 1981, p. 12), depression is a pervasive and persistent disorder that relies heavily on verbal reports of subjective states and highly inferential observer-based estimates for its diagnosis (N. S. Jacobson, 1981). In addition, depression is often the companion of other mental disorders, such as schizophrenia (Endicott & Spitzer, 1978) and anxiety (Fowles & Gersh, 1979; Gersh & Fowles, 1979). Considerable disagreement exists as to whether these disorders represent distinctive diagnostic categories (Derogatis, Klerman, & Lipman, 1972; Downing & Rickles, 1974; Garmany, 1956) or simply different points on the same continuum (Mapother, 1926).

Akiskal (1979) suggests that there may be four types of depressions. Normal depression is a relatively brief, situational response. Very often this type of depression is the result of a normal psychobiological process, such as during premenstrual (Dalton, 1984) or postpartum (Pitt,

1973) periods. Situational depression lasts longer than normal depression (from several weeks to several months) and may, in fact, reflect good reality testing (Fenichel, 1945). Secondary depression, on the other hand, is a demoralized state following a chronic psychiatric or medical problem (Klein, 1974; Lipowski, 1975; Robins & Guze, 1972). Primary depression arises in the absence of preexisting medical or psychiatric problems (Kocsis, 1981), is grossly out of proportion to any life event, and affects cognitive, psychomotor, and vegetative responding (i.e., all three modes).

Diagnosis

Diagnostic Issues

Determining specific diagnostic criteria for the depressive disorders is clouded by several unresolved issues. Andreasen (1982) notes that these issues have centered around three basic dichotomies—primary-secondary, endogenous-reactive, and bipolar-unipolar distinctions.

The Primary-Secondary Distinction. As in the case of anxiety, there are a number of medical conditions that present with depressive symptoms. When these symptoms result from such a condition, the depression is said to be secondary. Some of these conditions include hyperthyroidism (if slow in onset), hyperparathyroidism (with apathy and withdrawal), adrenocortical insufficiency (Addison's disease), and pernicious anemia (Addisonian anemia).

The primary-secondary distinction runs into problems, however, when the illness and the depressed state contribute to each other. This is often the case of incapacitating psychiatric disorders, such as schizophrenia, which can cause as well as be exacerbated by depression. A growing awareness of the interrelatedness of medical and psychological problems (cf. Depue, 1979) makes absolute distinctions between primary and secondary depression increasingly difficult.

The Endogenous-Reactive Distinction. In 1893, Mobius introduced the idea that some depressive states are biological in nature, whereas other types occur in response to environmental events (Becker, 1974). (Sometimes this is referred to as the "psychotic-neurotic" distinction.) Diagnosis of an endogenous depression depends on symptoms such as agitation, insomnia, anorexia, visceral symptoms, psychomotor retardation, and other "vegetative signs" said to reflect limbic-hypothalamic dis-regulation of mood and appetitive functions (Goodwin, 1977; Kocsis, 1981; S. H. Rosenthal & Klerman, 1966). This picture differs from so-called reactive depression that is more externally oriented and that focuses on one's interpersonal or role inadequacies.

The endogenous-reactive distinction received a good bit of support in the late 1950s and 1960s with the advent of high-speed computers, electroconvulsive therapy (ECT), and antidepressant medications. The computers permitted factor-analytic studies that usually identified two factors, one corresponding to endogenous depression and the other to its reactive counterpart (Carney, Roth, & Garside, 1965; Kiloh & Garside, 1963; Paykel, Klerman, & Prusoff, 1970). During the same period, studies employing ECT claimed greater success with endogenous patients than with reactive ones (Carney *et al.*, 1965; Carney & Sheffield, 1972, 1974; Mendels, 1965). In addition, use of antidepressant medications supported the distinction by identifying the "modal responder"— "an endogenous depressive with vegetative signs and a good premorbid personality who is anhedonic and nondelusional and has experienced few previous episodes or none" (Kocsis, 1981, p. 301; also see Bielski & Friedel, 1976; Kuhn, 1958).

Critics of this evidence, however, were not far behind. Fowles and Gersh (1979) noted that factor-analytic studies use clinical ratings thus biasing the results in favor of the anticipated distinction. Also factor structures vary across studies and account for only a modest portion of the total variance. This problem led Kendell to conclude that the endogenous-reactive distinction does "not do justice to the variety and diversity of depressive illness" (1976, p. 19).

The problem of selection bias is even more evident in the ECT studies (Fowles & Gersh, 1979, p. 65). The effectiveness of the ECT is normally determined by comparison to a placebo condition. Nonspecific (i.e., placebo) factors are known to have more of an effect on less severely depressed subjects. Consequently, it may be easier to document the relative gains of any treatment group consisting of seriously depressed individuals than differences between treatment and placebo conditions when the subjects are mildly depressed. Thus, the differential effectiveness of ECT for endogenous (i.e., serious) depressives may be due primarily to selection factors than to a biological basis for that subtype.

Studies involving antidepressant medication were also questioned after several double blind investigations found no evidence for differences between the two subgroups (Burt, Gordon, Holt, & Hordern, 1962; Greenblat, Grosser, & Wechsler, 1964; Hordern, Burt, & Holt, 1965; Paykel, 1972; Raskin & Crook, 1976). As a result, the contradictory evidence in all three areas led to debate between the "monists" such as Mapother (1926) and Lewis (1934, 1938) who believe that the only difference is one of severity, and the "dualists" who argue for two diagnostically meaningful groups.

By 1970, the weight of evidence tended to indicate that there is no clear-cut boundary between the two subtypes (Kendell, 1969, 1976; Kendell & Gourlay, 1970), suggesting that the distinction is of little value (Akiskal, Bitar, Puzantian, Rosenthal, & Walker, 1978). And because the endogenous label implies that this type of depression occurs independently of environmental influences, such as precipitating stress, the term was dropped from the DSM-III and survives only as an optional fifth digit ("with melancholia") in the diagnostic code for major depressive episode.

The Unipolar-Bipolar Distinction. A diagnostic dichotomy that did survive when the DSM-II was revised is the unipolar-bipolar distinction. The distinction was originally proposed by Leonhard (e.g., Leonhard, Kroff, & Schultz, 1962) and strongly supported by other investigators in the 1960s (Perris, 1966, 1968, 1969, 1971; Winokur, Clayton, & Reich, 1969). Although not everyone agrees with the distinction (e.g., Gershon, Baron, & Leckman, 1975), the evidence is extensive and derives from genetic and family studies, biological (i.e., metabolic) studies, differential response to treatment studies, and clinical observation of course and prognosis (see Andreasen, 1982, for a review). The prevailing view is that some type of biochemical imbalance(s) accounts for the emotional lability of bipolar depression (Perris, 1982). In many ways, it is appropriate to think of the bipolar-unipolar distinction as having replaced the endogenous-reactive construct.

DSM-III Diagnosis

The DSM-III uses the term *affective disorders* to refer to depression. Although a footnote suggests that this diagnostic grouping should more appropriately be thought of as "mood disorders," the historical term is retained for reasons of continuity. Within the diagnostic category itself, the affective disorders are organized along two dimensions—pure or unipolar depression and mixed or bipolar depression.

The unipolar states are divided into three subcategories—major depressive episode, dysthymic (chronic) disorder, and atypical depression. Of these, the *major depressive episode* is the most serious. It involves a dysphoric mood characterized as being depressed, sad, blue, hopeless, low, down in the dumps, or irritable. Accompanying dysphoric mood is the loss of interest or pleasure in all or almost all usual activities or pastimes. For a major depressive episode to be diagnosed, the individual must experience at least four of the following eight symptoms

daily for 2 weeks—poor appetite, insomnia or hypersomnia, psychomotor agitation or retardation, loss of interest or pleasure in usual activities, loss of energy (fatigue), feelings of worthlessness, and the like,
reduced ability to think or concentrate, or recurrent thoughts of death or
suicidal ideation.

Dysthymic disorder is similar to a major depressive episode except
that it is not of sufficient severity or duration to meet the criteria for the
latter. A major characteristic of this diagnosis is the persistence of symptoms over at least 2 years. During this period, the depressive symptomatology may be interrupted by brief periods of normal mood that last
a few days to a few weeks but no more than a few months at a time.

Atypical depression is diagnosed when the individual meets the criteria for dysthymic disorder but with periods of normal mood lasting for
more than several months. In many instances, this state may be attributed to schizophrenia. However, if the depressive episode (which
also must not meet the criteria for a major depressive illness) is in reaction to psychosocial stress, it is classified as an adjustment disorder.

The mixed or bipolar grouping also includes three diagnostic classifications. If both manic and depressive episodes are present (with the
depressive symptoms prominent for at least a full day) a diagnosis of
bipolar depression is assigned. *Cyclothymic disorder* is similar to bipolar
depression but lacks the severity of the latter. This disorder must also be
in evidence for at least 2 years with the depressive and hypomanic
periods separated by periods of normal mood. *Atypical bipolar disorder,*
on the other hand, is diagnosed if the periods of normal mood extend
for periods longer than a few months.

Finally, there is the diagnosis of an *adjustment disorder with depressed
mood*. As with anxiety, this disorder is in response to an identifiable
psychosocial stressor within 3 months of its occurrence. Such a reaction
becomes diagnosable if there is impairment of social or occupational
functioning and if the symptoms are in excess of the normal, expected
reaction to the stressor. It is assumed that the disturbance will remit
after the stressor has been removed or when a new level of functioning
is achieved.

Incidence

It has been estimated that 13 to 20% of the population in the United
States has experienced an affective disorder during their lifetime (Boyd
& Weissman, 1982; Craighead, 1981). In that depression accounts for
75% of all psychiatric hospitalizations, it is considered to be second only
to schizophrenia as a national mental health problem (Secunda, Katz,

Friedman, & Schuyler, 1973). And when one considers that up to 15% of depressives kill themselves, the seriousness of the disorder is clear.

Of the two types of depression (unipolar and bipolar), the former is more prevalent. Females are two to three times more likely to experience this type of disorder than males, and of all the unipolar cases, approximately two-thirds are considered to be "neurotic" (i.e., dysthymic) rather than biological in origin (Paykel, Klerman, & Prusoff, 1974; S. H. Rosenthal, 1966). The incidence of a unipolar, manic illness is rare and is usually classified under a bipolar code (Tryer & Shopsin, 1982). Major bipolar affective disorders are also uncommon (Kocsis, 1981), with an individual's lifetime risk of experiencing a first episode of that illness estimated at less than 1 in a 110 (Boyd & Weissman, 1982; James & Chapman, 1975). However, one's chances are doubled if one includes nonhospitalized cases of cyclothymic disorder (Krauthammer & Klerman, 1979).

Triple Modes of Depression

As with anxiety, depression is not a "lump" (Craighead, 1980). Nevertheless, many of the models we use to explain it and most of the measures we use to assess it contribute to viewing depression in this manner. For example, although most of the traditional theories of depression recognize different subtypes of the disorder, these variations are seen essentially as different manifestations of a single process. Thus, psychoanalytic theory attempts to define *a* pattern of unconscious processing that results in depressive symptomatology (Izard, 1972; Klerman, 1975). Likewise, medical explanations of depression often posit the existence of a "final common pathway" (Akiskal, 1979; Akiskal & McKinney, 1975). And finally, even behavioral approaches to the disorder, although recognizing its multidimensional nature, focus on *a* primary causative factor from which the other dimensions stem, such as environments (Lewinsohn, 1974), cognitive deficits (Beck, 1967), or learned helplessness (Seligman, 1975).

In a similar manner, assessment techniques used for depression usually provide a global score or single cutoff for classification purposes. Examples of some of the instruments defining depression in this manner include the Beck Depression Inventory (Beck, Ward, Mendelson, Mock, & Erbaugh, 1961), the MMPI (Lewinsohn, Biglan, & Zeiss, 1976), the Hamilton Observation Scale (Hamilton, 1967), and the Zung Self-Rating Depression Scale (G. L. Brown & Zung, 1972; Zung, 1974). Even an assessment procedure such as the Schedule for Affective Disorders and

Schizophrenia (SADS; Endicott & Spitzer, 1978) is more concerned with differentiating depression from other disorders, such as anxiety states, than with identifying subtypes of depression that can be tied to different treatment modalities (Fowles & Gersh, 1979).

One way of making a functional diagnosis so that the treatment can be tailored to the individual problem is to use the triple modes approach (Craighead, 1980). Depression is expressed by the motoric mode in a number of ways. Some of these responses include crying spells (Beck, 1967), increased EMG activity in response to sad or depressing statements (G. E. Schwartz, Fair, Greenberg, Mandel, & Klerman, 1975; Teasdale & Bancroft, 1977), and the ability to benefit from feedback and reinforcement of adaptive performance. Depression also interferes with the performance of appropriate social skills (Libet & Lewinsohn, 1973). One reason for this is the tendency for depressed persons to focus the conversation on themselves and their problems (Coyne, 1976; Lewinsohn, 1976). In general, depression results in a person's exhibiting fewer behaviors that are likely to be reinforced or be seen as reinforcing (Lewinsohn & Libet, 1972; MacPhillamy & Lewinsohn, 1974).

Manifestations of depression via the autonomic mode include sleep disturbances (Mendelson, Gillin, & Wyatt, 1977), loss of appetite and interest in sex (Beck, 1967), and reduced catecholamine levels (Sweeney & Maas, 1979). The cognitive mode, on the other hand, is characterized by maladaptive self-statements and an unfavorable view of oneself, the world, or the future (Beck, 1974, 1976). Ineffective self-reinforcement and self-punishment skills may also be present (R. E. Nelson & Craighead, 1977). In addition, depressed individuals are more likely to distort favorable feedback and focus on critical information (DeMonbreun & Craighead, 1977; Hammen & Krantz, 1976; Lewinsohn, Mischel, Chaplin, & Barton, 1980; R. E. Nelson & Craighead, 1977) as well as recall negatively toned material more readily than positively toned information (Lishman, 1972; Lloyd & Lishman, 1975). Other aspects of the cognitive mode include excessive self-blame (Abramson & Sackeim, 1977) and self-reports of dejected mood (Beck, 1967).

Suicide and Parasuicide

An interesting application of the triple modes to depression is seen in Linehan's (1981) analysis of suicidal and parasuicidal behavior. Drawing on the large literature in the area, Linehan identifies a number of response patterns characteristic of the individual who attempts to end his or her life.

In terms of the cognitive mode, there are two major components.

The first of these is a cognitive style that is defined as a characteristic manner of processing, organizing, and using information. The suicidal individual is differentiated from others by a cognitive style that is rigid rather than flexible (Neuringer, 1964; Patsiokas, Clum, & Luscomb, 1979; Vinoda, 1966), impulsive instead of reflective (Farberow *et al.*, 1970; Fox & Weissman, 1975; Kessel & McCulloch, 1966), and ineffective as opposed to effective in terms of problem solving (Levenson & Neuringer, 1971). The second area involves the content of the suicidal person's thinking that is characterized by hopelessness (Barraclough, Bunch, Nelson, & Sainsbury, 1974; Farberow & MacKinnon, 1974; Farberow & McEvoy, 1966) and being "one down" (Neuringer, 1974).

Suicidal individuals are also differentiated from those who are simply depressed in terms of being more likely to have serious health problems (Andress & Corey, 1977; Bagley, Jacobson, & Rehin, 1976; Dorpat & Ripley, 1960). In addition, they are more likely to have somatic complaints (Litman, 1974) and suffer from insomnia (Bagley *et al.*, 1976; Barraclough *et al.*, 1974; Farberow *et al.*, 1970). These problems constitute a physiological (i.e., autonomic) contribution to suicide.

The suicidal person's overt motor responses are also characterized by two styles—poor interpersonal patterns and maladaptive life-styles. The former involves low levels of social involvement (Breed, 1966; Crook, Raskin, & Davis, 1975; Farberow & MacKinnon, 1974; Farberow & McEvoy, 1966; Farberow *et al.*, 1970) as well as a demanding, argumentative way of interacting with people (Birtchnell & Alarcon, 1971; Greer, Gunn, & Koller, 1966; Paykel, Prusoff, & Myers, 1975; Weissman, Fox, & Klerman, 1973). Also frequently present are maladaptive habits that include alcoholism and drug addiction (Frankel, Ferrence, Johnson, & Whitehead, 1976; Kreitman, 1977; Miles, 1977) as well as a history of previous suicide attempts (Ettlinger, 1964; Paerregaard, 1975).

Treatment Strategies[1]

A discussion of treatments for depression implies an understanding of the nature and cause of the disorder. Unfortunately, there is yet much to be learned regarding the etiology of depressive states.

---

[1]No attempt will be made to review different treatment modalities in detail. Readers interested in a comprehensive presentation of behavior therapy for depression are referred to two recent books on the topic—those of Clarkin and Glazer (1981) and Rehm (1981b).

Etiological Models

There are basically two models of depression, one biological and the other social. Needless to say, the two views are not mutually exclusive and, in fact, contribute to an understanding of each other. Nevertheless, there is a spirited rivalry between treatment approaches based on the opposing views (cf. Rush, Hollon, Beck, & Kovacs, 1978).

Biological Models. Biological models focus primarily on limbic-diencephalic dysfunction as a primary cause for depression (Kraines, 1966; Pollitt, 1965). One explanation of this dysfunction has been termed the "catecholamine hypothesis" (Sweeney & Maas, 1979). The catecholamines are a family of neurotransmitters, primarily norepinephrine (NE) and epinephrine (EP), both of which exert peripheral and central effects. In the periphery (i.e., outside the CNS), these agents act to maintain the physiological balance of the body and to prepare it for "fight or flight" activity. Centrally, the catecholamines have been implicated in a number of emotional disorders, including schizophrenia, and apparently act directly on the pleasure centers of the brain (Gerald, 1981).

Some of the more convincing evidence for the catecholamine hypothesis comes from a series of studies on a metabolic by-product of NE—3-methoxy-4-hydroxy-phenethyleneglycol (MHPG). It has been found that a heterogeneous group of depressed patients excrete significantly less urinary MHPG, indicating lower levels of NE, than healthy comparison subjects (Deleon-Jones, Maas, Dekirmenjian, & Sanchez, 1975; Maas, Fawcett, & Dekirmenjian, 1968). Also, bipolar depressives can be differentiated on the basis of MHPG excretion from other depressives or comparable groups (Goodwin & Post, 1975; Maas, Dekirmenjian, & Jones, 1973; Schildkraut, Keeler, Papousek, & Hartmann, 1973). And finally, there is some evidence to suggest that MHPG excretion levels are predictive of responsiveness to medical treatments (Sweeney & Maas, 1979).

It is known that the basal levels of catecholamine synthesis and degradation are inherited (Stolk & Nisula, 1979), thus supporting the existence of a genetic component to the disorder (Depue & Monroe, 1979). Further, it has been hypothesized that a deficiency in catecholaminergic activity impairs the normal functioning of the pleasure centers resulting in depression (Akiskal & McKinney, 1973; Klein, 1974). Consequently, medical treatments for depression tend to act directly on the synthesis, release, or inactivation of NE and EP (Gerald, 1981). ECT, for example, is thought to increase the synthesis and release of NE. The monoamine oxidase (MAO) inhibitors (an antidepressant medication) prevent the inactivation of NE in the synaptic cleft by preventing its breakdown. And the tricyclic antidepressants, such as imipramine, prevent the reuptake of NE from the synaptic cleft thus allowing for a prolongation of its effects.

In spite of advances in determining a biological basis for depression, it is doubtful that an explanation from this perspective alone will suffice. One reason is that treatments based on the biological model leave much to be desired. ECT, for example, involves a substantial risk of relapse, results in a high incidence of undesirable side effects, and is frequently unacceptable to individual patients or segments of society. Treatment with antidepressant medications alone does not help from 35 to 40% of patients needing it (Coleman & Beck, 1981) and is particularly susceptible to placebo effects making demonstration of its effectiveness difficult (Kocsis, 1981). In addition, the success of nonbiological interventions, such as the cognitive-behavioral treatments, raise questions concerning the adequacy of a medical approach only (Blaney, 1981; Hollon & Beck, 1978; Rehm & Kornblith, 1979). In short, the search for "the 'Holy Grail' of biological psychiatry—the biochemically homogeneous subgroup of patients" (Buschbaum, 1979, p. 238)—goes on.

Social-Environmental Models. Some investigators believe that social-environmental factors are the single most important cause of depression (G. W. Brown, 1979; G. W. Brown & Harris, 1978). Most of the treatments based on social-environmental models fall into one of two groups—those that emphasize behavior and those that emphasize cognition. The former group of interventions emphasizes behavioral or performance deficits (Lewinsohn, 1974; McLean, 1981) and focuses on maladaptive person–environment interactions. Treatments developed from this perspective rely heavily on social learning theory (Bandura, 1977; Lewinsohn, Teri, & Wasserman, 1983).

The second group of treatments emphasizes dysfunctional cognitions, such as "illusions of incompetence" (Becker, 1979), lowered self-esteem (Beach, Abramson, & Levine, 1981), "expectancy" of uncontrollability (Garber, Miller, & Seaman, 1979), faulty attributions (Seligman, 1975), or thoughts that "function at a private, illogical level" (Coleman & Beck, 1981). Seligman summarizes the general thrust of the cognitive approaches nicely when he states:

> Put in a nutshell, depression will occur when the individual expects that bad events will occur, expects that he or she can do nothing to prevent their occurrence, and construes the cause of this state of affairs as resulting from internal, stable, and global factors. (1981, p. 124)

Thus, according to Seligman, depression is the result of blaming oneself for one's misfortune, believing it will last forever, and perceiving it to affect all aspects of one's life.

Cognitive-Behavioral Interventions

Although different types of social-environmental interventions can be distinguished in terms of the relative emphasis placed on behavior versus cognitions, there is much similarity across cognitive-behavioral treatments regardless of label (Biglan & Dow, 1981; Seligman, 1981). For example, the assessment phase for behavioral interventions focuses on social/interpersonal problems, frequency of pleasant activities, and occurrence of unpleasant events as well as depressive cognitions (Lewinsohn *et al.*, 1983). Some of the behavioral tactics implemented following the assessment phase include changing environmental conditions, teaching new skills, increasing pleasant and decreasing unpleasant activities in addition to cognitive-restructuring and self-management techniques (Lewinsohn & Arconad, 1981).

More cognitively oriented approaches focus on depressive thought processes and general problem-solving skills. Beck's cognitive therapy, however, also includes behavioral components such as activity scheduling, mastery and pleasure techniques, and graded task assignments as well as cognitive strategies such as identifying and modifying "automatic thoughts" (Coleman & Beck, 1981). Seligman's cognitively oriented treatment protocol calls for environmental enrichment, resignation (acceptance) training, and attribution retraining. An additional component is "personal control training" that includes the development of motor skills in social and environmental management areas as well as cognitive skills such as problem solving and decision making.

Outcomes, as might be expected, are similar across treatment types, although their relative effectiveness in comparison with medical interventions is less certain. Blaney concluded his review by stating that

> clear evidence exists for the efficacy of both cognitive and behavioral treatments of depression; moreover, evidence indicates that both may be more effective than either antidepressant medication or traditional psychotherapy. (1981, p. 27)

A similar conclusion has been reached by other reviewers of the literature in this area (Hollon & Beck, 1978; Rehm & Kornblith, 1979).

There is disagreement, however, as to whether the cognitive-behavioral strategies work as well with bipolar (i.e., endogenous) depressives. Rush and his associates (1978) argue that cognitive therapy does as well as drugs for patients with a greater preponderance of vegetative symptoms. Harpin (1979), on the other hand, found that behavioral procedures did not do as well with a chronically depressed population. Fortunately, the answer may be forthcoming as the result of a major comparison outcome study now in progress (National Institute of Mental Health, 1980).

Depression as a System

Although the relative importance of biological versus social-environmental contributions to depression may be a matter of debate, it is generally agreed that neither position is sufficient in and of itself (Paykel, 1979). There are at least two good reasons for this assertion. First, the presence of genetic or biological factors in some forms of depression need not inhibit the development of learning-based interventions for those subtypes. After all, in spite of one's genotype, one still has to live and function in the real world. A second reason is the emergence of interactive models that view depression as the consequence of a genetic predisposition *and* environmental factors (Buschbaum, 1979; Depue, Monroe, & Shackman, 1979; Mendels, 1965). This view, commonly known as a diathesis-stress model of depression (D. Rosenthal, 1970), states that a biological vulnerability, although necessary (diathesis means "predisposition"), is not sufficient to cause depression by itself.

Treatment, therefore, should take into account the *relative* contribution of different factors. This view has led to the proposal that different treatment models are differentially effective with various subtypes of depression (Beach *et al.*, 1981; Depue, 1979). For example, the catecholamine hypothesis suggests that depressive states that load heavily on the autonomic mode might be more responsive to interventions, such as medication, that affect that system directly (Sweeney & Maas, 1979; Weiss, Glazer, Pohorecky, Bailey, & Schneider, 1979). Depression with a stronger motoric component, however, might benefit more from strategies that attempt to increase instrumental responding (Averill, 1979; Lewinsohn, Youngren, & Grosscup, 1979). Depression stemming from maladaptive or faulty cognitions, on the other hand, might respond more readily to interventions that specifically target appraisal, expectations, attributions, cognitive coping responses, and the like (Averill, 1979; Becker, 1979; Garber *et al.*, 1979).

Support for differential treatment effects, however, is lacking. There may be at least two reasons for this. For one, most procedures involve a "smorgasbord of treatment components" (McLean, 1981, p. 205). This means that usually there is something for everybody, making identification of specific treatment by person interactions difficult. Second, the nonspecific (i.e., placebo) effect of most interventions "simply overwhelms any therapeutic gains made by optimal client-treatment matching."

Whatever the case, the multiple pathways by which depression can occur require attention to individual needs. Rehm (1981a) points to the interaction of coping skills, environmental stress, and biological vulnerability as affecting the onset and course of depression. Paykel (1979, p. 260) identifies 4 factors that mediate between an "event" and the "specific treated disease." His analysis includes social supports and stressors, vulnerability to events, specific illness vulnerability, and treatment-seeking factors. Akiskal (1979) proposes that there are as many as 10 etiological factors in depression. These include multiple social stressors, lack of social support, deficient social skills, developmental object loss, monoamine depletion, increasing monoamine oxidase with age, borderline hypothyroid functioning, puerperalism (i.e., following childbirth), alcoholism, and familial and genetic factors. Clearly, not every depressed individual is expected to share all 10 factors, making at least some effort to identify the most potent contributors necessary. Consequently, the modification of depression calls for "individualizing treatment based on functional relationship of depressed persons' symptom picture and its environmental antecedents and consequences" (Liberman, 1981, p. 251). Biglan and Dow (1981) refer to this approach as the "problem-specific model." The model attempts to avoid *a priori* assumptions, is reluctant to base conclusions on self-report data only, tries to link specific treatments to specific problem areas, and is open to feedback and evaluation.

Kanfer and Hagerman's (1981) self-control model of depression is offered as a good example of a problem-specific approach (Biglan & Dow, 1981). The approach is based on a flexible and multimodal program that sees depression as resulting from a cumulation of failure experiences due to any one of a number of factors, such as skill deficits, loss of support, or biological dysfunction. Attempts by the individual to remedy the situation apparently have failed and may be due to personal deficiencies or lack of support. This, in turn, can lead either to resignation or self-blame. The result is a preoccupation or focus on negative events and thoughts. The treatment program attempts to halt the "downward spiral" using a combination of medical and psychological interventions such as those discussed earlier.

Depression, from this perspective, is the product of complex systems operating on many levels and incorporating both physiological and psychological factors. As suggested earlier in the book, clinical syndromes such as depression may have many causes and, in turn, may be approached along multiple pathways. Consequently,

> it seems important to emphasize that depression is not an isolated phenomenon that has a life and existence of its own. To think of it in such a way would be to falsely reify it, analogous to reification of such psychoanalytic constructs as ego and id. On the contrary, depression in the narrow sense is a particular mood, and in the broader sense it is a syndrome of related

throughts, feelings, and behaviors. It rarely occurs alone; rather it is a thread woven into the context of a person interacting with an environment. This means that the assessment of depression never occurs in isolation but rather is an aspect of a more complete assessment of the person in an environment. By the same token, when the person becomes more effective in one area of life, positive changes often occur in relation to other areas even though they have not been specifically targeted for treatment." (Glazer *et al.*, 1981, p. 26)

Capitalizing on this possibility, the astute clinician may design and implement treatment strategies that extend beyond the particular focus of the initiating problem itself and thus affect greater gains than either the client or the therapist expected. This is what makes the treatment of emotional disorders such as depression both a formidable challenge and welcome opportunity at the same time.

Recommended Readings

Clarkin, J. F., & Glazer, H. I. (Eds.). (1981). *Depression: Behavioral and directive intervention strategies.* New York: Garland STPM Press.

Rehm, L. P. (Ed.). (1981). *Behavior therapy for depression: Present status and future directions.* New York: Academic Press.

These edited works appeared in the same year and cover much of the same ground. (In fact, they even share several of the same authors.) Both provide a good overview of the more viable current interventions for depression. With many of the more notable names in the depression literature as contributors, both volumes have much to offer the reader interested in the assessment and treatment of depression.

CHAPTER **10**

Physiology and Behavior Therapy

Our look at behavior therapy from a physiological perspective is about to end. We have reviewed some preliminary concepts, discussed some basic issues, and applied this thinking to several clinical problems. The central theme has been that behavior is a complex, multidetermined, interactive phenomenon for which no single explanation is sufficient.

Behavior Therapy

Behavior therapy is an approach to treatment that recognizes the importance of a comprehensive assessment leading to multidimensional interventions tailored to fit individual needs. Although behavioral approaches cannot be seen as offering a panacea for all emotional ills, the assumptions upon which they are based make their integration with physiological concepts a natural and comfortable union.

Definition

To begin, one may define behavior therapy in terms of what it is *not*. For example, behavior therapy is not an identifiable set of techniques based on a unified theory (Rachman & Wilson, 1980). Behavior therapy, therefore, cannot be defined in terms of its procedures, nor can it be identified with any one person or "school" (Ross, 1978, p. 591). Rather, behavior therapy is a way of thinking, "an approach to clinical problems, a system for collecting, organizing, and evaluating clinical data and then designing individual treatment programs tailored to specific presenting problems" (Melamed & Siegel, 1980, p. 3).

Essentially, behavior therapy is the application of the scientific method to clinical problems (Borkovec & Bauer, 1982; McFall, 1985). As such, it shares the methodology common to most forms of scientific inquiry (cf. Platt, 1964). More specifically, this basic process includes (a) devising a number of alternative hypotheses as to what is causing the problem; (b) designing an intervention that addresses these hypotheses directly; (c) implementing the treatment in a manner that allows one to determine which hypotheses are more plausible than others; and (d) recycling the procedure so that the remaining hypotheses are refined and set up to be tested again. The approach is problem oriented rather than method oriented in that no particular explanation or intervention is favored before it is tested.

A key aspect of a problem-solving approach is an appreciation of disconfirmation as a logical basis of knowledge (Mahoney, 1976). This means that one looks for evidence that fails to support his or her hypothesis as intently as one seeks data to confirm it. Assessment is thus a process of ruling out possible explanations as much as it is supporting others. Consequently, one approaches clinical problems with multiple working hypotheses and attempts to evaluate each on its own merits rather than moving quickly to accept the first that comes to mind (cf. Chamberlin, 1965).

This process is illustrated by Gottman and Markman's (1978) distinction between a "mastery" and a "mystery" approach to treatment evaluation.

> A mastery approach is one in which the researcher is out to demonstrate that the program being evaluated can master the problem it addresses. A mystery approach is one in which the research question is more complex, in which the interest is perhaps, "What kind of people make what kinds of specific gains in which specific settings with the program"? The distinction is nontrivial in a major sense that two different attitudes are created in the mind of the investigator by these two approaches. The mastery investigator is likely to become angry at data that disconfirm the program's effectiveness and to be repulsed by a phenomenon that demonstrates itself to be complex. The mystery investigator enjoys the data; failure indicates that there is unexpected information in the phenomenon. (pp. 56–57)

Therapists married to a single model generally fail to appreciate the value of this type of approach and attempt to apply their theory as widely as possible. The result is, as Maslow writes, "If the only tool you have is a hammer, [you tend] to treat everything as if it were a nail" (1966, pp. 15–16). Behavior therapy's grounding in the scientific method provides a flexibility that enables it to take into account multiple explanations, including those that incorporate physiological factors.

Eclecticism

In many ways, this definition of behavior therapy may appear synonymous with eclecticism. After all, eclecticism is *the* most common treatment orientation in psychology. In the mid-1970s Garfield and Kurtz (1976) surveyed 855 members and fellows from Division 12 (Clinical Psychology) of the American Psychological Association and found that over half (55%) reported that their theoretical orientation was "eclectic." Several years later, D. Smith (1982) surveyed members and fellows from Division 12 and Division 17 (Counseling Psychology). Results indicated that an eclectic approach was endorsed by 41% of the 422 respondents. (The difference between the two figures is probably due to a wider range of theoretical choices [9 versus 13] available on the later questionnaire.) Eclecticism is clearly the most frequently endorsed theoretical stance among professional psychologists.

By definition, eclectic means "choosing what appears to be best from diverse sources, systems, or styles" (*American Heritage Dictionary of the English Language,* 1971, p. 412). In practice, eclectic therapists align themselves with no particular school or model and choose those techniques and methods that appear best to fit the client's needs.

It would seem difficult to argue against eclecticism as an approach to treatment given its flexibility and emphasis on what works best. However, the term is often viewed "as being synonymous with 'muddle-headedness' or minimal brain damage" (Garfield, 1982b, p. 12). The reason is because most explanations of eclectic psychotherapy have been idiosyncratic and nonsystematic (Garfield & Kurtz, 1977). Also, because eclecticism does not represent an integrated approach but rather a combination of therapeutic procedures and models, it is difficult to define. Consequently,

> although an eclectic approach allows the therapist great flexibility and access to a wider range of procedures than is the case of most other therapies, it is nonsystematic, covers a multitude of sins, and is difficult to evaluate. (Garfield, 1982b, p. 13)

Ironically, the more one attempts to meet these criticisms, the less "eclectic" his or her approach becomes. To make the approach more systematic, one must hold certain values and assumptions constant. The consistent application of values and assumptions, however, constitutes an identifiable treatment orientation. Thus, if one believes that certain things are more important than others in working with clients, these biases deserve to be acknowledged rather than veiled with the cloak of eclecticism. For example, if one is interested in behavior change more than cognitive change, then one is applying a specific set of values to clinical practice that distinguishes him or her from the therapist for whom cognition is of primary importance. Although both may employ a variety of therapeutic strategies to meet their individual ends, it would seem misleading to lump them under the ambiguous rubric of eclecticism.

Support for this assertion comes, interestingly enough, from one of the foremost advocates of a flexible and integrative approach to treatment. Jerome Frank in *Persuasion and Healing* (1963) notes that:

> It seems probable that certain approaches are better for some types of patients or problems than for others. Until this question is clarified, the advance of both knowledge and practice is probably better served by members of different schools defending their own positions, while being tolerant of other schools, than by being uncritical eclectics. (p. 342)

Behavior therapy continues to be distinguished from eclecticism and other approaches by its emphasis on behavior and its adherence to a data-based process for selecting and implementing treatment strategies (Barlow, 1980; Wilson, 1982). This constitutes a core of assumptions based on the scientific method (Agras, Kazdin, & Wilson, 1979; Wilson & O'Leary, 1980) and includes a reliance on testable theories, empirical support, and treatment specificity (Wilson, 1982, p. 292). To the degree that this set of assumptions allows for the open-ended consideration of many contributions to behavior change, then it is "eclectic," at least in terms of technique. To the degree it serves to promote an approach to treatment that stands apart from other orientations, these values remain the hallmark of behavior therapy and provide a basis upon which it is able to integrate physiological concerns.

Integrative Strengths

The Scientific Method. In a very real sense, behavior therapists and physiologists speak the same language—the language of science. Although psychology as a science may be less secure than other sciences (cf. Boulding, 1980) and although many psychologists have followed decidedly nonscientific approaches to human problems (cf. Sarason, 1981), the scientific heritage of psychology continues as one of its major strengths. One example of this is the adoption of the scientist-practitioner training model (Raimy, 1950) that continues to be a significant factor that distinguishes psychologists from other health-care providers (Barlow, Hayes, & Nelson, 1984; Wollersheim, 1974; Zehr, 1982).

Perhaps no other approach within psychology is tied as closely to its scientific roots as behavior therapy.

> What is novel in the behavior therapies is their adoption of methods that shift from laboratory to clinic and back to the laboratory in self-conscious testing of

the utility and validity of their operation, and with a data-oriented, hypothesis-testing frame of reference within the treatment setting itself. (Kanfer & Phillips, 1970, p. 16)

Today the "laboratory" is often the clinical setting itself, leading to the integration of science and practice in the form of the "empirical clinician" (Barlow, 1980). This commitment to a scientific basis for one's practice provides a common ground upon which constructs and data from psychology and physiology can be integrated.

The Functional Analysis of Behavior. The application of the scientific method to clinical problems takes the form of a functional analysis of behavior. A functional analysis is the step beyond diagnostic classification that allows for a tailoring of a treatment regimen to suit the individual case (Kanfer & Saslow, 1965). Unlike topographical classifications such as those found in the DSM-III, a functional diagnosis

seeks to classify and comprehend behaviors and their significance in terms of what actually controls them, not in terms of how they look; it seeks to classify stimulus contexts in terms of which behaviors they actually control and how, not in terms of their presumed a priori significance. (Glazer, Clarkin & Hunt, 1981, p. 9)

Kanfer and Nay (1982) propose that this process consists of two steps. The first is the discovery component or hypothesis-formulation phase that "relies heavily on the clinician's experience, skill, familiarity with psychological principles, prevailing sociocultural norms, and awareness of non-psychological variables (e.g., biological, sociological, economic)" (p. 370). This step is followed by the verification component, a phase that involves the collection of data that support or fail to support the hypotheses generated by the first step. The two steps together provide for an open-ended process of exploration that facilitates the inclusion of many considerations, including those physiological in nature.

The Focus on Behavior. A final integrative strength of behavior therapy is its emphasis on behavior itself. One of the ironies of psychology's focus on cognition is an appreciation of the role of behavior in affecting cognitions. Although it may be argued that cognition is basic to all behavior change, "cognitive" interventions are not always the most effective means of achieving that change (Rachman, 1980, 1981). This is the "therapeutic paradox" discussed earlier (Chapter 7) in reference to Bandura (1977, p. 78) who suggests that although therapeutic change may be mediated through cognitive processes, the processes themselves are induced or altered most readily by experiences based on successful performance (i.e., behavior).

Like the behavior therapist, the physiologist is also interested in behavior. Although many physiological systems can be studied in isolation, overt behavior activates physiological systems on all levels and thus becomes a logical endpoint for physiology. For example, heart rate, blood pressure, and respiration are linked so closely to motor activity that the slightest, even unobservable, motor response will serve to alter these variables significantly (Obrist, 1981). Thus, behavior can be seen as a major focus of physiology just as it is for psychotherapy.

Integrative Problems

In spite of these advantages, some aspects of behavior therapy may interfere with the incorporation of physiological constructs. These difficulties reflect some of the differences in philosophy and style that occur within behavior therapy itself.

Behavioral Epistemology. Epistemology is the study of human knowledge, its nature, origins, methods, and limits. The epistemological assumptions one makes determines what he or she accepts as a legitimate basis for knowing.

Some forms of behavioral epistemology argue against the consideration of variables that cannot be actually observed. For example, the behaviorism of Skinner (1974) and others (e.g., Rachlin, 1977) is based on the premise that the objective and accessible facts of behavior constitute the only proper subject for psychological study. This view is sometimes referred to as *metaphysical* or *radical* behaviorism (Mahoney & Arnkoff, 1978).

Historically, this argument was directed toward the highly inferential constructs derived from psychoanalytic theory. Nevertheless, the same cautions have been applied to biomedical data as well. Skinner (1938) has referred to the central nervous system as the conceptual nervous system because "mental events" are not directly observable. Although Skinner (1950) does not argue against the study of the CNS, he does question whether knowledge of this sort is *necessary* for the understanding and prediction of behavior. Further, Skinner contends that attention to physiological explanations of behavior may provide a false sense of security and thus keep us from pursuing more observable and thus more powerful predictors of behavior.

A competing view, termed *methodological* behaviorism, is also concerned with "the importance of objectivity and experimental rigor in the analysis of behavior" (Mahoney & Arnkoff, 1978, p. 711) but differs from metaphysical behaviorism in its willingness to consider variables that are not directly observable. Nevertheless, methodological behaviorists are also primarily interested in behavior to the degree that unobservable processes, including physiological ones, add to one's predictive power

(p. 713). For example, an appreciation for a physiological contribution to anxiety is useful if it saves time and effort by directing attention to appropriate medical remedies rather than belaboring the client with learning-based interventions. Or, the question of the biological contributions to learning (see Chapter 4) may serve a useful purpose generally in helping select target behaviors and designing treatment programs.

Behavioral Belligerence. Behavior therapy has been and still is in a struggle with other orientations over political influence and professional acceptance. On occasion, the result of this struggle has been a belligerence that has tended to emphasize differences rather than similarities. For example, the emphasis of psychodynamic theory on internal causes has led behavior therapists to attack the "medical" or "disease" model of behavior. Although there may be many good reasons to do so, it is also clear that the medical contribution to our understanding behavior cannot be casually dismissed.

There is often the tendency, however, to assume an either/or attitude in which medical and behavioral approaches are seen as mutually exclusive. As a result, the usefulness of medical interventions for many behavior problems and the contribution of biomedical knowledge to the understanding of behavior has been, at times, ignored. Often, there is an antimedical bias that can interfere with acceptance of the fact that psychologists are not the only ones capable of helping people (Hersen, 1979; Hollandsworth, 1985a).

In recent years, the development of behavioral medicine has tended to ease earlier antagonisms. It is common now for the behavior therapist to function as a member of a larger treatment team that includes health care professionals from medicine as well as other areas. Although this is often the case for medical problems that exhibit psychological components, there may be a growing acceptance of the role of medicine as a companion treatment for many disorders often seen as primarily psychogenic in nature, such as depression and agoraphobia (Becker & Schuckit, 1978; Rush, Hollon, Beck, & Kovacs, 1978; Telch, Agras, Taylor, Roth, & Gallen, 1985; also see Chapters 8 and 9). The degree to which these old antagonisms persist, however, will serve to hinder the integration of behavioral procedures with physiological knowledge.

Behavioral Medicine

Behavioral medicine is an excellent example of how physiology and behavior therapy can form a mutually beneficial alliance. In its broadest sense, behavioral medicine is concerned with how behaviors and attitudes effect the development and course of medical disorders. In a more specific sense, it signifies the application of a behavioral methodology to medical problems (Pomerleau & Brady, 1979). In both instances, behavioral medicine represents "an emerging network of communication among an array of disciplines not previously connected" (Agras, 1982, p. 797).

The need for greater communication across traditional boundaries resulted from a growing awareness that many problems could not be dealt with satisfactorily from one perspective alone. The success of medical science in stamping out major killers of the past (e.g., infectious diseases) resulted in an extended life span so that by the 1960s chronic disorders, such as cardiovascular disease and cancer, became the leading causes of death. Unlike earlier medical problems, however, these disorders are "managed" rather than "cured," highlighting the role of behavior (i.e., life-style) as a major factor contributing to health (Blanchard, 1982).

The growing awareness of behavior's role in the development and progression of many medical disorders was accompanied by the emergence during the late 1960s and early 1970s of behavior therapy as an effective treatment approach. Soon these and related strategies were applied to various "psychosomatic" problems, such as hypertension (Patel, 1973), headache (Benson, Klemchuk, & Graham, 1974), and chronic pain (Fordyce et al., 1973). In addition, the widespread interest in biofeedback during the same period (see Chapter 6) caught the attention of the medical community and stimulated some of the first applications of behavioral medicine (Birk, 1973).

Behavioral medicine's success pushed both medicine and psychology in unexpected directions. On the medical side of things, behavior's role has grown to involve much more than the management of chronic illness. Now, behavior is implicated in the onset of a wide range of disorders, including many (such as allergies, upper respiratory infections and cancer) whose etiology was once thought to be entirely medical in origin (Jemmott & Locke, 1984; Levy, Herberman, Maluish, Schlien, & Lippman, 1985). In terms of psychology, the increased interaction with the medical community did much to break down barriers that had separated behavioral from biological approaches to treatment and resulted in a new view of health and illness that incorporates both medical as well as psychological factors. In a very real sense, the present book could not have been written without the extensive foundation laid down by nearly a decade of fruitful collaboration across the two disciplines.

Modalities

Behavioral medicine encompasses a wide range of treatment modalities, some that attempt to modify the disease process directly and others that attempt to do so indirectly by supporting the application of medical regimens (Pomerleau & Brady, 1979). The direct approach attempts to alter behaviors that contribute to the natural progression of a disorder before it reaches the disease state (*prevention*) or to modify the course of the disease once it has occurred (*treatment*). The indirect approach supports medical interventions by providing the patient with behaviors that allow him or her to cooperate more fully with the treatment protocol (*adherence*) or by assisting medical health providers in the application their science (*consultation*).

All four roles can be illustrated in relation to almost any disorder. For example, chronic obstructive pulmonary disease (COPD; S. A. Turner, Daniels, & Hollandsworth, 1985) is a persistent impairment of respiratory function as a result of damage to the lungs, usually from prolonged cigarette smoking. If one attempts to get a person to stop smoking before this medical problem arises, one is applying prevention. However, if smoking cessation is a part of the overall medical regimen designed to halt or reverse the disease process, then one is providing treatment. Actions that encourage the COPD patient to participate fully with the medical intervention by keeping appointments, taking medication, and following instructions is seen as increasing adherence, whereas assisting the physician in considering psychological factors in the treatment decision-making process is an example of consultation.

Interventions

Behavior therapy and related strategies can be useful in all four modalities. For example, prevention or treatment strategies may be designed to reduce autonomic nervous system (ANS) reactivity, given its role in accelerating or exacerbating the disease process. Examples of this type of intervention include the use of relaxation and/or biofeedback in the treatment of hypertension (Shapiro & Goldstein, 1982), migraine headache (Blanchard & Andrasik, 1982), vascular disease (e.g., Raynuad's syndrome; Surwit, 1982), arthritis (Achterberg-Lawlis, 1982), and a variety of other stress-related disorders (Stoyva, 1979). In addition, the reduction of ANS reactivity among individuals with established patterns of coronary prone behavior has been advocated (Suinn, 1982). Other interventions, such as exercise (Martin & Dubbert, 1982), that tend to ameliorate exaggerated responding may serve to replace or augment any of these procedures.

In other cases, behavior itself is of primary interest. This is true in areas such as chronic pain (Fordyce & Steger, 1979) and some gastrointestinal disorders (Whitehead & Basmajian, 1982) in which the problem involves motoric as well as physiological components. For example, operant procedures can be extremely useful in treating pain behavior or training sphincter control for fecal incontinence.

In terms of adherence, operant strategies related to self-control are also useful for disorders, such as diabetes (Fisher, Delamater, Bertelson, & Kirkley, 1982), that require strict compliance to a prescribed treatment regimen (see Epstein & Cluss, 1982). However, ANS reactivity can also play a role in adherence, as when elevated autonomic arousal interferes with participation in the treatment itself. When this occurs, steps are taken to alleviate this "anxiety" using modeling, information, relaxation, or other fear-reduction techniques (Kendall & Watson, 1981; Pinto & Hollandsworth, 1983).

Interactions

There are a number of problem areas that fall under the general rubric of behavioral medicine that provide particularly good examples of the reciprocal interaction of physiological with behavioral systems. Some of these include obesity, smoking, and alcoholism.

In each case, physiological as well as psychological factors appear to play an important role. For example, the treatment of obesity must take into account the possible contribution of elevated set points and fat cell composition in determining the physiologic regulation of weight (Brownell, 1982). Rodin (1985) examined the interaction of insulin levels, hunger, and food intake in relation to weight control and concluded that "'overeating' is caused by a complex feedback system of environmental, behavioral, and biological factors" (p. 1).

Smoking also appears to involve important physiological elements. Schachter (1980), for example, argues that nicotine addiction is the primary determinant of smoking behavior. Even when one takes into account social-environmental variables, the persistence of smoking appears closely tied to maintaining a state of physiological homeostasis (Pomerleau, 1980). Consequently, most smoking-cessation programs usually attend to the physiological contribution by attempting to reduce nicotine dependence using procedures involving brand fading or nicotine substitutes as well as focus on the important psychosocial contributions (Lichetenstein, 1982).

Finally, the physiological attraction of alcohol has generally been cited as its most important feature, leading many to view alcoholism entirely as a physiological (i.e., medical) disorder. However, research on the effects of psychological variables, such as expectancy, reveal drinking behavior to be influenced by much more than a simple craving for alcohol. Nathan and Goldman (1979) emphasize the interaction of psychological, environmental, and pharmacolgcial factors when they note that

> a complex interaction of factors determines what many have long considered to be simply the pharmacological effects of alcohol. These factors include the actions of the drug on physiological functioning, the individual's expectancy of what the effects of the drug will be, his/her prior history of drug use, and the environment in which the ingestion takes place. (pp. 256–257)

Consequently, most investigators advocate a multidimensional approach to the treatment so that psychological as well as pharmacological factors are considered. Even Alcoholics Anonymous, with its strong bias toward alcoholism as a disease state, relies heavily on psychosoical factors such as peer support (i.e., weekly if not daily meetings) and the mainpulation of expectancy (i.e., a commitment to total abstinence achieved one day at time).

Although the addictive behaviors clearly illustrate the interaction of behavior with physiology, in almost every area of behavioral medicine, the complementary roles of behavior and physical health are represented. Behavioral medicine, therefore, demonstrates the potential for applying behavior therapy to physiological processes. In addition, the role of physiology in facilitating or hindering behavior change is illustrated. In both cases, behavioral medicine involves the interaction of multiple factors in a systems model that supports the multidimensional, flexible approach to treatment presented earlier.

John Hunter: A Reprise

We began this book with an accounting of John Hunter's death. That event served to illustrate the complexity of physiological regulation on multiple levels throughout the body, some of which we can control voluntarily and some of which we cannot. Subsequent chapters developed this thinking further and provided some ideas as to how this perspective can affect one's approach to treatment. It is appropriate at this point to return to John Hunter in an attempt to apply what we have learned. To do this, we will consider Dr. Hunter as if he were alive today at the age of 60, a few years before his death. It will be useful to remember that Dr. Hunter has a serious problem with his anger and his heart and that he is at the height of his professional career.

Initial Stages of Treatment

Getting Dr. Hunter into Treatment. Getting John Hunter into treatment will be the first of several challenges. In spite of the seriousness of his problem, it is probable that Dr. Hunter will be a reluctant client. His professional success, his visibility in the community, and his heavy work schedule might act to dissuade him from seeking psychological treatment. In addition, being a physician, Dr. Hunter may prefer to deal with his problem medically. For example, his angina might be controlled pharmacologically, or even surgically (i.e., bypass), thus reducing his motivation to deal with the problem of anger control.

On the other hand, if we do get Dr. Hunter into treatment, he is likely to prefer a behavior therapist. As an active researcher, the problem-solving orientation of a behavior therapist will likely please him. In addition, the rationale for an approach that shares his values of parsimony, functionalism, and empiricism should be accepted rapidly.

Establishing a Therapeutic Relationship. A therapeutic relationship with Dr. Hunter will be essential as well as somewhat of a challenge. We know that his arrogant and rude manner will test our patience and require our best talents as a "skilled helper" (Egan, 1982). On the other hand, his directness will be an advantage. If he is displeased with his treatment, most likely he will let us know about it directly rather than resort to passive-aggressive stratagems. This will make resolving conflicts in the relationship or differences of opinion over treatment easier to handle (Parsons & Wicks, 1983).

In terms of an approach to the relationship, we might want to avoid being too nondirective. Given his impatience and expertise, an approach that is too reflective may prove frustrating. Instead, we will want to assume the sort of professional attitude that communicates a certain degree of direction as is fitting an expert in an area. It is possible that Dr. Hunter will respond most favorably if treated as a colleague rather than a client. As part of the process, the provision of sufficient information, particularly as it relates to our rationale for treatment, will be important.

Diagnosis. For purposes of record keeping and third-party payment, we will want to assign a diagnosis from the DSM-III early in treatment. Although it is dangerous to assign a diagnostic code on the basis of insufficient information, we will speculate that the most likely diagnosis for Dr. Hunter is *psychological factors affecting physical condition* (316.00). The diagnostic criteria for this disorder include the presence of a situation that is temporally related to the initiation or exacerbation of a physical condition. In this case, Dr. Hunter's angry episodes leading to acute angina attacks fulfill this diagnostic requirement. Further, his coronary condition, which will be recorded on Axis III, meets the diagnostic requirement that the physical condition have demonstrable organic pathology.

Assessment

Autonomic/Medical Mode. Given the clear indication of angina, a review of his medical records will be essential. In that Dr. Hunter is a physician, it will be particularly important to use him as a source of information concerning his own illness. Self-monitoring will probably constitute a major assessment approach for this mode. In that Dr. Hunter is personally involved in research, it is likely that he will respond favorably to this type of data collection. Of primary interest will be the frequency and severity of his angina attacks. In addition, identifying the circumstances under which these attacks occur will be important.

Dr. Hunter's autonomic reactivity also suggests that he may be a hyperresponder (Obrist, 1981). Consequently, we might consider the use of other self-report measures to determine his awareness of this responsivity, particularly as it relates to his angry outbursts. The Autonomic Perception Questionnaire reworded for anger situations (APQ; Mandler, Mandler, & Uviller, 1958) might be useful in this context. Information from the APQ can be incorporated into anger-control training so that Dr. Hunter can learn to use autonomic cues as a signal to take compensatory action in the early stages of anger.

Psychophysiological assessment using a polygraph might also be in order if the instrumentation is available. Of particular relevance will be cardiovascular responses such as heart rate and blood pressure under conditions of active coping (e.g., Ellender & Hollandsworth, 1986; Ginter, Hollandsworth, & Intrieri, 1984; Rectanus & Hollandsworth, 1985). This assessment information will be especially useful as a pre-post index of treatment effectiveness.

Cognitive Mode. There is a possibility that Dr. Hunter's quickness to anger is tied to his perceptions of the way the world *should* be. In other words, Dr. Hunter's strong opinions and biases might serve to make even trivial situations major opportunities for an emotional response. This possibility can be checked in a number of ways. The interview itself will provide information concerning the presence of irrational thoughts or faulty thinking patterns that contribute to his angry outbursts. Also, standardized instruments, such as the *Irrational Beliefs Test* (Jones, 1968), can be employed.

As with the autonomic mode, self-monitoring will be useful. But unlike the recording of angina attacks, the self-assessment of cognitions should be open ended, allowing for Dr. Hunter to elaborate the nature of his thoughts in situations that make him angry and/or lead to angry outbursts. Also, part of the cognitive assessment will be eliciting information concerning the type of coping strategies Dr. Hunter uses in situations that raise his ire.

Motoric Mode. Focus on the motoric mode will involve essentially two different problem areas. The first concerns his interpersonal style. It is likely that Dr. Hunter's lack of social skills is setting the stage for situations that precipitate angry encounters. Given that Dr. Hunter may be viewed as more aggressive than assertive, the usual measures for unassertive behavior (e.g., Gay, Hollandsworth, & Galassi, 1975) will be of little value. These measures are designed to identify the low assertive individual and demonstrate questionable validity in terms of differentiating highly assertive individuals from those who are aggressive (Hollandsworth, Galassi, & Gay, 1977). Perhaps an aggression scale, such as the Buss-Durkee Inventory (Buss & Durkee, 1957), will be useful. This measure provides several indexes of aggressive behavior, including irritability and verbal aggression. Reports from individuals who observe and react to Dr. Hunter's behavior will be a particularly valuable source of assessment information. In addition, one might have Dr. Hunter role play in order to analyze his responses in terms of their coercive content (Hollandsworth, 1977, 1985b).

The second focus of the motoric mode will concern Dr. Hunter's life-style. Dietary habits, exercise, and recuperative activities will be the legitimate targets of this assessment. A number of standardized risk-factor inventories can be used (e.g., American Institute for Preventive Medicine, 1981). In addition, his coronary-prone behavior will deserve special attention. Although there are a number of self-report indexes of this construct, such as the Jenkins Activity Survey (Jenkins, Rosenman, & Friedman, 1967), the Structured Interview should be administered and rated by someone trained in its use in order to determine Dr. Hunter's Type A characteristics (Dembroski, 1978).

Treatment Goals. Depending on the results of the assessment, treatment goals will possibly cover three areas. (These goals, of course, apply to the behavioral interventions only and do not concern ongoing medical treatment for Dr. Hunter's coronary problems.) One goal might deal specifically with Dr. Hunter's angry outbursts given their relationship to his angina. This goal can be evaluated through his self-monitoring and the reports of colleagues at work. An ideal outcome for this goal would be to eliminate anger completely in his interactions with others. This is probably unrealistic, however, given the long-standing nature of this response style. A more realistic goal would be to reduce the frequency of outbursts by one-half, with the intensity of these responses decreased to the point that they occur without concomitant autonomic symptoms.

A second goal might deal with Dr. Hunter's manner of interacting with people generally. If his abrasive style contributes to those situations in which anger occurs, more harmonious interactions with others will serve a preventive function. An ideal outcome for this goal will be to have Dr. Hunter become appropriately assertive as opposed to aggressive in his dealings with others. Again, given the long-standing history of this behavior pattern, it is unlikely that major changes will result. A more realistic level for this goal might include the elimination of some of the more objectionable (i.e., coercive) aspects of his interpersonal style.

A final goal might involve life-style change. The specifics of this goal will follow a detailed review of his present habits and could include smoking cessation, dietary modification, weight reduction, and possibly alterations in coronary-prone behavior (Gentry & Williams, 1979; N. K. Wenger & Hellerstein, 1978).

Setting Priorities. Determining which of these goals should be the first target for change will take into account the seriousness of the problem as well as its potential for successful modification. Given Dr. Hunter's report that he is at the mercy of "any rogue who cares to tease me," his reactivity to provocation would be high on the list. Improving his relationships with others would also be important but perhaps tackled later given less certainty concerning the ability to affect this long-standing behavior. Life-style change, the most difficult of all to change, would become third in the order of priority. This does not mean, however, that it is unimportant. Although changes in life-style may play less of a role in preventing infraction once serious pathophysiology exists (as in the case of Dr. Hunter), behaviors such as smoking are clearly linked to increased mortality among coronary patients (e.g., Aberg *et al.*, 1983) and thus should be pursued.

Treatment

Anger-Control. To deal with the first goal, the use of an anger-control procedure as discussed in Chapter 5 (Novaco, 1978) could be explored. It will be remembered that this approach is patterned after Meichenbaum's (1977a) stress-inoculation model and involves three phases—cognitive preparation, skill acquisition, and practice. In the first phase, Dr. Hunter's assumptions will be explored with an eye to using cognitive restructuring if those assumptions appear to be contributing to his angry outbursts. Also, during the first phase, the relationship between these angry episodes and his coronary problems can be reviewed.

In the skills-acquisition phase, both cognitive and motoric components will be targeted. For example, the autonomic aspects of anger will be highlighted with an emphasis on using these responses as cues for coping strategies such as more adaptive self-statements and calming behaviors. The coping strategies themselves will be practiced during the third phase using role play. Homework assignments will also be used, as long as they involve situations Dr. Hunter feels he can handle successfully. It will be very important for Dr. Hunter to avoid major confrontations until his anger-control skills have been well integrated.

A final aspect of the anger-control intervention will be attention to the instrumental value of these responses in his work environment. It may be that angry outbursts enable Dr. Hunter to accomplish things that a less belligerent attitude does not. If that is the case, alternative ways of achieving these ends will need to be explored.

Social Skills. Anger control by itself will probably not be sufficient to deal with the problem, making the second goal a close companion of the first. Moon and Eisler (1983), for example, found that stress inoculation alone tends to foster withdrawal and does not support the use of more effective interpersonal skills. Given Dr. Hunter's position and responsibilities, it is doubtful that he will acquiesce to a change in his behavior that makes him less active in his daily life.

A basic social skills approach (Kelly, 1982) might be employed. This procedure involves instruction, modeling, role playing, feedback, and reinforcement of appropriate responses. Again, the importance of actual practice will be emphasized. In Dr. Hunter's case, it will be important to analyze both his nonverbal and verbal means of expression, focusing particularly on the coercive or punishing content of the latter.

Life-Style Change. Possible interventions could include targeting his dietary habits, particularly in terms of fat and sodium intake. Dr. Hunter's weight will also be a concern, and a weight-reduction program tailored to fit his needs and involving long-term life-style change rather than temporary diets will be considered (Stuart, Mitchell, & Jensen, 1981). In addition, we might consider whether his Type A behavior is a problem and use a strategy to reduce this behavior (Roskies, 1980). It should be noted, however, that the evidence linking Type A behavior to the risk of myocardial infarction once serious pathophysiology exists remains controversial (Case, Heller, Case, & Moss, 1985) and that Dr. Hunter's environment, not to mention the lifelong pattern of this type of responding, will make the meaningful modification of his coronary-prone behavior difficult at best.

In addition, Dr. Hunter's blood pressure will be monitored by medical personnel. Although antihypertensive medications are the treatment of choice for this problem, behavioral adjuncts to the medical treatment will be considered (Shapiro & Goldstein, 1982). And finally, attention to Dr. Hunter's way of dealing with stressful work situations will be explored. Although relaxation-type procedures may be considered, a person like Dr. Hunter might prefer a more active means of dealing with tension, such as a mild exercise (i.e., walking) program (Martin & Dubbert, 1982). Throughout every aspect of treatment, continuous and specific communication with Hunter's personal physician will be maintained. Considerations relating to malpractice will make such a collaboration essential (cf. Knapp & VandeCreek, 1981).

Evaluation and Follow-Up

The pretreatment assessments should provide sufficient information to allow for a posttreatment evaluation. Although Dr. Hunter's self-report of change will be important, particularly in terms of the social validity of the procedures (Wolf, 1978), physiological and observational measures will be needed to insure that meaningful changes have actually occurred. Reports from others who have the opportunity to interact with Dr. Hunter in the work setting will be important. In addition, laboratory measures, such as blood chemistries, might serve as additional indexes of a successful intervention.

As with any treatment, short-term change does not guarantee long-term success. Consequently, a follow-up of at least 6 months will be planned. Perhaps one of the most important factors in determining the maintenance and generalization of the skills learned during treatment will be the nature of the contingencies that exist for Dr. Hunter in his natural (particularly work) environment (Galassi & Galassi, 1984). If that environment is not supportive of these changes, Dr. Hunter is unlikely to change, too. This presents a major challenge in that we have little power to manipulate an environment as complex and institutionalized as the one in which Dr. Hunter operates. Consequently, special attention will need to be paid to helping Dr. Hunter function more effectively in the existing environment while changing his behavior in a more healthful direction at the same time.

Summary

The integration of physiology with behavioral procedures makes the clinician's job even more challenging than it already is. Extending the functional analysis of behavior to include physiological variables requires increased sophistication and additional knowledge.

Initially, this prospect may seem a bit frightening if not overwhelming. However, this need not be the case. Through the use of appropriate referrals and good working relations with colleagues in other disciplines, the behavior therapist can extend his or her competency many times over that available on the basis of his or her training alone. Specific knowledge as to how the human body works is less important than a flexible and curious approach to assessment that allows for the consideration of multiple hypotheses concerning the client's problems. The point of this book, therefore, is not to make psychologists into physiologists but to highlight their common heritage as scientists who can work together to alleviate human concerns.

Recommended Readings

Barlow, D. H., Hayes, S. C., & Nelson, R. O. (1984). *The scientist practitioner: Research and accountability in clinical and educational settings.* New York: Pergamon Press.

> If there is a companion volume to the present work, this is it. Although *Physiology and Behavior Therapy* attempts to provide a rationale for a multidimensional, investigative approach to clinical problems, *The Scientist Practitioner* tells you how to do it. Not a treatment manual, this book is concerned with applying the rigors of scientific thinking to clinical problems and, in turn, using an experimental approach with individual cases. Consequently, the work provides a conceptual framework upon which treatments can be based and thus complements the present effort nicely. There is no dearth of applied treatment guides, but relatively less is written about the thinking that undergirds the clinical decision-making process. *The Scientist Practitioner* fills in many gaps that have separated the application of science to the art of practice and thus offers a powerful alternative to the "crystal ball gazing" (Wollersheim, 1974) of the past.

Garfield, S. L. (Ed.). (1982a). Behavioral medicine [Special issue]. *Journal of Consulting and Clinical Psychology, 50*(6).

> A flood of books related to behavioral medicine have hit the market over the past few years. Although many of these volumes are worthy of mention here, no single collection of readings is as good as that appearing in this special issue. The 19 articles cover a wide range of topics that relate behavior to physiology, such as asthma, insomnia, gastrointentinal disorders, arthritis, vascular disorders, and diabetes. In addition, most of the standard topics are represented, including obesity, smoking, hypertension, headache, chronic pain, and cancer. Better still, the issue can be ordered separately for $10 by writing the Order Department, American Psychological Association, 1400 North Uhle Street, Room 403, Arlington, Virginia 22201.

References

Aberg, A., Bergstrand, R., Johansson, S., Ulvenstam, G., Vedin, A., Wedel, H., Wihelmsson, C., & Wilhelmsen, L. (1983). Cessation of smoking after myocardial infarction: Effects on mortality after 10 years. *British Heart Journal, 49,* 416–422.

Abrams, D. B. (1983). Assessment of alcohol-stress interaction: Bridging the gap between laboratory and treatment outcome research. In L. A. Pohorecky & J. Brick (Eds.), *Stress and alcohol use* (pp. 61–86). New York: Elsevier.

Abramson, L. Y., & Sackeim, H. A. (1977). A paradox in depression: Uncontrollability and self-blame. *Psychological Bulletin, 84,* 838–851.

Achterberg-Lawlis, J. (1982). The psychological dimensions of arthritis. *Journal of Consulting and Clinical Psychology, 50,* 984–992.

Agras, W. S. (1982). Behavioral medicine in the 1980s: Nonrandom connections. *Journal of Consulting and Clinical Psychology, 50,* 797–803.

Agras, S., & Jacob, R. (1979). Hypertension. In O. F. Pomerleau & J. P. Brady (Eds.), *Behavioral medicine: Theory and practice* (pp. 205–232). Baltimore: Williams & Wilkins.

Agras, S., Kazdin, A. E., & Wilson, G. T. (1979). *Behavior therapy: Toward an applied clinical science.* San Francisco: W. H. Freeman.

Agras, W. S., Taylor, C. B., Kraemer, H. C., Allen, R. A., & Schneider, J. A. (1980). Relaxation training: Twenty-four hour blood pressure reductions. *Archives of General Psychiatry, 37,* 859–863.

Akins, T., Hollandsworth, J. G., & O'Connell, S. J. (1982). Visual and verbal modes of information processing and their relation to the effectiveness of cognitively-based anxiety-reduction techniques. *Behaviour Research and Therapy, 20,* 261–268.

Akins, T., Hollandsworth, J. G., & Alcorn, J. D. (1983). Visual and verbal modes of information processing and cognitively-based coping strategies: An extension and replication. *Behaviour Research and Therapy, 21,* 69–73.

Akiskal, H. S. (1979). A biobehavioral approach to depression. In R. A. Depue (Ed.), *The psychobiology of the depressive disorders: Implications for the effects of stress* (pp. 409–437). New York: Academic Press.

Akiskal, H. S., & McKinney, W. T. (1973). Depressive disorders: Toward a unified hypothesis. *Science, 182,* 20–29.

Akiskal, H. S., & McKinney, W. T. (1975). Overview of recent research in depression: Integration of ten conceptual models into a comprehensive clinical frame. *Archives of General Psychiatry, 32,* 285–305.

Akiskal, H. S., Bitar, A. H., Puzantian, V. R., Rosenthal, T. L., & Walker, P. W. (1978). The nosological status of neurotic depression: A prospective 3–4 year follow-up examination in the light of the primary-secondary and the unipolar-bipolar dichotomies. *Archives of General Psychiatry, 35,* 756–766.

Alberti, R. E., & Emmons, M. L. (1974). *Your perfect right: A guide to assertive behavior.* San Luis Obispo, CA: Impact.

American College Dictionary (C. L. Barnhart, Ed.). (1958). New York: Random House.

American Heritage Dictionary of the English Language (W. Morris, Ed.). (1976). Boston: Houghton Mifflin.

American Institute for Preventive Medicine. (1981). *Health risk appraisal.* (Available from Author, 19111 West 10 Mile Road, Suite 101, Southland, Michigan 48075)

Andrasik, F., Blanchard, E. B., Edlund, S. R., & Rosenblum, E. L. (1982). Autogenic feedback in the treatment of two children with migraine headache. *Child and Family Behavior Therapy, 4*(4), 13–23.

Andrasik, F., Blanchard, E. B., Edlund, S. R., & Attanasio, V. (1983). EMG biofeedback treatment of a child with muscle contraction headache. *American Journal of Clinical Biofeedback, 6,* 96–102.

Andreasen, N. C. (1982). Concepts, diagnosis and classification. In E. S. Paykel (Ed.). *Handbook of affective disorders* (pp. 24–44). New York: Guilford Press.

Andress, V. R., & Corey, D. M. (1977). Suicide motives: Comparison of assignment of motives by coroners and psychologists. *Psychological Reports, 40,* 11–14.

Andrews, J. M. (1964). Neuromuscular re-education of the hemiplegic with the aid of the electromyograph. *Archives of Physical Medicine and Rehabilitation, 45,* 530–532.

Arnold, M. B. (1950). The excitatory theory of emotion. In M. L. Reymert (Ed.), *Feelings and emotions: The Moosehart symposium* (pp. 11–33). New York: McGraw-Hill.

Arnold, M. B. (1960). *Emotion and personality* (2 vols.). New York: Columbia University Press.

Arnold, M. B. (1970). Brain function in emotion: A phenomenological analysis. In P. Black (Ed.), *Physiological correlates of emotion* (pp. 261–285). New York: Academic Press.

Arrington, R. E. (1932). Some technical aspects of observer reliability as indicated in studies of the "Talkies." *The American Journal of Sociology, 38,* 409–417.

Astrand, P. O., & Rodahl, K. (1970). *Textbook of work physiology.* New York: McGraw-Hill.

Averill, J. R. (1975). A semantic atlas of emotional concepts. *Catalog of Selected Documents in Psychology, 5,* 330. (Ms. No. 421)

Averill, J. R. (1979). A selective review of cognitive and behavioral factors involved in the regulation of stress. In R. A. Depue (Ed.), *The psychobiology of the depressive disorders: Implications for the effects of stress* (pp. 365–387). New York: Academic Press.

Averill, J. R. (1982). *Anger and aggression: An essay on emotion.* New York: Springer-Verlag.

Averill, J. R. (1983). Studies on anger and aggression: Implications for theories of emotion. *American Psychologist, 38,* 1145–1160.

Ax, A. F. (1953). The physiological differentiation between fear and anger in humans. *Psychosomatic Medicine, 15,* 433–442.

Bagley, C., Jacobson, S., & Rehin, A. (1976). Completed suicide: A taxonomic analysis of clinical and social data. *Psychological Medicine, 6,* 429–438.

Bakal, D. A. (1979). *Psychology and medicine: Psychobiological dimensions of health and illness.* New York: Springer.

Baldwin, A. L. (1969). A cognitive theory of socialization. In D. A. Goslin (Ed.), *Handbook of socialization theory and research* (pp. 325–346). Chicago: Rand McNally.

Bandura, A. (1967). Behavioral psychotherapy. *Scientific American, 216*(3), 78–86.

Bandura, A. (1973). *Aggression: A social learning analysis.* Englewood Cliffs, NJ: Prentice-Hall.

Bandura, A. (1974). Behavior theory and the models of man. *American Psychologist, 29,* 859–869.

Bandura, A. (1977). *Social learning theory*. Englewood Cliffs, NJ: Prentice-Hall.

Barlow, D. H. (1980). Behavior therapy: The next decade. *Behavior Therapy, 11*, 315–328.

Barlow, D. H., Cohen, A. S., Waddell, M. T., Vermilyea, B. B., Klosko, J. S., Blanchard, E. B., & Di Nardo, P. A. (1984). Panic and generalized anxiety disorders: Nature and treatment. *Behavior Therapy, 15*, 431–449.

Barlow, D. H., Hayes, S. C., & Nelson, R. O. (1984). *The scientist practitioner: Research and accountability in clinical and educational settings*. New York: Pergamon Press.

Barraclough, B., Bunch, J., Nelson, B., & Sainsbury, P. (1974). A hundred cases of suicide: Clinical aspects. *British Journal of Psychiatry, 125*, 355–373.

Basmajian, J. V., & Hatch, J. P. (1979). Biofeedback and the modification of skeletal muscular dysfunctions. In R. J. Gatchel & K. P. Price (Eds.), *Clinical applications of biofeedback: Appraisal and status* (pp. 97–111). New York: Pergamon. Press.

Baum, A., Grunberg, N. E., & Singer, J. E. (1982). The use of psychological and neuroendocrinological measurements in the study of stress. *Health Psychology, 1*, 217–236.

Beach, S. R. H., Abramson, L. Y., & Levine, F. M. (1981). Attributional reformulation of learned helplessness and helplessness: Therapeutic implications. In J. F. Clarkin & H. I. Glazer (Eds.), *Depression: Behavioral and directive intervention strategies* (pp. 131–165). New York: Garland STPM Press.

Beary, J. F., & Benson, H. (1974). A simple psychophysiologic technique which elicits the hypometabolic changes of the relaxation response. *Psychosomatic Medicine, 36*, 115–120.

Beck, A. T. (1967). *Depression: Causes and treatment*. Philadelphia: University of Pennsylvania Press.

Beck, A. T. (1973). *The diagnosis and management of depression*. Philadelphia: University of Pennsylvania Press.

Beck, A. T. (1974). The development of depression: A cognitive model. In R. J. Friedman & M. M. Katz (Eds.), *The psychology of depression: Contemporary theory and research* (pp. 3–20). New York: Winston-Wiley.

Beck, A. T. (1976). *Cognitive therapy and the emotional disorders*. New York: International Universities Press.

Beck, A. T., & Emery, G. (1979). *Cognitive therapy of anxiety and phobic disorders*. Philadelphia: Center for Cognitive Therapy.

Beck, A. T., Ward, C. H., Mendelson, M., Mock, J., & Erbaugh, J. (1961). An inventory for measuring depression. *Archives of General Psychiatry, 4*, 561–571.

Becker, J. (1974). *Depression: Theory and research*. Washington, DC: Winston.

Becker, J. (1979). Vulnerable self-esteem as a predisposing factor in depressive disorders. In R. A. Depue (Ed.), *The psychobiology of the depressive disorders: Implications for the effects of stress* (pp. 317–334). New York: Academic Press.

Becker, J., & Schuckit, M. A. (1978). The comparative efficacy of cognitive therapy and pharmacotherapy in the treatment of depressions. *Cognitive Therapy and Research, 2*, 193–197.

Bellack, A. S., & Hersen, M. (1977). Self-report inventories in behavioral assessment. In J. D. Cone & R. P. Hawkins (Eds.), *Behavioral assessment: New directions in clinical psychology* (pp. 52–76). New York: Brunner/Mazel.

Bellet, S., Roman, L., DeCastro, O., Kim, K. E., & Keushbaum, A. (1969). *Metabolism, 18*, 288–291.

Bennett, R. (1973). Social isolation and isolation-reducing programs. *Bulletin of the New York Academy of Medicine, 49*, 1143–1163.

Benson, H. (1975). *The relaxation response*. New York: Morrow.

Benson, H. A., Beary, J. F., & Carol, M. P. (1974). The relaxation response. *Psychiatry, 37*, 37–46.

Benson, H., Klemchuk, H. P., & Graham, J. R. (1974). The usefulness of the relaxation response in the therapy of headache. *Headache, 14,* 49–52.

Berger, M., & Passingham, R. E. (1973). Early experience and other environmental factors: An overview. In H. J. Eysenck (Ed.), *Handbook of abnormal psychology* (2nd ed., pp. 604–644). San Diego, CA: Robert R. Knapp.

Bergin, A. E., & Lambert, M. J. (1978). The evaluation of therapeutic outcomes. In S. L. Garfield & A. E. Bergin (Eds.), *Handbook of psychotherapy and behavior change: An empirical analysis* (2nd ed., pp. 139–190). New York: Wiley.

Bergmann, G. (1956). The contribution of John B. Watson. *Psychological Review, 63,* 265–276.

Best, P. J., & Zuckerman, K. (1971). Subcortical mediation of learned taste aversion. *Physiology and Behavior, 7,* 317–320.

Bielski, R. J., & Friedel, R. O. (1976). Prediction of tricyclic antidepressant response: A critical review. *Archives of General Psychiatry, 33,* 1479–1489.

Biglan, A., & Dow, M. G. (1981). Toward a second-generation model: A problem-specific approach. In L. P. Rehm (Ed.), *Behavior therapy for depression: Present status and future directions* (pp. 97–121). New York: Academic Press.

Bindra, D. (1970). Emotion and behavior theory: Current research in historical perspective. In P. Black (Ed.), *Physiological correlates of emotion* (pp. 3–20). New York: Academic Press.

Birk, L. (1973). Biofeedback—Furor therapeuticus. In L. Birk (Ed.), *Biofeedback: Behavioral medicine* (pp. 1–4). New York: Grune & Stratton.

Birtchnell, J., & Alarcon, J. (1971). Depression and attempted suicide: A study of 91 cases seen in a casualty department. *British Journal of Psychiatry, 118,* 289–296.

Bitterman, M. E. (1965). Phyletic differences in learning. *American Psychologist, 20,* 396–410.

Bitterman, M. E. (1975). The comparative analysis of learning. *Science, 188,* 699–709.

Bitterman, M. E. (1976). Flavor aversion studies. *Science, 192,* 266–267.

Blanchard, E. B. (1979). Biofeedback and the modification of cardiovascular dysfunctions. In R. J. Gatchel & K. P. Price (Eds.), *Clinical applications of biofeedback: Appraisal and status* (pp. 28–51). New York: Pergamon Press.

Blanchard, E. B. (1982). Behavioral medicine: Past, present, and future. *Journal of Consulting and Clinical Psychology, 50,* 795–796.

Blanchard, E. B., & Andrasik, F. (1982). Psychological assessment and treatment of headache: Recent developments and emerging issues. *Journal of Consulting and Clinical Psychology, 50,* 859–879.

Blanchard, E. B., & Epstein, L. H. (1978). *A biofeedback primer.* Reading, MA: Addison-Wesley.

Blanchard, E. B., Scott, R. W., Young, L. D., & Edmundson, E. D. (1974). Effect of knowledge of response on the self-control of heart rate. *Psychophysiology, 11,* 251–264.

Blaney, P. H. (1981). The effectiveness of cognitive and behavioral therapies. In L. P. Rehm (Ed.), *Behavior therapy for depression: Present status and future directions* (pp. 1–32). New York: Academic Press.

Boll, T. J., O'Leary, D. S., & Barth, J. T. (1981). A quantitative and qualitative approach to neuropsychological evaluation. In C. K. Prokop & L. A. Bradley (Eds.), *Medical psychology: Contributions to behavioral medicine* (pp. 67–80). New York: Academic Press.

Bolles, R. C. (1970). Species-specific defense reactions and avoidance learning. *Psychological Review, 77,* 32–48.

Bolles, R. C., & Seelbach, S. E. (1964). Punishing and reinforcing effects of noise onset and termination for different responses. *Journal of Comparative and Physiological Psychology, 58,* 127–131.

Borkovec, T. D. (1973). The role of expectancy and physiological feedback in fear research: A review with special references to subject characteristics. *Behavior Therapy, 4,* 491–505.

Borkovec, T. D. (1976). Physiological and cognitive processes in the regulation of anxiety. In G.E. Schwartz & D. Shapiro (Eds.), *Consciousness and self-regulation: Advances in research* (Vol. 1) (pp. 261–312). New York: Plenum Press.

Borkovec, T. D. (1982). Insomnia. *Journal of Consulting and Clinical Psychology, 50,* 880–895.

Borkovec, T. D., & Bauer, R. M. (1982). Experimental design in group outcome research. In A. S. Bellack, M. Hersen, & A. E. Kazdin (Eds.), *International handbook of behavior modification and therapy* (pp. 139–165). New York: Plenum Press.

Borkovec, T. D., Robinson, E., Pruzinsky, T., & DePree, J. A. (1983). Preliminary exploration of worry: Some characteristics and processes. *Behaviour Research and Therapy, 21,* 9–16.

Borkovec, T. D., Wilkinson, L., Folensbee, R., & Lerman, C. (1983). Stimulus control applications to the treatment of worry. *Behaviour Research and Therapy, 21,* 247–251.

Born, J. O., & Hollandsworth, J. G. (1985, November). *Actual versus perceived fitness in relation to mood states.* Paper presented at the 19th Annual Convention of the Association for Advancement of Behavior Therapy, Houston.

Bornstein, P. H. (1985). Self-instructional training: A commentary and state-of-the-art. *Journal of Applied Behavior Analysis, 18,* 69–72.

Boulding, K. E. (1980). Science: Our common heritage. *Science, 207,* 831–836.

Boyd, J. H., & Weissman, M. M. (1982). Epidemiology. In E. S. Paykel (Ed.), *Handbook of affective disorders* (pp. 109–125). New York: Guilford Press.

Bradley, M. T., & Janisse, M. P. (1981). Accuracy demonstrations, threat, and the detection of deception: Cardiovascular, electrodermal, and pupillary measures. *Psychophysiology, 18,* 307–315.

Brecher, E. M. (1972). *Licit and illicit drugs.* Boston: Little, Brown.

Breed, W. (1966). Suicide, migration, and race: A study of suicide in New Orleans. *Journal of Social Issues, 22,* 30–43.

Brener, J. A. (1974). A general model of voluntary control applied to the phenomena of learned cardiovascular change. In P. A. Obrist, A. H. Black, J. Brener, & L. V. DiCara (Eds.), *Cardiovascular psychophysiology* (pp. 365–391). Chicago: Aldine.

Broadbent, D. E. (1977). The hidden preattentive processes. *American Psychologist, 32,* 109–118.

Brogden, W. J., & Gantt, W. H. (1942). Intraneural conditioning: Cerebellar conditioned reflexes. *Archives of Neurological Psychiatry, 48,* 437–455.

Brower, L. P. (1969). Ecological chemistry. *Scientific American, 220*(2), 22–29.

Brown, B. B. (1970). Recognition of aspects of consciousness through association with EEG alpha activity represented by a light signal. *Psychophysiology, 6,* 442–452.

Brown, B. B. (1971). Awareness of EEG-subjective relationships detected within a closed feedback system. *Psychophysiology, 7,* 451–464.

Brown, B. B. (1974). *New mind, new body: Biofeedback, new directions for the mind.* New York: Harper & Row.

Brown, G. L., & Zung, W. W. K. (1972). Depression scales: Self or physician rating? A validation of certain clinically observable phenomena. *Comprehensive Psychiatry, 13,* 361–367.

Brown, G. W. (1979). The social etiology of depression—London studies. In R. A. Depue (Ed.), *The psychobiology of the depressive disorders: Implications for the effects of stress* (pp. 263–289). New York: Academic Press.

Brown, G. W., & Harris, T. O. (1978). *Social origins of depression: A study of psychiatric disorder in women.* New York: Free Press.

Brown, J. S., & Farber, I. E. (1951). Emotions conceptualized as intervening variables—with suggestions toward a theory of frustration. *Psychological Bulletin, 48*, 465–495.

Brown, P. L., & Jenkins, H. M. (1968). Auto-shaping of the pigeon's key-peck. *Journal of the Experimental Analysis of Behavior, 11*, 1–8.

Brownell, K. D. (1982). Obesity: Understanding and treating a serious, prevalent, and refractory disorder. *Journal of Consulting and Clinical Psychology, 50*, 820–840.

Bruell, J. H. (1970). Heritability of emotional behavior. In P. Black (Ed.), *Physiological correlates of emotion* (pp. 23–36). New York: Academic Press.

Budzynski, T. H. (1977). Clinical implications of electromyographic training. In G. Schwartz & J. Beatty (Eds.), *Biofeedback: Theory and research* (pp. 433–448). New York: Academic Press.

Burish, T. G. (1981). EMG biofeedback in the treatment of stress-related disorders. In C. K. Prokop & L. A. Bradley (Eds.), *Medical psychology: Contributions to behavioral medicine* (pp. 395–421). New York: Academic Press.

Burt, C. G., Gordon, W. F., Holt, N. F., & Hordern, A. (1962). Amitriptyline in in depressive states: A controlled trial. *Journal of Mental Science, 108*, 711–730.

Buschbaum, M. S. (1979). Neurophysiological reactivity, stimulus intensity modulation and the depressive disorders. In R. A. Depue (Ed.), *The psychobiology of the depressive disorders: Implications for the effects of stress* (pp. 221–242). New York: Academic Press.

Buss, A. H., & Durkee, A. (1957). An inventory for assessing different kinds of hostility. *Journal of Consulting Psychology, 21*, 343–349.

Butler, R., & Lewis, M. (1977). *Aging and mental health: Positive psychological approaches* (2nd ed.). St. Louis: C. V. Mosby.

Cannon, W. B. (1915). *Bodily changes in pain, hunger, fear and rage.* New York: Appleton.

Cannon, W. B. (1927). The James-Lange theory of emotions: A critical examination and an alternative theory. *American Journal of Psychology, 39*, 106–124.

Cannon, W. B. (1939). *The wisdom of the body.* New York: W. W. Norton.

Carlson, J. G., Basilio, C. A., & Heaykulani, J. D. (1983). Transfer of EMG training: Another look at the general relaxation issue. *Psychophysiology, 20*, 530–536.

Carlson, N. R. (1977). *Physiology of behavior.* Boston: Allyn and Bacon.

Carney, M. W. P., & Sheffield, B. F. (1972). Depression and the Newcastle scales—Their relationship to Hamilton's scale. *British Journal of Psychiatry, 121*, 35–40.

Carney, M. W. P., & Sheffield, B. F. (1974). The effects of pulse ECT in neurotic and endogenous depression. *British Journal of Psychiatry, 125*, 91–94.

Carney, M. W. P., Roth, M., & Garside, R. F. (1965). The diagnosis of depressive syndromes and the prediction of E.C.T. response. *British Journal of Psychiatry, 111*, 659–674.

Carroll, D. (1977). Cardiac perception and cardiac control: A review. *Biofeedback and Self-Regulation, 2*, 349–369.

Carter, W. R., Johnson, M. S., & Borkovec, T. D. (1984, November). *Worry: An electrocortical analysis.* Paper presented at the 18th Annual Convention of the Association for Advancement of Behavior Therapy, Philadelphia.

Case, R. B., Heller, S. S., Case, N. B., & Moss, A. J. (1985). Type A behavior and survival after acute myocardial infarction. *New England Journal of Medicine, 312*, 737–741.

Chamberlin, T. C. (1965). The method of multiple working hypotheses. *Science, 148*, 754–759.

Chernigovskiy, V. N. (1967). *Interoceptors.* Washington, DC: American Psychological Association.

Chomsky, N. (1968). *Language and mind.* New York: Harcourt Brace & World.

Chomsky, N. (1975). *Reflections in language.* New York: Pantheon Books.

Ciminero, A. R., Calhoun, K. S., & Adams, H. E. (Eds.). (1977). *Handbook of behavioral assessment*. New York: Wiley.

Clarizio, H. F., & McCoy, G. F. (1983). *Behavior disorders in children* (3rd ed.). New York: Harper & Row.

Clarkin, J. F., & Glazer, H. I. (Eds.). (1981). *Depression: Behavioral and directive intervention strategies*. New York: Garland STPM Press.

Coleman, R. E., & Beck, A. T. (1981). Cognitive therapy for depression. In J. F. Clarkin & H. I. Glazer (Eds.), *Depression: Behavioral and directive intervention strategies* (pp. 111–130). New York: Garland STPM Press.

Cone, J. D., & Hawkins, R. P. (Eds.). (1977). *Behavioral assessment: New directions in clinical psychology*. New York: Brunner/Mazel.

Counts, D. K., Hollandsworth, J. G., & Alcorn, J. D. (1978). Use of electromyographic feedback and cue-controlled relaxation in the treatment of test anxiety. *Journal of Consulting and Clinical Psychology, 46*, 990–996.

Cowley, A. W. (1980). The concept of autoregulation of total blood flow and its role in hypertension. *American Journal of Medicine, 68*, 906–916.

Coyne, J. C. (1976). Toward an interactional description of depression. *Psychiatry, 39*, 28–40.

Craighead, W. E. (1980). Away from a unitary model of depression. *Behavior Therapy, 11*, 122–128.

Craighead, W. E. (1981). Issues resulting from treatment studies. In L. P. Rehm (Ed.), *Behavior therapy for depression: Present status and future directions* (pp. 73–96). New York: Academic Press.

Cravens, H. (1978). *The triumph of evolution*. Philadelphia: University of Pennsylvania Press.

Crook, T., Raskin, A., & Davis, D. (1975). Factors associated with attempted suicide among hospitalized depressed patients. *Psychological Medicine, 5*, 381–388.

Dalton, K. (1984). *The premenstrual syndrome and progesterone therapy* (2nd ed.). Chicago: Year Book Medical.

D'Amato, M., & Schiff, D. (1964). Long-term discriminated avoidance performance in the rat. *Journal of Comparative and Physiological Psychology, 57*, 123–126.

Darrow, C. W. (1932). The relation of the galvanic skin reflex recovery curve to reactivity, resistance level, and perspiration. *Journal of General Psychology, 7*, 261–272.

Darsee, J. R., Mikolich, J. R., Nicoloff, N. B., & Lesser, L. E. (1979). Prevalence of mitral valve prolapse in presumably healthy young men. *Circulation, 59*, 619–622.

Darwin, C. (1979). *The expression of emotion in man and animals*. London: Julian Friedmann. (Original work published 1872)

Davidson, R. J. (1978). Specificity and patterning in biobehavioral systems: Implications for behavior change. *American Psychologist, 33*, 430–436.

Davidson, R. J., & Schwartz, G. E. (1976). The psychobiology of relaxation and related states: A multi-process theory. In D. I. Mostofsky (Ed.), *Behavior control and modification of physiological activity* (pp. 399–442). Englewood Cliffs, NJ: Prentice-Hall.

Davidson, R. J., & Schwartz, G. E. (1977). Brain mechanisms subserving self-generated imagery: Electrophysiological specificity and patterning. *Psychophysiology, 14*, 598–602.

Davidson, R. J., Schwartz, G. E., & Rothman, L. P. (1976). Attentional style and the self-regulation of mode-specific attention: An electroencephalographic study. *Journal of Abnormal Psychology, 85*, 611–621.

Davis, J. O. & Freeman, R. H. (1976). Mechanisms regulating renin release. *Physiological Review, 56*, 1–56.

Dawson, M. E. (1980). Physiological detection of deception: Measurement of responses to questions and answers during countermeasure maneuvers. *Psychophysiology, 17*, 8–17.

Deffenbacher, J. L. (1978). Worry, emotionality, and task-generated interference in test anxiety: An empirical test of attentional theory. *Journal of Educational Psychology, 70*, 248–254.

Deffenbacher, J., & Suinn, R. (1982). The self-control of anxiety. In P. Karoly & F. H. Kanfer (Eds.), *The psychology of self-management: From theory to practice* (pp. 393–442). Elmsford, NY: Pergamon Press.

Deleon-Jones, F., Maas, J. W., Dekirmenjian, H., & Sanchez, J. (1975). Diagnostic subgroups of affective disorders and their urinary excretion of catecholamine metabolites. *American Journal of Psychiatry, 132*, 1141–1148.

Delgado, J. M. R. (1967). Social rank and radio-stimulated aggressiveness in monkeys. *Journal of Nervous and Mental Disease, 144*, 383–390.

Delgado, J. M. R. (1970). Modulation of emotions by cerebral radio stimulation. In P. Black (Ed.), *Physiological correlates of emotion* (pp. 189–202). New York: Academic Press.

Delgado, J. M. R., & Mir, D. (1969). Fragmental organization of emotional behavior in the monkey brain. *Annals of the New York Academy of Sciences, 159*, 731–751.

Delprato, D. J. (1980). Hereditary determinants of fears and phobias: A critical review. *Behavior Therapy, 11*, 79–103.

Delprato, D. J., & McGlynn, F. D. (1984). Behavioral theories of anxiety disorders. In S. M. Turner (Ed.), *Behavioral theories and treatment of anxiety* (pp. 1–49). New York: Plenum Press.

Dembroski, T. M. (1978). Reliability and validity of methods used to assess coronary-prone behavior. In T. M. Dembroski, S. M. Weiss, J. L. Shields, S. G. Haynes, & M. Feinleib (Eds.), *Coronary-prone behavior* (pp. 95–106). New York: Springer-Verlag.

DeMonbreun, B. G., & Craighead, W. E. (1977). Distortion of perception and recall of positive and neutral feedback in depression. *Cognitive Therapy and Research, 1*, 311–329.

Denny, D. R. (1978). Self-control approaches to the treatment of test anxiety. In I. G. Sarason (Ed.), *Test anxiety: Theory, research, and applications.* Hillsdale, NJ: Erlbaum.

Depue, R. A. (Ed.). (1979). *The psychobiology of the depressive disorders: Implications for the effects of stress.* New York: Academic Press.

Depue, R. A., & Monroe, S. M. (1979). The unipolar-bipolar distinction in the depressive disorders: Implications for stress-onset interaction. In R. A. Depue (Ed.), *The psychobiology of the depressive disorders: Implications for the effects of stress* (pp. 23–53). New York: Academic Press.

Depue, R. A., Monroe, S. M., & Shackman, S. L. (1979). The psychobiology of human disease: Implications for conceptualizing the depressive disorders. In R. A. Depue (Ed.), *The psychobiology of the depressive disorders: Implications for the effects of stress* (pp. 3–20). New York: Academic Press.

Derogatis, L. R., Klerman, G. L., & Lipman, R. S. (1972). Anxiety states and depressive neuroses. *Journal of Nervous and Mental Disease, 155*, 392–403.

De Silva, P., Rachman, S., & Seligman, M. E. P. (1977). Prepared phobias and obsessions: Therapuetic outcome. *Behaviour Research and Therapy, 15*, 65–77.

Deutsch, K. W. (1951). Mechanism, organism, and society: Some models in natural and social science. *Philosophy of Science, 18*, 230–252.

Dewey, J. (1896). The reflex arc concept in psychology. *Psychological Review, 3*, 357–370.

Diamond, S., & Franklin, M. (1975). Autogenic training with biofeedback in the treatment of children with migraine. *Therapy in Psychosomatic Medicine*, 190–195.

DiCara, L. V., & Miller, N. E. (1968). Changes in heart rate instrumentally learned by curarized rats as avoidance responses. *Journal of Comparative Physiological Psychology, 65,* 8–12. (a)

DiCara, L. V., & Miller, N. E. (1968). Instrumental learning of systolic blood pressure responses in curarized rats: Dissociation of cardiac and vascular changes. *Psychosomatic Medicine, 30,* 489–494. (b)

Di Nardo, P. A., O'Brien, G. T., Barlow, D. H., Waddell, M. T., & Blanchard, E. B. (1983). Reliability of DSM-III anxiety disorder categories using a new structured interview. *Archives of General Psychiatry, 40,* 1070–1074.

Dixon, N. F. (1971). *Subliminal perception: The nature of a controversy.* London: McGraw-Hill.

Dixon, N. F. (1981). *Preconscious processing.* Chichester, England: Wiley.

Dobrzecka, C., Szwejkowska, G., & Konorski, J. (1966). Qualitative versus directional cues in two forms of differentiation. *Science, 153,* 87–89.

Dorpat, T. L., & Ripley, H. S. (1960). A study of suicide in the Seattle area. *Comparative Psychiatry, 1,* 349–359.

Downing, R. W., & Rickles, K. (1974). Mixed anxiety-depression—Fact or myth? *Archives of General Psychiatry, 30,* 312–317.

Drachman, D. A., & Hart, C. W. (1972). An approach to the dizzy patient. *Neurology, 22,* 323–334.

Duffy, E. (1941). The conceptual categories of psychology: A suggestion for revision. *Psychological Review, 48,* 177–203.

Duffy, E. (1948). Leeper's "motivational theory of emotion." *Psychological Review, 55,* 324–328.

Duffy, E. (1972). Activation. In N. S. Greenfield & R. A. Sternbach (Eds.), *Handbook of psychophysiology* (pp. 577–622). New York: Holt, Rinehart & Winston.

Dush, D. M., Hirt, M. L., & Schroeder, H. (1983). Self-statement modification with adults: A meta-analysis. *Psychological Bulletin, 94,* 408–422.

Dworkin, B. (1982). Instrumental learning for the treatment of disease. *Health Psychology, 1,* 45–59.

D'Zurilla, T. J., & Goldfried, M. R. (1971). Problem solving and behavior modification. *Journal of Abnormal Psychology, 78,* 107–126.

Edelstein, B. A., Keaton-Brasted, C., & Burg, M. M. (1983). The effects of caffeine withdrawal on cardiovascular and gastrointestinal responses. *Health Psychology, 2,* 343–352.

Egan, G. (1982). *The skilled helper: Model, skills, and methods for effective helping* (2nd ed.). Monterey, CA: Brooks/Cole.

Eisler, R. M., & Frederiksen, L. W. (1980). *Perfecting social skills: A guide to interpersonal behavior development.* New York: Plenum Press.

Ekman, P., Friesen, W. V., & Ellsworth, P. (1972). *Emotion in the human face: Guidelines for research and an integration of findings.* New York: Pergamon Press.

Ellender, B. S., & Hollandsworth, J. G. (1986). *Heart rate reactivity during signaled and unsignaled reaction-time tasks using shock and aversive noise.* Manuscript submitted for publication.

Ellis, A. (1962). *Reason and emotion in psycholtherapy.* New York: Lyle-Stuart.

Ellis, A. (1968). What *really* causes psychotherapeutic change? *Voices, 4*(12), 90–95.

Ellis, A. (1979). A note on the treatment of agoraphobics with cognitive modification versus prolonged exposure *in vivo. Behaviour Research and Therapy, 17,* 162–164.

Ellis, A. (1985). Cognition and affect in emotional disturbance. *American Psychologist, 40,* 471–472.

Ellis, A., & Grieger, R. (1977). *Handbook of rational-emotive therapy*. New York: Springer.

Emmelkamp, P. M. G. (1975). Effect of expectancy on systematic desensitization and flooding. *European Journal of Behavior Analysis and Modification, 1*, 1–11.

Emmelkamp, P. M. G., & Emmelkamp-Benner, A. (1983). Anxiety-based disorders. In M. Hersen (Ed.), *Outpatient behavior therapy: A clinical guide* (pp. 45–108). New York: Grune & Stratton.

Emmelkamp, P. M. G., & Wessels, H. (1975). Flooding in imagination versus flooding *in vivo*: A comparison with agoraphobics. *Behaviour Research and Therapy, 13*, 7–15.

Emmelkamp, P. M. G., Kuipers, A. C. M., & Eggeraat, J. B. (1978). Cognitive modification versus prolonged exposure *in vivo*: A comparison with agoraphobics as subjects. *Behaviour Research and Therapy, 16*, 33–41.

Encyclopedia Americana: International edition (B. S. Cayne, Ed.). (1985). New York: Americana Corporation.

Endicott, J., & Spitzer, R. L. (1978). A diagnostic interview: The Schedule for Affective Disorders and Schizophrenia. *Archives of General Psychiatry, 35*, 837–844.

Engel, G. L. (1977). The need for a new medical model: A challenge for biomedicine. *Science, 196*, 129–136.

Epstein, L. (1976). Symposium on age differentiation in depressive illness: Depression in the elderly. *Journal of Gerontology, 31*, 278–282.

Epstein, L., & Cluss, P. A. (1982). A behavioral medicine perspective on adherence to long-term medical regimens. *Journal of Consulting and Clinical Psychology, 50*, 950–971.

Erdelyi, M. H. (1974). A new look at the New Look: Perceptual defense and vigilance. *Psychological Review, 81*, 1–25.

Erlenmeyer-Kimling, L. (1972). Gene–environment interactions and the variability of behavior. In L. Ehrman, G. S. Omenn, & E. Caspari (Eds.), *Genetics, environment, and behavior: Implications for educational policy* (pp. 181–208). New York: Academic Press.

Ettlinger, R. W. (1964). Suicides in a group of patients who had previously attempted suicide. *Acta Psychiatrica Scandinavica, 40*, 363–378.

Evans, I. M., & Busch, C. J. (1974). The effectiveness of visual and gustatory conditioned stimuli in human classical aversion conditioning with electric shock. *Behaviour Research and Therapy, 12*, 129–140.

Eysenck, H. J. (1979). The conditioning model of neurosis. *The Behavioral and Brain Sciences, 2*, 155–199.

Eysenck, H. J. (1982). Neobehavioristic (S-R) theory. In G. T. Wilson & C. M. Franks (Eds.), *Contemporary behavior therapy: Conceptual and empirical foundations* (pp. 205–276). New York: Guilford Press.

Farberow, N. L., & MacKinnon, D. (1974). Prediction of suicide in neuropsychiatric hospital patients. In C. Neuringer (Ed.), *Psychological assessment of suicidal risk* (pp. 186–224). Springfield, IL: Charles C Thomas.

Farberow, N. L., & McEvoy, T. L. (1966). Suicide among patients with diagnoses of anxiety reaction or depressive reaction in general medical and surgical hospitals. *Journal of Abnormal Psychology, 71*, 287–299.

Farberow, N. L., McKelligott, J., Cohn, S., & Darbonne, A. (1970). Suicide among cardiovascular patients. In E. S. Schneidman, N. L. Farberow, & R. E. Litman (Eds.), *The psychology of suicide* (pp. 369–384). New York: Science House.

Fenichel, O. (1945). *The psychoanalytic theory of neurosis*. New York: Norton.

Fenwick, P. B. C., Donaldson, S., Gillis, L., Bushman, J., Fenton, G. W., Tilsley, I. P., & Serafinowicz, H. (1977). Metabolic and EEG changes during transcendental meditation: An explanation. *Biological Psychology, 5*, 101–118.

Féré, C. (1976). Note on changes in electrical resistance under the effect of sensory stimulation and emotion. In S. W. Porges & M. G. H. Coles (Eds.), *Psychophysiology* (pp. 21–22). Stroudsburg, PA: Dowden, Hutchinson & Ross. (Original work published 1888)

Finger, R., & Galassi, J. P. (1977). Effects of modifying cognitive versus emotionality responses in the treatment of test anxiety. *Journal of Consulting and Clinical Psychology, 45,* 280–287.

Fisher, E. B., Delamater, A. M., Bertelson, A. D., & Kirkley, B. G. (1982). Psychological factors in diabetes and its treatment. *Journal of Consulting and Clinical Psychology, 50,* 993–1003.

Ford, C. V., Bray, G. A., & Swerdloff, R. S. (1976). A psychiatric study of patients referred with a diagnosis of hypoglycemia. *American Journal of Psychiatry, 133,* 290–294.

Fordyce, W. E., & Steger, J. C. (1979). Chronic pain. In O. F. Pomerleau & J. P. Brady (Eds.), *Behavioral medicine: Theory and practice* (pp. 125–153). Baltimore: Williams & Wilkins.

Fordyce, W. E., Fowler, R. S., Lehmann, J. F., DeLateur, B. J., Sand, P. L., & Trieschmann, R. B. (1973). Operant conditioning in the treatment of chronic pain. *Archives of Physical Medicine and Rehabilitation, 54,* 399–408.

Fowler, R. L., & Kimmel, H. D. (1962). Operant conditioning of the GSR. *Journal of Experimental Psychology, 63,* 563–587.

Fowles, D. C., & Gersh, F. S. (1979). Neurotic depression: The endogenous-neurotic distinction. In R. A. Depue (Ed.), *The psychobiology of the depressive disorders: Implications for the effects of stress* (pp. 55–80). New York: Academic Press.

Fox, K., & Weissman, M. (1975). Suicide attempts and drugs: Contradiction between method and intent. *Social Psychiatry, 10,* 31–38.

Frank, J. D. (1963). *Persuasion and healing.* Baltimore: Johns Hopkins Press.

Frankel, B. G., Ferrence, R. G., Johnson, F. G., & Whitehead, P. C. (1976). Drinking and self-injury: Toward untangling the dynamics. *British Journal of Addiction, 71,* 299–306.

Freud, S. (1953). The unconscious (C. M. Baines, Trans.). In E. Jones (Ed.), *Collected papers* (Vol. 4, pp. 98–136). London: Hogarth Press. (Original work published 1915)

Freud, S. (1953). Turnings in the ways of psychoanalytic therapy (J. Riviere, Trans.). In E. Jones (Ed.), *Collected papers* (Vol. 2, pp. 3xx–4xx). London: Hogarth Press. (Original work published 1919)

Frick, R. W. (1985). Communicating emotion: The role of prosodic features. *Psychological Bulletin, 97,* 412–429.

Fridlund, A. J., Fowler, S. C., & Pritchard, D. A. (1980). Striate muscle tensional patterning in frontalis EMG biofeedback. *Psychophysiology, 17,* 47–55.

Fridlund, A. J., Cottam, G. L., & Fowler, S. C. (1982). In search of the general tension factor: Tensional patterning during auditory stimulation. *Psychophysiology, 19,* 136–145.

Fridlund, A. J., Schwartz, G. E., & Fowler, S. C. (1984). Pattern recognition of self-reported emotional state from multiple-site facial EMG activity during affective imagery. *Psychophysiology, 21,* 622–637.

Fuller, G. D. (1978). Current status of biofeedback in clinical practice. *American Psychologist, 33,* 39–48.

Fuller, J. L. (1973). Genetics and vulnerability to experiential depression. In J. P. Scott (Ed.), *Separation and depression: Clinical and research aspects* (Publication No. 94, pp. 113–124). Washington, DC: American Association for the Advancement of Science.

Furth, H. G. (1969). *Piaget and knowledge: Theoretical foundations.* Englewood Cliffs, NJ: Prentice-Hall. (Originally published in French, Paris: Gallimard, 1967).

Gaarder, K. R., & Montgomery, P. S. (1977). *Clinical biofeedback: A procedural manual.* Baltimore: Williams & Wilkins.

Galassi, J. P., & Galassi, M. D. (1984). Promoting transfer and maintenance of counseling outcomes: How do we do it and how do we study it? In S. D. Brown & R. W. Lent (Eds.), *Handbook of counseling psychology* (pp. 397–434). New York: Wiley.

Gambrill, E. D., & Richey, C. A. (1975). An assertion inventory for use in assessment and research. *Behavior Therapy, 6,* 550–561.

Gantt, W. H. (1953). The physiological basis of psychiatry: The conditional reflex. In J. Wortis (Ed.), *Basic problems in psychiatry* (pp. 52–89). New York: Grune & Stratton.

Gantt, W. H. (1966). Reflexology, schizokinesis and autokinesis. *Conditional Reflex, 1,* 57–68.

Garber, J., Miller, W. R., & Seaman, S. F. (1979). Learned helplessness, stress, and the depressive disorders. In R. A. Depue (Ed.), *The psychobiology of the depressive disorders: Implications for the effects of stress* (pp. 335–363). New York: Academic Press.

Garcia, J., & Koelling, R. A. (1966). Relation of cue to consequence in avoidance learning. *Psychonomic Science, 4,* 123–124.

Garcia, J., Ervin, F. R., & Koelling, R. A. (1966). Learning with prolonged delay of reinforcement. *Psychonomic Science, 5,* 121–122.

Garcia, J., McGowan, B. K., & Green, K. F. (1972). Biological constraints on conditioning. In A. H. Black & W. F. Prokasy (Eds.), *Classical conditioning II: Current research and theory* (pp. 3–27). New York: Appleton-Century-Crofts.

Garcia, J., Hankins, W. G., & Rusiniak, K. W. (1976). Flavor aversion studies. *Science, 192,* 265–266.

Garfield, S. L. (Ed.). (1982). Behavioral medicine [Special issue]. *Journal of Consulting and Clinical Psychology, 50*(6). (a)

Garfield, S. L. (1982). Eclecticism and integration in psychotherapy. *Behavior Therapy, 13,* 610–23. (b)

Garfield, S. L., & Kurtz, R. (1976). Clinical psychologists in the 1970s. *American Psychologist, 31,* 1–9.

Garfield, S. L., & Kurtz, R. (1977). A study of eclectic views. *Journal of Consulting and Clinical Psychology, 45,* 78–83.

Garmany, G. (1956). Anxiety states. *British Medical Journal, 1,* 943–946.

Gatchel, R. J., & Price, K. P. (1979). *Clinical applications of biofeedback: Appraisal and status.* New York: Pergamon Press.

Gay, M. L., Hollandsworth, J. G., & Galassi, J. P. (1975). An assertiveness inventory for adults. *Journal of Counseling Psychology, 22,* 340–344.

Geer, J. H. (1979). Biofeedback and the modification of sexual dysfunctions. In R. J. Gatchel & K. P. Price (Eds.), *Clinical applications of biofeedback: Appraisal and status* (pp. 52–64). New York: Pergamon Press.

Gentry, W. D., & Williams, R. B. (Eds.). (1979). *Psychological aspects of myocardial infarction and coronary care* (2nd ed.). St. Louis: Mosby.

Gerald, M. C. (1981). *Pharmacology: An introduction to drugs* (2nd ed.). Englewood Cliffs, NJ: Prentice-Hall.

Gersh, F. S., & Fowles, D. C. (1979). Neurotic depression: The concept of anxious depression. In R. A. Depue (Ed.), *The psychobiology of the depressive disorders* (pp. 81–104). New York: Academic Press.

Gershon, E. S., Baron, M., & Leckman, J. F. (1975). Genetic models of the transmission of affective disorders. *Journal of Psychiatric Research, 12,* 301–317.

Gintner, G. G., Hollandsworth, J. G., & Intrieri, R. (1984, November). *Predictors of cardiovascular response during active coping.* Paper presented at the 18th Annual Convention of the Association for Advancement of Behavior Therapy, Philadelphia.

Glass, A. L., Holyoak, K. J., & Santa, J. L. (1979). *Cognition.* Reading, MA: Addison-Wesley.

Glazer, H. I., Clarkin, J. F., & Hunt, H. F. (1981). Assessment of depression. In J. F. Clarkin & H. I. Glazer (Eds.), *Depression: Behavioral and directive intervention strategies* (pp. 3–30). New York: Garland STPM Press.

Glazeski, R. C., Hollandsworth, J. G., & Jones, G. E. (in press). An investigation of the role of physiological arousal in test anxiety. *Educational and psychological research.*

Goldfried, M. R. (1980). Psychotherapy as coping skills training. In M. Mahoney (Ed.), *Psychotherapy process: Current issues and future directions* (pp. 89–119). New York: Plenum Press. (a)

Goldfried, M. R. (1980). Toward the delineation of therapeutic change principles. *American Psychologist, 35,* 991–999. (b)

Goldfried, M. R., & Goldfried, A. P. (1975). Cognitive change methods. In F. H. Kanfer & A. P. Goldstein (Eds.), *Helping people change* (pp. 89–116). Elmsford, NY: Pergamon Press.

Goldfried, M. R., & Merbaum, M. (Eds.). (1973). *Behavior change through self-control.* New York: Holt, Rinehart & Winston.

Goldstein, I. B., Shapiro, D., Thananopavarn, C., & Sambhi, M. P. (1982). Comparison of drug and behavioral treatments of essential hypertension. *Health Psychology, 1,* 7–26.

Goodman, E. (1985, June 18). Don't blame victim for cancer. *The Clarion-Ledger* [Jackson, MS], pp. 9A.

Goodwin, F. K. (1977). Biologic basis of drug action in the affective disorders. In M. E. Jarvik (Ed.), *Psychopharmacology in the practice of medicine* (pp. 231–238). New York: Appleton-Century-Crofts.

Goodwin, F. K., & Post, R. M. (1975). Studies of amine metabolites in affective illness and in schizophrenia: A comparative analysis. In D. X. Freedman (Ed.), *Biology of the major psychoses: A comparative analysis* (pp. 299–332). New York: Raven Press.

Gottman, J. M., & Markman, H. J. (1978). Experimental designs in psychotherapy research. In S. L. Garfield & A. E. Bergin (Eds.), *Handbook of psychotherapy and behavior change: An empirical analysis* (2nd ed., pp. 23–62). New York: Wiley.

Gottschalk, C. W. (1979). Renal nerves and sodium excretion. *Annual Review of Physiology, 41,* 229–240.

Greden, J. F. (1974). Anxiety or caffeinism: A diagnostic dilemma. *American Journal of Psychiatry, 131,* 1089–1092.

Greden, J. F. (1979). Coffee, tea and you. *The Sciences, 19*(1), 6–11.

Greenblatt, M., Grosser, G. H., & Wechsler, H. (1964). Differential response of hospitalized depressed patients to somatic therapy. *American Journal of Psychiatry, 120,* 935–943.

Greer, S., Gunn, J. C., & Koller, K. M. (1966). Aetiological factors in attempted suicide. *British Medical Journal, 2,* 1352–1355.

Guyton, A. C. (1980). *Arterial pressure and hypertension.* Philadelphia: W. B. Saunders.

Guyton, A. C. (1981). *Textbook of medical physiology* (6th ed.). Philadelphia: W. B. Saunders.

Guyton, A. C., Jones, C. E., & Coleman, T. G. (1973). *Circulatory physiology: Cardiac output and its regulation* (2nd ed.). Philadelphia: W. B. Saunders.

Guyton, A. C., Taylor, A. E., & Granger, H. J. (1975). *Circulatory physiology II: Dynamics and control of the body fluids.* Philadelphia: W. B. Saunders.

Hafner, J., & Marks, I. (1976). Exposure *in vivo* of agoraphobics: Contributions of diazepam, group exposure, and anxiety evocation. *Psychological Medicine, 6,* 71–88.

Hall, G. S. (1897). A study of fears. *American Journal of Psychology, 8,* 147–249.

Hamilton, M. (1967). Development of a rating scale for primary depressive illness. *British Journal of Social and Clinical Psychology, 6,* 278–296.

Hammen, C. L., & Krantz, S. (1976). Effect of success and failure on depressive cognitions. *Journal of Abnormal Psychology, 85,* 577–586.

Hand, I., Lamontagne, Y., & Marks, I. (1974). Group exposure (flooding) *in vivo* for agoraphobics. *British Journal of Psychiatry, 124,* 588–602.

Harlow, H. F., & Harlow, M. K. (1970). Developmental aspects of emotional behavior. In P. Black (Ed.), *Physiological correlates of emotion* (pp. 37–58). New York: Academic Press.

Harpin, R. E. (1970). A psychosocial treatment for some forms of depression? *Dissertation Abstracts International, 39,* 2499B. (University Microfilms No. 78-20,832)

Harré, R., & Secord, P. F. (1972). *The explanation of social behavior.* Totown, NJ: Rowman and Littlefield.

Harrow, M., Colbert, J., Detre, T., & Bakeman, R. (1966). Symptomatology and subjective experiences in current depressive states. *Archives of General Psychiatry, 14,* 203–212.

Harvey, A. M., Johns, R. J., Owens, A. H., & Ross, R. S. (Eds.). (1972). *The principles and practice of medicine* (18th ed.). New York: Appleton-Century-Crofts.

Hasher, L., & Zacks, R. T. (1984). Automatic processing of fundamental information: The case of frequency of occurrence. *American Psychologist, 39,* 1372–1388.

Hassett, J. (1978). *A primer of psychophysiology.* San Francisco: W. H. Freeman.

Hastrup, J. L., & Katkin, E. S. (1976). Electrodermal lability: An attempt to measure its psychological correlates. *Psychophysiology, 13,* 296–301.

Hebb, D. O. (1946). On the nature of fear. *Psychological Review, 53,* 259–276.

Hebb, D. O. (1949). *The organization of behavior: A neuropsychological theory.* New York: Wiley.

Hebb, D. O. (1958). *A textbook of psychology.* Philadelphia: W. B. Saunders.

Heisler, G. H., & McCormack, J. (1982). Situational and personality influences on the reception of provocative responses. *Behavior Therapy, 13,* 743–750.

Hermansson, K., Larson, M., Kallskog, O., & Wolgast, M. (1981). Effects of renal nerve activity on arteriolar resistance, ultrafiltration dynamics, and fluid reabsorption. *Pfluger Archiv, 389,* 85–90.

Herrnstein, R. J. (1977). The evolution of behaviorism. *American Psychologist, 32,* 593–603.

Hersen, M. (1973). Self-assessment of fear. *Behavior Therapy, 4,* 241–257.

Hersen, M. (1979). Limitations and problems in the clinical application of behavioral technique in psychiatric settings. *Behavior Therapy, 10,* 65–80.

Hersen, M., & Bellack, A. S. (Eds.). (1976). *Behavioral assessment: A practical handbook.* New York: Pergamon Press.

Hersh, S. P. (1977). Epilogue: Future considerations and directions. In J. G. Schulterbrandt & A. Raskin (Eds.), *Depression in childhood: Diagnosis, treatment, and conceptual models* (pp. 147–149). New York: Raven Press.

Himadi, W. G., Boice, R., & Barlow, D. H. (1985). Assessment of agoraphobia: Triple response measurement. *Behaviour Research and Therapy, 23,* 311–323.

Hnatiow, M., & Lang, P. J. (1965). Learned stabilization of cardiac rate. *Psychophysiology, 1,* 330–336.

Hodges, J. L., & Hollandsworth, J. G. (1980, November). *Use of the skin potential response as a source for therapist feedback during systematic desensitization.* Paper presented at the 14th Annual Convention of the Association for Advancement of Behavior Therapy, New York.

Hodgson, R., & Rachman, S. (1974). Desynchrony in measures of fear. II. *Behaviour Research and Therapy, 12,* 319–326.

Hollandsworth, J. G. (1977). Differentiating assertion and aggression: Some behavioral guidelines. *Behavior Therapy, 8,* 347–351.

Hollandsworth, J. G. (1979). Some thoughts on distance running as training in biofeedback. *Journal of Sport Behavior, 2*, 71–82.

Hollandsworth, J. G. (1982, November). Long-term versus short-term regulation of blood pressure: Implications for behavioral treatments of hypertension. In J. Martin (Chair), *Advances in the behavioral management of high blood pressure: Toward life-style modification.* Symposium conducted at the 19th Annual Convention of the Association for Advancement of Behavior Therapy, Los Angeles.

Hollandsworth, J. G. (1985). Counseling psychology, health psychology, and beyond: A reply to Klippel and DeJoy. *Journal of Counseling Psychology, 32*, 150–153. (a)

Hollandsworth, J. G. (1985). Social validation of a construct for differentiating assertion and aggression. *The Behavior Therapist, 8*, 136–138. (b)

Hollandsworth, J. G., & Cooley, M. L. (1978). Provoking anger and gaining compliance with assertive versus aggressive responses. *Behavior Therapy, 9*, 640–646.

Hollandsworth, J. G., & Jones, G. E. (1979). Perceptions of arousal and awareness of physiological responding prior to and after running 20 kilometers. *Journal of Sport Psychology, 1*, 291–300.

Hollandsworth, J. G., & Sandifer, B. A. (1979). Behavioral training for increasing job-interview skills: Follow-up and evaluation. *Journal of Counseling Psychology, 26*, 448–450.

Hollandsworth, J. G., Dressel, M. E., & Stevens, J. (1977). Use of behavioral versus traditional procedures for increasing job interview skills. *Journal of Counseling Psychology, 24*, 503–510.

Hollandsworth, J. G., Galassi, J. P., & Gay, M. L. (1977). The Adult Self Expression Scale: Validation by the multitrait–multimethod procedure. *Journal of Clinical Psychology, 33*, 407–415.

Hollandsworth, J. G., Glazeski, R. C., & Dressel, M. E. (1978). Use of social-skills training in the treatment of extreme anxiety and deficient verbal skills in the job-interview setting. *Journal of Applied Behavior Analysis, 11*, 259–269.

Hollandsworth, J. G., Glazeski, R. C., Kirkland, K., Jones, G. E., & Van Norman, L. R. (1979). An analysis of the nature and effects of test anxiety: Cognitive, behavioral and physiological components. *Cognitive Therapy and Research, 3*, 165–180.

Hollandsworth, J. G., Kazelskis, R., Stevens, J., & Dressel, M. E. (1979). Relative contributions of verbal, articulative, and nonverbal communication to employment decisions in the job interview setting. *Personnel Psychology, 32*, 359–367.

Hollandsworth, J. G., Gintner, G. G., Ellender, B. S., & Rectanus, E. F. (1984). O$_2$ consumption, heart rate and subjective ratings under conditions of relaxation and active coping. *Behaviour Research and Therapy, 22*, 281–288.

Hollon, S. D., & Beck, A. T. (1978). Psychotherapy and drug therapy: Comparisons and combinations. In S. L. Garfield & A. E. Bergin (Eds.), *Handbook of psychotherapy and behavior change: An empirical analysis* (2nd ed., pp. 437–490). New York: Wiley.

Holmes, D. S. (1984). Meditation and somatic arousal reduction: A review of the experimental evidence. *American Psychologist, 39*, 1–10.

Holroyd, K. A. (1979). Stress, coping and the treatment of stress-related illness. In J. R. McNamara (Ed.), *Behavioral approaches to medicine: Application and analysis* (pp. 191–226). New York: Plenum Press.

Holroyd, K. A., & Andrasik, F. (1978). Coping and the self-control of chronic tension headache. *Journal of Consulting and Clinical Psychology, 46*, 1036–1045.

Holroyd, K. A., Westbrook, T., Wolf, M., & Badhorn, E. (1978). Performance, cognition, and physiological responding in test anxiety. *Journal of Abnormal Psychology, 87*, 442–451.

Holroyd, K. A., Andrasik, F., & Noble, J. (1980). A comparison of EMG biofeedback and a credible pseudotherapy in treating tension headache. *Journal of Behavioral Medicine, 3,* 29–39.

Hordern, A., Burt, C. G., & Holt, N. F. (1965). *Depressive states: A pharmacological study.* Springfield, IL: Charles C Thomas.

Hosford, R. (1969). Overcoming fear of speaking in a group. In J. Krumboltz & C. Thoresen (Eds.), *Behavioral counseling: Cases and techniques* (pp. 80–82). New York: Holt, Rinehart & Winston.

Houts, A. C. (1982). Relaxation and thermal feedback treatment of child migraine headache: A case study. *American Journal of Clinical Biofeedback, 5,* 154–157.

Hugdahl, K. (1981). The three-systems-model of fear and emotion: A critical examination. *Behaviour Research and Therapy, 19,* 75–85.

Hull, C. L. (1943). *Principles of behavior.* New York: Appleton.

Ikeda, Y., & Hirai, H. (1976). Voluntary control of electrodermal activity in relation to imagery and internal perception scores. *Psychophysiology, 13,* 330–333.

Izard, C. E. (1972). *Patterns of emotion: A new analysis of anxiety and depression.* New York: Academic Press.

Izard, C. E. (Ed.). (1977). *Human emotions.* New York: Plenum Press.

Izard, C. E. (1984). Emotion–cognition relationships and human development. In C. E. Izard, J. Kagan, & R. B. Zajonc (Eds.), *Emotions, cognition, and behavior* (pp. 17–37). New York: Cambridge University Press.

Jacob, R. G., & Rapport, M. D. (1984). Panic disorder: Medical and psychological parameters. In S. M. Turner (Ed.), *Behavioral theories and treatment of anxiety* (pp. 187–237). New York: Plenum Press.

Jacob, R. G., & Turner, S. M. (1984). Somatoform disorders. In S. M. Turner & M. Hersen (Eds.), *Adult psychopathology and diagnosis.* New York: Wiley.

Jacob, R. G., Moller, M. B., Turner, S. M., & Wall, C. (1983, December). *Oto-vestibular dysfunction in panic disorder or agoraphobia with panic attacks.* Paper presented at the 17th Annual Convention of the Association for Advancement of Behavior Therapy, Washington.

Jacobson, E. (1938). *Progressive relaxation.* Chicago: University of Chicago Press.

Jacobson, N. S. (1981). The assessment of overt behavior. In L. P. Rehm (Ed.), *Behavior therapy for depression: Present status and future directions* (pp. 279–300). New York: Academic Press.

James, N. M., & Chapman, C. J. (1975). A genetic study of bipolar affective disorder. *British Journal of Psychiatry, 126,* 449–456.

James, W. (1884). What is emotion? *Mind, 9* (Series I), 188–204.

James, W. (1890). *The principles of psychology* (Vol. 2). New York: Henry Holt.

Jemmott, J. B., & Locke, S. E. (1984). Psychosocial factors, immunologic mediation, and human susceptibility to infectious diseases: How much do we know? *Psychological Bulletin, 95,* 78–108.

Jenkins, C. D., Rosenman, R. H., & Friedman, M. (1967). Development of an objective psychological test for the determination of the coronary-prone behavior pattern in employed men. *Journal of Chronic Disease, 20,* 371–379.

Jones, F., Maas, J. W., Dekirmenjian, H., & Sanchez, J. (1975). Diagnostic subgroups of affective disorders and their urinary excretion of catecholamine metabolites. *American Journal of Psychiatry, 132,* 1141–1148.

Jones, G. E., & Hollandsworth, J. G. (1981). Heart rate discrimination before and after exercise-induced augmented cardiac activity. *Psychophysiology, 18,* 252–257.

Jones, R. (1968). A factored measure of Ellis' irrational belief system, with personality and maladjustment correlates. *Dissertation Abstracts International, 29,* 4379B. (University Microfilms No. 69-6443)

Julien, R. M. (1981). *A primer of drug action* (3rd ed.). San Francisco: W. H. Freeman.

Kahnerman, D. (1973). *Attention and effort.* Englewood Cliffs, NJ: Prentice-Hall.

Kamiya, J. (1968). Conscious control of brain waves. *Psychology today, 1*(11), 56–61.

Kamiya, J. (1969). Operant control of the EEG alpha rhythm and some of its reported effects on consciousness. In C. Tart (Ed.), *Altered states of consciousness* (pp. 507–517). New York: Wiley.

Kanfer, F. H., & Hagerman, S. (1981). The role of self-regulation. In L. P. Rehm (Ed.), *Behavior therapy for depression: Present status and future directions* (pp. 143–179). New York: Academic Press.

Kanfer, F. H., & Nay, W. R. (1982). Behavioral assessment. In G. T. Wilson & C. M. Franks (Eds.), *Contemporary behavior therapy: Conceptual and empirical foundations* (pp. 367–402). New York: Guilford Press.

Kanfer, F. H., & Phillips, J. S. (1970). *Learning foundations of behavior therapy.* New York: Wiley.

Kanfer, F. H., & Saslow, G. (1965). Behavior analysis. *Archives of General Psychiatry, 12,* 529–538.

Kantor, J. S., Zitrin, C. M., & Zeldis, S. M. (1980). Mitral valve prolapse syndrome in agoraphobic patients. *American Journal of Psychiatry, 137,* 467–469.

Karacan, I., Thornby, J. I., Anch, A. M., Booth, G. H., Williams, R. L., & Salis, P. J. (1977). Dose related sleep disturbances induced by coffee and caffeine. *Clinical Pharmacology and Therapeutics, 20,* 682–689.

Katkin, E. S. (1985). Blood, sweat, and tears: Individual differences in autonomic self-perception. *Psychophysiology, 22,* 125–137.

Katkin, E. S., & Murray, E. N. (1968). Instrumental conditioning of autonomically-mediated behavior: Theoretical and methodological issues. *Psychological Bulletin, 70,* 52–68.

Kausler, D. H. (1982). *Experimental psychology and human aging.* New York: Wiley.

Kazdin, A. E. (1980). *Behavior modification in applied settings* (Rev. ed.). Homewood, IL: Dorsey Press.

Kazdin, A. E. (1982). Symptom substitution, generalization, and response covariation: Implications for psychotherapy outcome. *Psychological Bulletin, 91,* 349–365.

Keane, T. M., Fairbank, J. A., Caddell, J. M., Zimering, R. T., & Bender, M. E. (1985). A behavioral approach to assessing and treating post traumatic stress disorders in Vietnam veterans. In C. R. Figley (Ed.), *Trauma and its wake: The assessment and treatment of post traumatic stress disorders* (pp. 257–294). New York: Brunner/Mazel.

Keane, T. M., Zimering, R. T., & Caddell, J. M. (1985). A behavioral formulation of posttraumatic stress disorder in Vietnam veterans. *The Behavior Therapist 8,* 9–12.

Kelly, J. A. (1982). *Social-skills training: A practical guide for interventions.* New York: Springer.

Kendall, P. C. (1982). Integration: Behavior therapy and other schools of thought. *Behavior Therapy, 13,* 559–571.

Kendall, P. C., & Watson, D. (1981). Psychological preparation for stressful medical procedures. In C. K. Prokop & L. A. Bradley (Eds.), *Medical psychology: Contributions to behavioral medicine* (pp. 197–221). New York: Academic Press.

Kendell, R. E. (1969). The continuum model of depressive illness. *Proceedings of the Royal Society of Medicine, 62,* 335–339.

Kendell, R. E. (1976). The classifications of depressions: A review of contemporary confusion. *British Journal of Psychiatry, 129,* 15–28.

Kendell, R. E., & Gourlay, J. (1970). The clinical distinction between psychotic and neurotic depressions. *British Journal of Psychiatry, 117,* 257–266.

Kendler, T. S. (1963). Development of mediating responses in children. *Monographs of the Society for Research in Child Development, 28*(2) (Serial No. 86). (pp. 33–52).

Kessel, N., & McCulloch, W. (1966). Repeated acts of self-poisoning and self-injury. *Proceedings of the Royal Society of Medicine, 59,* 89–92.

Kety, S. S. (1970). Neurochemical aspects of emotional behavior. In P. Black (Ed.), *Physiological correlates of emotion* (pp. 61–72). New York: Academic Press.

Kiloh, L. G., & Garside, R. F. (1963). The independence of neurotic depression and endogenous depression. *British Journal of Psychiatry, 109,* 451–463.

Kimmel, E., & Kimmel, H. D. (1963). A replication of operant conditioning of the GSR. *Journal of Experimental Psychology, 65,* 212–213.

Kimmel, H. D. (1967). Instrumental conditioning of autonomically mediated behavior. *Psychological Bulletin, 67,* 337–345.

Kimmel, H. D. (1974). Instrumental conditioning of autonomically mediated responses in human beings. *American Psychologist, 29,* 325–335.

Kimmel, H. D., & Hill, F. A. (1960). Operant conditioning of the GSR. *Psychological Reports, 7,* 555–562.

Kincey, J., & Benjamin, S. (1984). Desynchrony following the treatment of pain behavior. *Behaviour Research and Therapy, 22,* 85–86.

King, N. J., & Montgomery, R. B. (1980). Biofeedback-induced control of human peripheral temperature: A critical review of the literature. *Psychological Bulletin, 88,* 738–752.

Kirkland, K., & Hollandsworth, J. G. (1979). Test anxiety, study skills, and academic performance. *Journal of College Student Personnel, 20,* 431–435.

Kirkland, K., & Hollandsworth, J. G. (1980). Effective test-taking: Skills-acquisition versus anxiety-reduction techniques. *Journal of Consulting and Clinical Psychology, 48,* 431–439.

Klein, D. F. (1974). Endogenomorphic depression: A conceptual and terminological revision. *Archives of General Psychiatry, 31,* 447–454.

Kleinginna, P. R., & Kleinginna, A. M. (1985). Cognition and affect: A reply to Lazarus and Zajonc. *American Psychologist, 40,* 470–471.

Klerman, G. L. (1975). Overview of depression. In A. M. Freedman, H. I. Kaplan, & B. J. Sadock (Eds.), *Comprehensive textbook of psychiatry* (Vol. 1, 2d ed., pp. 1003–1012). Baltimore: Williams & Wilkins.

Knapp, S., & VandeCreek, L. (1981). Behavioral medicine: Its malpractice risks for psychologists. *Professional Psychology, 12,* 677–683.

Kocsis, J. (1981). Somatic treatment for depression. In J. F. Clarkin & H. I. Glazer (Eds.), *Depression: Behavioral and directive intervention strategies* (pp. 295–307). New York: Garland STPM Press.

Koeppen, A. (1974). Relaxation training for children. *Elementary School Guidance and Counseling, 9,* 14–21.

Kolb, B., & Whishaw, I. Q. (1980). *Fundamentals of human neuropsychology.* San Francisco: W. H. Freeman.

Konorski, J. (1967). *Integrative activity of the brain: An interdisciplinary approach.* Chicago: University of Chicago Press.

Korner, P. I. (1974). Control of blood flow to special vascular areas: Brain, kidney, muscle, skin, liver and intestine. In A. C. Guyton & C. E. Jones (Eds.), *MTP International Review of Science: Physiology Series One* (Vol. 1, pp. 123–162). Baltimore: University Park Press.

Kraines, S. H. (1966). Manic depressive syndrome: A physiologic disease. *Diseases of the Nervous System, 27*, 573–582.

Krantz, D. S., & Manuck, S. B. (1984). Acute psychophysiologic reactivity and risk of cardiovascular disease: A review and methodological critique. *Psychological Bulletin, 96*, 435–464.

Krauthammer, C., & Klerman, G. L. (1979). The epidemiology of mania. In B. Shopsin (Ed.), *Manic illness* (pp. 11–28). New York: Raven Press.

Kreitman, N. (Ed.). (1977). *Parasuicide*. London: Wiley.

Kuhn, R. (1958). The treatment of depressive states with G 22355 (imipramine hydrochloride). *American Journal of Psychiatry, 115*, 459–464.

Kuo, Z. Y. (1967). *The dynamics of behavior development: An epigenetic view*. New York: Random House.

Labbé, E., & Williamson, D. (1983). Temperature biofeedback in the treatment of children with migraine headache. *Journal of Pediatric Psychology, 8*, 317–326.

Lacey, J. I. (1950). Individual differences in somatic response patterns. *Journal of Comparative and Physiological Psychology, 43*, 338–350.

Lacey, J. I. (1967). Somatic response patterning and stress: Some revisions of activation theory. In M. H. Appley & R. Trumbull (Eds.), *Psychological stress: Issues in research* (pp. 14–42). New York: Appleton-Century-Crofts.

Lader, M. H. (1967). Palmar skin conductance measures in anxiety and phobic states. *Journal of Psychosomatic Research, 11*, 271–281.

Lader, M. (1978). Benzodiazepines—The opium of the masses? *Neuroscience, 3*, 159–165.

Lamon, S., Wilson, G. T., & Leaf, R. C. (1977). Human classical aversion conditioning: Nausea versus electric shock in the reduction of target beverage consumption. *Behaviour Research and Therapy, 15*, 313–320.

Lampedusa, G. di (1960). *The leopard*. (A. Colquhoun, Trans.). New York: Pantheon. (Original work published 1958)

Landers, D. M. (1979). Motivation and performance: The role of arousal and attentional factors. In W. F. Straub (Ed.), *Sport psychology: An analysis of athlete behavior* (2d ed., pp. 91–103). Ithaca, NY: Movement Publications.

Lang, P. J. (1964). Experimental studies of desensitization psychotherapy. In J. Wolpe, A. Salter, & L. J. Reyna (Eds.), *The conditioning therapies: The challenge in psychotherapy* (pp. 38–53). New York: Holt, Rinehart & Winston.

Lang, P. J. (1971). The application of psychophysiological methods to the study of psychotherapy and behavior modification. In A. E. Bergin & S. L. Garfield (Eds.), *Handbook of psychotherapy and behavior change: An empirical analysis* (pp. 75–125). New York: Wiley.

Lang, P. J. (1977). Physiological assessment of anxiety and fear. In J. D. Cone & R. P. Cone (Eds.), *Behavioral assessment: New directions in clinical psychology* (pp. 178–195). New York: Brunner/Mazel. (a)

Lang, P. J. (1977). Imagery in therapy: An information processing analysis of fear. *Behavior Therapy, 8*, 862–886. (b)

Lang, P. J. (1979). A bio-informational theory of emotional imagery. *Psychophysiology, 16*, 495–512.

Lang, P. J., & Hnatiow, M. (1962). Stimulus repetition and the heart rate response. *Journal of Comparative and Physiological Psychology, 55*, 781–785.

Lang, P. J. & Lazovik, A. D. (1963). Experimental desensitization of a phobia. *Journal of Abnormal and Social Psychology, 66*, 519–525.

Lang, P. J., Geer, J., & Hnatiow, M. (1963). Semantic generalization of conditioned autonomic responses. *Journal of Experimental Psychology, 65*, 552–558.

Lang, P. J., Sroufe, L. A., & Hastings, J. E. (1967). Effects of feedback and instructional set on the control of cardiac-rate variability. *Journal of Experimental Psychology, 75,* 425–431.

Lang, P. J., Rice, D. G., & Sternbach, R. A. (1972). The psychophysiology of emotion. In N. S. Greenfield & R. A. Sternbach (Eds.), *Handbook of psychophysiology* (pp. 623–643). New York: Holt, Rinehart & Winston.

Lang, P. J., Levin, D. N., Miller, G. A., & Kozak, M. J. (1983). Fear behavior, fear imagery, and the psychophysiology of emotion: The problem of affective response integration. *Journal of Abnormal Psychology, 92,* 276–306.

Lange, A. J., & Jakubowski, P. (1976). *Responsible assertive behavior: Cognitive/behavioral procedures for trainers.* Champaign, IL: Research Press.

Lazarus, A. A. (1968). Aversion therapy and sensory modalities: Clinical impressions. *Perceptual and Motor Skills, 27,* 178.

Lazarus, R. S. (1966). *Psychological stress and the coping process.* New York: McGraw-Hill.

Lazarus, R. S. (1975). A cognitively oriented psychologist looks at biofeedback. *American Psychologist, 30,* 553–561.

Lazarus, R. S. (1982). Thoughts on the relations between emotion and cognition. *American Psychologist, 37,* 1019–1024.

Lazarus, R. S. (1984). On the primacy of cognition. *American Psychologist, 39,* 124–129.

Lazovik, A. D., & Lang, P. J. (1960). A laboratory demonstration of systematic desensitization psychotherapy. *Journal of Psychological Studies, 11,* 238–247.

Lehrer, P. M., Schoicket, S., Carrington, P., & Woolfolk, R. L. (1980). Physiological and cognitive responses to stressful stimuli in subjects practicing progressive relaxation and clinically standardized meditation. *Behaviour Research and Therapy, 18,* 293–303.

Lenneberg, E. (1967). *Biological foundations of language.* New York: Wiley.

Lenneberg, E. H. (1969). On explaining language. *Science, 164,* 635–643.

Leonhard, K., Kroff, I., & Schultz, H. (1962). Temperaments in the families of monopolar and bipolar phasic psychoses. *Psychiatria et Neurologia, 143,* 416–434.

Levenson, M., & Neuringer, C. (1971). Problem-solving behavior in suicidal adolescents. *Journal of Consulting and Clinical Psychology, 37,* 433–436.

Levi, L. (1967). Effect of coffee on the function of the sympatho-adrenomedullary system in man. *Acta Medica Scandinavica, 181,* 431–438.

Levis, D. J., & Malloy, P. F. (1982). Research in infrahuman and human conditioning. In G. T. Wilson & C. M. Franks (Eds.), *Contemporary behavior therapy: Conceptual and empirical foundations* (pp. 65–118). New York: Guilford Press.

Levitt, E. E., Lubin, B., & Brooks, J. M. (1983). *Depression: Concepts, controversies and some new facts.* Hillside, NJ: Erlbaum.

Levy, S. M. (1981). The psychosocial assessment of the chronically ill geriatric patient. In C. K. Prokop & L. A. Bradley (Eds.), *Medical psychology: Contributions to behavioral medicine* (pp. 119–137). New York: Academic Press. (a)

Levy, S. M. (1981). Treatment of the chronically ill geriatric patient. In C. K. Prokop & L. A. Bradley (Eds.), *Medical psychology: Contributions to behavioral medicine* (pp. 307–328). New York: Academic Press. (b)

Levy, S. M., Herberman, R. B., Maluish, A. M., Schlien, B., & Lippman, M. (1985). Prognostic risk assessment in primary breast cancer by behavioral and immunological parameters. *Health Psychology, 4,* 99–113.

Lewinsohn, P. M. (1974). A behavioral approach to depression. In R. J. Friedman & M. M. Katz (Eds.), *The psychology of depression: Contemporary theory and research* (pp. 157–185). New York: Winston-Wiley.

Lewinsohn, P. M. (1976). Activity schedules in treatment of depression. In J. D. Krumboltz

& C. E. Thoresen (Eds.), *Counseling methods* (pp. 74–83). New York: Holt, Rinehart & Winston.

Lewinsohn, P. M., & Arconad, M. (1981). Behavioral treatment of depression: A social learning approach. In J. F. Clarkin & H. I. Glazer (Eds.), *Depression: Behavioral and directive intervention strategies* (pp. 33–67). New York: Garland STPM Press.

Lewinsohn, P. M., & Libet, J. (1972). Pleasant events, activity schedules, and depression. *Journal of Abnormal Psychology, 79,* 291–295.

Lewinsohn, P. M., Biglan, A., & Zeiss, A. M. (1976). Behavioral treatment of depression. In P. O. Davidson (Ed.), *The behavior management of anxiety, depression and pain* (pp. 91–146). New York: Brunner/Mazel.

Lewinsohn, P. M., Youngren, M. A., & Grosscup, S. J. (1979). Reinforcement and depression. In R. A. Depue (Ed.), *The psychobiology of the depressive disorders: Implications for the effects of stress* (pp. 291–316). New York: Academic Press.

Lewinsohn, P. M., Mischel, W., Chaplin, W., & Barton, R. (1980). Social competence and depression: The role of illusory self-perceptions. *Journal of Abnormal Psychology, 89,* 203–212.

Lewinsohn, P. M., Teri, L., & Wasserman, D. (1983). Depression. In M. Hersen (Ed.), *Outpatient behavior therapy: A clinical guide* (pp. 81–108). New York: Grune & Stratton.

Lewis, A. J. (1934). Melancholia: A clinical survey of depressive states. *Journal of Mental Science, 80,* 277–378.

Lewis, A. J. (1938). States of depression: Their clinical and aetiological differentiation. *British Medical Journal, 2,* 875–878.

Ley, R. (1985). Agoraphobia, the panic attack and the hyperventilation syndrome. *Behaviour Research and Therapy, 23,* 79–81.

Liberman, R. P. (1981). A model for individualizing treatment. In L. P. Rehm (Ed.), *Behavior therapy for depression: Present status and future directions* (pp. 231–253). New York: Academic Press.

Libet, J. M., & Lewinsohn, P. M. (1973). Concept of social skill with special reference to the behavior of depressed persons. *Journal of Consulting and Clinical Psychology, 40,* 304–312.

Libow, L. (1977). Senile dementia and "pseudosenility": Clinical diagnosis. In C. Eisdorfer & R. Freidel (Eds.), *Cognitive and emotional disturbance in the elderly: Clinical issues* (pp. 75–88). Chicago: Yearbook Medical Publishers.

Lichtenstein, E. (1982). The smoking problem: A behavioral perspective. *Journal of Consulting and Clinical Psychology, 50,* 804–819.

Lick, J. R., & Katkin, E. S. (1976). Assessment of anxiety and fear. In M. Hersen & A. S. Bellack (Eds.), *Behavioral assessment: A practical handbook* (pp. 175–206). New York: Pergamon Press.

Light, K. C., Koepke, J. P., Obrist, P. A., & Willis, P. W. (1983). Psychological stress induces sodium and fluid retention in men at high risk for hypertension. *Science, 220,* 429–431.

Lindsley, D. B. (1951). Emotion. In S. S. Stevens (Ed.), *Handbook of experimental psychology* (pp. 473–516). New York: Wiley.

Lindsley, D. B. (1970). The role of nonspecific reticulo-thalamo-cortical systems in emotion. In P. Black (Ed.), *Physiological correlates of emotion* (pp. 147–188). New York: Academic Press.

Linehan, M. M. (1977). Issues in behavioral interviewing. In J. D. Cone & R. P. Hawkins (Eds.), *Behavioral assessment: New directions for clinical psychology* (pp. 30–51). New York: Brunner/Mazel.

Linehan, M. M. (1981). A social-behavioral analysis of suicide and parasuicide: Implications for clinical assessment and treatment. In J. F. Clarkin & H. I. Glazer (Eds.), *Depression: Behavioral and directive intervention strategies* (pp. 229–294). New York: Garland STPM Press.

Lipowski, Z. J. (1975). Psychiatry of somatic diseases: Epidemiology, pathogenesis, classification. *Comprehensive Psychiatry, 16,* 105–124.

Lipowski, Z. J. (1977). Psychosomatic medicine in the seventies: An overview. *American Journal of Psychiatry, 134,* 233–244.

Lipton, M. (1976). Age differentiation in depression: Biochemical aspects. *Journal of Gerontology, 31,* 293–299.

Lishman, W. A. (1972). Selective factors in memory: II. Affective disorder. *Psychological Medicine, 2,* 248–253.

Litman, R. E. (1974). Models for predicting suicide risk. In C. Neuringer (Ed.), *Psychological assessment of suicide risk* (pp. 177–185). Springfield, IL: Charles C Thomas.

Lloyd, G. G., & Lishman, W. A. (1975). Effect of depression on the speed of recall of pleasant and unpleasant experiences. *Psychological Medicine, 5,* 173–180.

Luria, A. R. (1973). *The working brain: An introduction to neuropsychology.* (B. Haigh, Trans.). New York: Basic Books.

Maas, J. W., Fawcett, J., & Dekirmenjian, H. (1968). 3-methoxy-4-hydroxy phenylglycol (MHPG) excretion in depressive states: A pilot study. *Archives of General Psychiatry, 19,* 129–134.

Maas, J. W., Dekirmenjian, H., & Jones, F. (1973). The identification of depressed patients who have a disorder of norepinephrine metabolism and/or disposition. In E. Usdin & S. Snyder (Eds.), *Frontiers in catecholamine research* (pp. 1091–1096). New York: Pergamon Press.

Mackworth, J. F. (1969). *Vigilance and habituation: A neuropsychological approach.* Baltimore: Penguin Books.

MacLean, P. D. (1970). The limbic brain in relation to the psychoses. In P. Black (Ed.), *Physiological correlates of emotion* (pp. 130–146). New York: Academic Press.

MacLean, P. D. (1973). *A triune concept of the brain and behaviour.* Toronto: University of Toronto Press.

MacPhillamy, D. J., & Lewinsohn, P. M. (1974). Depression as a function of levels of desired and obtained pleasure. *Journal of Abnormal Psychology, 83,* 651–657.

Mahoney, M. J. (1974). *Cognition and behavior modification.* Cambridge, MA: Ballinger.

Mahoney, M. J. (1976). *Scientist as subject: The psychological imperative.* Cambridge, MA: Ballinger.

Mahoney, M. J., & Arnkoff, D. (1978). Cognitive and self-control therapies. In S. L. Garfield & A. E. Bergin (Eds.), *Handbook of psychotherapy and behavior change: An empirical analysis* (2nd ed., pp. 689–722). New York: Wiley.

Mandler, G., & Sarason, S. B. (1952). A study of anxiety and learning. *Journal of Abnormal and Social Psychology, 47,* 166–173.

Mandler, G., Mandler, J. M., & Uviller, E. T. (1958). Autonomic feedback: The perception of autonomic activity. *Journal of Abnormal and Social Psychology, 56,* 367–373.

Manning, A. (1972). *An introduction to animal behavior* (2nd ed.). Reading, MA: Addison-Wesley.

Mapother, E. (1926). Discussion on manic-depressive psychosis. *British Medical Journal, 2,* 872–879.

Marinacci, A. A., & Horande, M. (1960). Electromyogram in neuromuscular reeducation. *Bulletin of the Los Angeles Neurological Society, 25,* 57–71.

Markiewicz, W., Stoner, J., London, E., Hunt, S. A., & Popp, R. L. (1976). Mitral valve prolapse in 100 presumably healthy young females. *Circulation, 53*, 464–473.

Marks, I. (1978). Behavioral psychotherapy of adult neurosis. In S. L. Garfield & A. E. Bergin (Eds.), *Handbook of psychotherapy and behavior change: An empirical analysis* (2nd ed., pp. 443–548). New York: Wiley.

Marshall, G. D., & Zimbardo, P. G. (1979). Affective consequences of inadequately explained physiological arousal. *Journal of Personality and Social Psychology, 37*, 970–988.

Marsland, D. W., Wood, M., & Mayo, F. (1976). A data bank for patient care, curriculum, and research in family practice: 526,196 patient problems. *Journal of Family Practice, 3*, 25–28.

Martin, J. E., & Dubbert, P. M. (1982). Exercise applications and promotion in behavioral medicine: Current status and future directions. *Journal of Consulting and Clinical Psychology, 50*, 1004–1017.

Marzillier, J. S. (1980). Cognitive therapy and behavioural practice. *Behaviour Research and Therapy, 18*, 249–258.

Maslach, C. (1979). Negative emotional biasing of unexplained arousal. *Journal of Personality and Social Psychology, 37*, 953–969.

Maslow, A. H. (1966). *The psychology of science: A reconnaissance.* New York: Harper & Row.

Mason, E. B. (1983). *Human Physiology.* Menlo Park, CA: Benjamin/Cummings.

Mason, J. W. (1975). A historical view of the stress field. *Journal of Human Stress, 1*(1), 6–12, 1(2), 22–36.

Mavissakalian, M., & Barlow, D. H. (1981). *Phobia: Psychological and pharmacological treatment.* New York: Guilford Press.

Mavissakalian, M., & Michelson, L. (1982). Patterns of psychophysiological change in the treatment of agoraphobia. *Behaviour Research and Therapy, 20*, 347–356.

McCaul, K. D., & Malott, J. M. (1984). Distraction and coping with pain. *Psychological Bulletin, 95*, 516–533.

McCord, W., Porta, J., & McCord, J. (1962). The familial genesis of psychoses. *Psychiatry, 25*, 60–71.

McDougall, W. (1908). *An introduction to social psychology.* London: Methuen.

McFall, R. M. (1985). Neobehavioral training for behavioral clinicians. *The Behavior Therapist, 8*, 27–30.

McLean, P. D. (1981). Matching treatment to patient characteristics in an outpatient setting. In L. P. Rehm (Ed.), *Behavior therapy for depression: Present status and future directions* (pp. 197–207). New York: Academic Press.

Mechanic, D. (1974). *Politics, medicine, and social science.* New York: Wiley.

Meichenbaum, D. (1972). Cognitive modification of test anxious college students. *Journal of Consulting and Clinical Psychology, 39*, 370–380.

Meichenbaum, D. (1975). Self-instructional methods. In F. H. Kanfer & A. P. Goldstein (Eds.), *Helping people change* (pp. 357–392). New York: Pergamon Press.

Meichenbaum, D. (1977). *Cognitive-behavior modification: An integrative approach.* New York: Plenum Press. (a)

Meichenbaum, D. (1977, December). [Untitled address]. In G. T. Wilson (Chair), *Comparative outcome research.* Symposium conducted at the 11th Annual Convention of the Association for Advancement of Behavior Therapy, Atlanta. (b)

Meichenbaum, D., & Goodman, J. (1971). Training impulsive children to talk to themselves: A means of developing self-control. *Journal of Abnormal Psychology, 77*, 115–126.

Meichenbaum, D., & Jaremko, M. E. (Eds.). (1983). *Stress reduction and prevention.* New York: Plenum Press.

Meichenbaum, D., & Turk, D. (1973). *Stress inoculation: A skills training approach to anxiety management.* Unpublished manuscript, University of Waterloo, Ontario, Canada.

Melamed, B. G., & Siegel, L. J. (1980). *Behavioral medicine: Practical applications in health care.* New York: Springer.

Mendels, J. (1965). Electroconvulsive therapy and depression. II. Significance of endogenous and reactive syndromes. *British Journal of Psychiatry, 111,* 682–686.

Mendelson, W. B., Gillin, J. C., & Wyatt, R. J. (1977). *Human sleep and its disorders.* New York: Plenum Press.

Miles, C. P. (1977). Condition predisposing to suicide: A review. *Journal of Nervous and Mental Disease, 164,* 231–246.

Miller, G. A. (1956). The magical number seven, plus or minus two: Some limits on our capacity for processing information. *Psychological Review, 63,* 81–97.

Miller, J. G. (1978). *Living systems.* New York: McGraw-Hill.

Miller, N. E. (1981). An overview of behavioral medicine: Opportunities and dangers. In S. M. Weiss, J. A. Herd, & B. H. Fox (Eds.), *Perspectives on behavioral medicine* (pp. 3–24). New York: Academic Press.

Miller, S., & Konorski, J. (1928). On a particular type of conditioned reflex. *Proceedings of the Biological Society* (Polish Section, Paris), *9,* 1155–1157.

Mischel, W. (1968). *Personality and assessment.* New York: Wiley.

Moates, D. R., & Schumacher, G. M. (1980). *An introduction to cognitive psychology.* Belmont, CA: Wadsworth.

Monroe, L. (1967). Psychological and physiological differences between good and poor sleepers. *Journal of Abnormal Psychology, 72,* 255–264.

Moon, J. R., & Eisler, R. M. (1983). Anger control: An experimental comparison of three behavioral treatments. *Behavior Therapy, 14,* 493–505.

Morrell, E. M. (in press). Meditation and somatic arousal. *American Psychologist.*

Morrell, E. M., & Hollandsworth, J. G. (1984, November). *The effect of a regularly practiced relaxation procedure on stressed and resting plasma norepinephrine levels, heart rate, and blood pressure.* Paper presented at the 18th Annual Convention of the Association for Advancement of Behavior Therapy, Philadelphia.

Morrell, E. M. & Hollandsworth, J. G. (in press). Norepinephrine alterations under stress conditions following the regular practice of meditation. *Psychosomatic Medicine.*

Mowrer, O. H. (1947). On the dual nature of learning: A reinterpretation of "conditioning" and "problem-solving." *Harvard Educational Review, 17,* 102–148.

Mulholland, T. B., & Peper, E. (1971). Occipital alpha and accommodative vergence, pursuit tracking, and fast eye movements. *Psychophysiology, 8,* 556–575.

Murray, E. J., & Jacobson, L. I. (1978). Cognition and learning in traditional and behavioral psychotherapy. In S. L. Garfield & A. E. Bergin (Eds.), *Handbook of psychotherapy and behavior change: An empirical analysis* (2nd ed., pp. 661–688). New York: Wiley.

Nachman, M. (1970). Limited effects of electroconvulsive shock on memory of taste stimulation. *Journal of Comparative and Physiological Psychology, 73,* 31–37.

Nathan, P. E., & Goldman, M. S. (1979). Problem drinking and alcoholism. In O. F. Pomerleau & J. P. Brady (Eds.), *Behavioral medicine: Theory and practice* (pp. 255–277). Baltimore: Williams & Wilkins.

National Institute of Mental Health. (1980). *NIMH treatment of depression, collaborative research program (pilot phase), revised research plan, January, 1980, Psychosocial Treatments Research Branch.* Bethesda: Author.

Nelson, R. E., & Craighead, W. E. (1977). Selective recall of positive and negative feedback, self-control behaviors, and depression. *Journal of Abnormal Psychology, 86,* 379–388.

Neuringer, C. (1964). Rigid thinking in suicidal individuals. *Journal of Consulting and Clinical Psychology, 28,* 54–58.

Neuringer, C. (1974). Self-and other-appraisals by suicidal, psychosomatic and normal hospitalized patients. *Journal of Consulting and Clinical Psychology, 42,* 306.

Newton, J. E., & Gantt, W. H. (1960). Curare reveals central rather than peripheral factor determining cardiac orienting reflex. *American Journal of Physiology, 199,* 978–980.

Nicholas, D. R., & Hollandsworth, J. G. (in press). The assessment of anticipatory nausea and vomiting in cancer chemotherapy: Theoretical and methodological considerations. *Journal of Psychosocial Oncology.*

Nisbett, R. E., & Wilson, T. D. (1977). Telling more than we can know: Verbal reports on mental processes. *Psychological Review, 84,* 231–259.

Novaco, R. W. (1975). *Anger control: The development and evaluation of an experimental treatment.* Lexington, MA: D. C. Heath.

Novaco, R. W. (1976). Treatment of chronic anger through cognitive and relaxation controls. *Journal of Consulting and Clinical Psychology, 44,* 681.

Novaco, R. W. (1977). A stress inoculation approach to anger management in the training of law enforcement officers. *American Journal of Community Psychology, 5,* 327–346.

Novaco, R. W. (1978). Anger and coping with stress: Cognitive behavioral interventions. In J. P. Foreyt & D. P. Rathjen (Eds.), *Cognitive behavior therapy: Research and application* (pp. 135–174). New York: Plenum Press.

Nowlis, D. P., & Kamiya, J. (1970). The control of electroencephalographic alpha rhythms through auditory feedback and the associated mental activity. *Psychophysiology, 6,* 476–484.

O'Brien, G. T., & Barlow, D. H. (1984). Agoraphobia. In S. M. Turner (Ed.), *Behavioral theories and treatment of anxiety* (pp. 143–185). New York: Plenum Press.

Obrist, P. A. (1981). *Cardiovascular psychophysiology: A perspective.* New York: Plenum Press.

O'Connor, R. D. (1969). Modification of social withdrawal through symbolic modeling. *Journal of Applied Behavior Analysis, 2,* 15–22.

Ohman, A., & Dimsberg, U. (1978). Facial expressions as conditioned stimuli for electrodermal responses: A case of "preparedness"? *Journal of Personality and Social Psychology, 36,* 1251–1258.

Ohman, A., Eriksson, A., & Olofsson, C. (1975). One-trial learning and superior resistance to extinction of autonomic responses conditioned to potentially phobic stimuli. *Journal of Comparative and Physiological Psychology, 88,* 619–627.

Ohman, A., Erixon, G., & Lofberg, I. (1975). Phobias and preparedness: Phobic versus neutral pictures as conditioned stimuli for human autonomic responses. *Journal of Abnormal Psychology, 84,* 41–45.

Ohman, A., Fredrikson, M., Hugdahl, K., & Rimmo, P. A. (1976). The premise of equipotentiality in human classical conditioning: Conditioned electrodermal responses to potentially phobic stimuli. *Journal of the Experimental Psychology: General, 105,* 313–337.

Osgood, C. E., Suci, G. T., & Tannenbaum, P. H. (1957). *The measurement of meaning.* Urbana: University of Illinois Press.

OSS Assessment Staff. (1948). *Assessment of men: Selection of personnel for the Office of Strategic Services.* New York: Rinehart & Company.

Ost, L. G., & Hugdahl, K. (1981). Acquisition of phobias and anxiety response patterns in clinical patients. *Behaviour Research and Therapy, 19,* 439–447.

Ost, L. G., & Hugdahl, K. (1983). Acquisition of agoraphobia, mode of onset and anxiety response patterns. *Behaviour Research and Therapy, 21,* 623–631.

Ost, L. G., & Hugdahl, K. (1985). Acquisition of blood and dental phobia and anxiety response patterns in clinical patients. *Behaviour Research and Therapy, 23,* 27–34.

Ost, L. G., Jerremalm, A., & Johansson, J. (1981). Individual response patterns and the effects of different behavioral methods in the treatment of social phobia. *Behaviour Research and Therapy, 19,* 1–16.

Ost, L. G., Johansson, J., & Jerremalm, A. (1982). Individual response patterns and the effects of different behavioral methods in the treatment of claustrophobia. *Behaviour Research and Therapy, 20,* 445–460.

Ost, L. G., Jerremalm, A., & Jansson, L. (1985). Individual response patterns and the effects of different behavioral methods in the treatment of agoraphobia. *Behaviour Research and Therapy, 22,* 697–707.

Oxendine, J. B. (1970). Emotional arousal and motor performance. *Quest, 13,* 23–32.

Paerregaard, G. (1975). Suicide among attempted suicides: A 10-year follow-up. *Suicide, 5,* 140–144.

Pallak, M. S. (Ed.). (1985). Comment [Special Section]. *American Psychologist, 40,* 717–731.

Pariser, S. F., Pinta, E. R., & Jones, B. A. (1978). Mitral valve prolapse syndrome and anxiety neurosis/panic disorder. *American Journal of Psychiatry, 135,* 246–247.

Parsons, R. D., & Wicks, R. J. (Eds.). (1983). *Passive-aggressiveness: Theory and practice.* New York: Brunner/Mazel.

Patel, C. H. (1973). Yoga and biofeedback in the management of hypertension. *Lancet, 2,* 1053–1055.

Patel, C. H. (1977). Biofeedback-aided relaxation and meditation in the management of hypertension. *Biofeedback and Self-Regulation, 2,* 1–41.

Patsiokas, A. T., Clum, G. A., & Luscomb, R. L. (1979). Cognitive characteristics of suicide attempters. *Journal of Consulting and Clinical Psychology, 47,* 478–484.

Paul, G. L. (1969). Outcome of systematic desensitization I: Background procedures, and uncontrolled reports of individual treatments. In C. M. Franks (Ed.), *Behavior therapy: Appraisal and status* (pp. 63–104). New York: McGraw-Hill.

Paul, G. L., & Bernstein, D. A. (1976). Anxiety and clinical problems: Systematic desensitization and related techniques. In J. T. Spence, R. C. Carson, & J. W. Thibaut (Eds.), *Behavioral approaches to therapy.* Morristown, NJ: General Learning Press.

Pavlov, I.P. (1928). *Lectures on conditioned reflexes* (W. H. Gantt, Trans. & Ed.). New York: International Publishers.

Paykel, E. S. (1972). Depressive typologies and response to amitriptyline. *British Journal of Psychiatry, 120,* 147–156.

Paykel, E. S. (1979). Recent life events in the development of the depressive disorders. In R. A. Depue (Ed.), *The psychobiology of the depressive disorders: Implications for the effects of stress* (pp. 245–262). New York: Academic Press.

Paykel, E. S., Klerman, G. L., & Prusoff, B. A. (1970). Treatment setting and clinical depression. *Archives of General Psychiatry, 22,* 11–21.

Paykel, E. S., Klerman, G. L., & Prusoff, B. A. (1974). Prognosis of depression and the endogenous-neurotic distinction. *Psychological Medicine, 4,* 57–64.

Paykel, E. S., Prusoff, B. A., & Myers, J. K. (1975). Suicide attempts and recent life events: A controlled comparison. *Archives of General Psychiatry, 32,* 327–333.

Permutt, M. A. (1980). Is it really hypoglycemia? If so, what should you do? *Medical Times, 108,* 35–43.

Perris, C. (1966). A study of bipolar (manic-depressive) and unipolar recurrent depressive psychoses. *Acta Psychiatrica Scandinavica, 42,* 7–189.

Perris, C. (1968). Genetic transmission of depressive psychoses. *Acta Psychiatrica Scandinavica, 44,* 238–248.

Perris, C. (1969). The separation of bipolar (manic-depressive) from unipolar recurrent depressive psychoses. *Behavioral Neuropsychiatry, 1,* 17–25.

Perris, C. (1971). Abnormality on paternal and maternal sides: Observations in bipolar (manic-depressive) and unipolar depressive psychoses. *British Journal of Psychiatry, 118*, 207–210.

Perris, C. (1982). The distinction between bipolar and unipolar affective disorders. In E. S. Paykel (Ed.), *Handbook of affective disorders* (pp. 45–58). New York: Guilford Press.

Peterson, L. (1984). A brief methodological comment on possible inaccuracies induced by multimodal measurement analysis and reporting. *Journal of Behavioral Medicine, 7*, 307–313.

Philips, C. (1980). Recent developments in tension headache research: Implications for understanding and management of the disorder. In S. Rachman (Ed.), *Contributions to medical psychology* (Vol. 2, pp. 113–130). New York: Pergamon Press.

Pinkerton, S. S., Hughes, H., & Wenrich, W. W. (1982). *Behavioral medicine: Clinical applications.* New York: Wiley.

Pinto, R. P., & Hollandsworth, J. G. (1983, December). *Preparing pediatric patients for surgery using videotape models.* Paper presented at the 17th Annual Convention of the Association for Advancement of Behavior Therapy, Washington.

Pitt, B. (1973). Maternity blues. *British Journal of Psychiatry, 122*, 431–433.

Platt, J. R. (1964). Strong inference. *Science, 146*, 347–353.

Plomin, R., DeFries, J. C., & McClearn, G. E. (1980). *Behavioral genetics: A primer.* San Francisco: W. H. Freeman.

Plotkin, W. B. (1976). On the self-regulation of the occipital alpha rhythm: Control strategies, states of consciousness, and the role of physiological feedback. *Journal of Experimental Psychology: General, 105*, 66–99.

Podlesny, J. A., & Raskin, D. C. (1977). Physiological measures and the detection of deception. *Psychological Bulletin, 84*, 782–799.

Podlesny, J. A., & Raskin, D. C. (1978). Effectiveness of techniques and physiological measures in the detection deception. *Psychophysiology, 15*, 344–359.

Pollitt, J. D. (1965). Suggestions for a physiological classification of depression. *British Journal of Psychiatry, 111*, 489–495.

Pomerleau, O. F. (1980). Why people smoke: Current psychobiological models. In P. O. Davidson & S. M. Davidson (Eds.), *Behavioral medicine: Changing health lifestyles* (pp. 94–115). New York: Brunner/Mazel.

Pomerleau, O. F., & Brady, J. P. (1979). Introduction: The scope and promise of behavioral medicine. In O. F. Pomerleau & J. P. Brady (Eds.), *Behavioral medicine: Theory and practice* (pp. xi–xxvi). Baltimore: Williams & Wilkins.

Price, D. J. de S. (1961). *Science since Babylon.* New Haven: Yale University Press.

Price, K. P. (1979). Biofeedback and migraine. In R. J. Gatchel & K. P. Price (Eds.), *Clinical applications of biofeedback: Appraisal and status* (pp. 134–147). New York: Pergamon Press.

Prokop, C. K., & Bradley, L. A. (1981). *Medical psychology: Contributions to behavioral medicine.* New York: Academic Press.

Rachlin, H. (1977). Reinforcing and punishing thoughts. *Behavior Therapy, 8*, 659–665.

Rachman, S. J. (1977). The conditioning theory of fear-acquisition: A critical examination. *Behaviour Research and Therapy, 15*, 375–387.

Rachman, S. J. (1978). *Fear and courage.* San Francisco: W. H. Freeman.

Rachman, S. J. (1980). Emotional processing. *Behaviour Research and Therapy, 18*, 51–60.

Rachman, S. J. (1981). The primacy of affect: Some theoretical implications. *Behaviour Research and Therapy, 19*, 279–290.

Rachman, S. J., & Hodgson, R. (1974). Synchrony and desynchrony in fear and avoidance: I. *Behaviour Research and Therapy, 12*, 311–318.

Rachman, S. J., & Hodgson, R. J. (1980). *Obsessions and compulsions.* Englewood Cliffs, NJ: Prentice-Hall.

Rachman, S. J., & Seligman, M. E. P. (1976). Unprepared phobias: "Be prepared." *Behaviour Research and Therapy, 14,* 333–338.

Rachman, S. J., & Wilson, G. T. (1980). *The effects of psychological therapy* (2nd ed.). New York: Pergamon Press.

Raimy, V. C. (Ed.). (1950). *Training in clinical psychology.* New York: Prentice-Hall.

Rapee, R. M. (1985). A case of panic disorder treated with breathing retraining. *Journal of Behavior Therapy and Experimental Psychiatry, 16,* 63–65.

Raskin, A., & Crook, T. H. (1976). The endogenous-neurotic distinction as a predictor of response to antidepressant drugs. *Psychological Medicine, 6,* 59–70.

Rathjen, D. P., Rathjen, E. D., & Hiniker, A. (1978). A cognitive analysis of social performance: Implications for assessment and treatment. In J. P. Foreyt & D. P. Rathjen (Eds.), *Cognitive behavior therapy: Research and application* (pp. 33–76). New York: Plenum Press.

Rectanus, E. F., & Hollandsworth, J. G. (1985). *An examination of a multimodal, multivariate predictor of laboratory induced cardiovascular hyperreactivity.* Manuscript submitted for publication.

Redd, W. H., & Andrykowski, M. A. (1982). Behavioral intervention in cancer treatment: Controlling aversion reactions to chemotherapy. *Journal of Consulting and Clinical Psychology, 50,* 1018–1029.

Rees, W. I. (1973). General aspects of anxiety: An introductory survey. In W. I. Rees (Ed.), *Symposium on anxiety factors in comprehensive patient care* (pp. 1–7). New York: American Elsevier.

Rehm, L. P. (1981). A self-control therapy program for treatment of depression. In J. F. Clarkin & H. I. Glazer (Eds.), *Depression: Behavioral and directive intervention strategies* (pp. 68–110). New York: Garland STPM Press. (a)

Rehm, L. P. (Ed.). (1981). *Behavior therapy for depression: Present status and future directions.* New York: Academic Press. (b)

Rehm, L. P., Kornblith, S. J. (1979). Behavior therapy for depression: A review of recent developments. In M. Hersen, R. M. Eisler, & P. M. Miller (Eds.), *Progress in behavior modification* (Vol. 7, pp. 277–318). New York: Academic Press.

Reisenzein, R. (1983). The Schachter theory of emotion: Two decades later. *Psychological Bulletin, 94,* 239–264.

Restak, R. M. (1984). *The brain.* New York: Bantam Books.

Revusky, S. (1977). Learning as a general process with an emphasis on data from feeding experiments. in N. W. Milgram, L. Kraines, T. M. Alloway (Eds.), *Food aversion learning* (pp. 1–51). New York: Plenum Press.

Rimm, D. C., & Masters, J. C. (1979). *Behavior therapy: Techniques and empirical findings* (2nd ed.). New York: Academic Press.

Rinn, W. E. (1984). The neuropsychology of facial expression: A review of the neurological and psychological mechanisms for producing facial expressions. *Psychological Bulletin, 95,* 52–77.

Ritchie, J. M. (1975). Central nervous system stimulants [Continued]: The xanthines. In L. S. Goodman & A. Gilman (Eds.), *The pharmacological basis of therapeutics* (5th ed., pp. 367–378). New York: Macmillan.

Robins, E., & Guze, S. B. (1972). Classification of affective disorders: The primary-secondary, the endogenous-reactive, and the neurotic-psychotic concepts. In T. A. Williams, M. M. Katz, & J. A. Shield (Eds.), *Recent advances in the psychobiology of the depressive illnesses* (DHEW Publication No. HSM 70-9053, pp. 283–293). Washington, DC: U.S. Government Printing Office.

Roll, D. L., & Smith, J. C. (1972). Conditioned taste aversion in anesthetized rats. In M. E. P. Seligman & J. L. Hager (Eds.), *Biological boundaries of learning* (pp. 98–102). New York: Appleton-Century-Crofts.

Rodin, J. (1985). Insulin levels, hunger and food intake: An example of feedback loops in body weight regulation. *Health Psychology, 4,* 1–24.

Rosenthal, D. (1970). *Genetic theory and abnormal behavior.* New York: McGraw-Hill.

Rosenthal, S. H. (1966). Changes in a population of hospitalized patients with affective disorders, 1945–1965. *American Journal of Psychiatry, 123,* 671–681.

Rosenthal, S. H., & Klerman, G. L. (1966). Content and consistency in the endogenous depressive pattern. *British Journal of Psychiatry, 112,* 471–484.

Roskies, E. (1980). Considerations in developing a treatment program for the coronary-prone (Type A) behavior pattern. In P. O. Davidson & S. M. Davidson (Eds.), *Behavioral medicine: Changing health lifestyles* (pp. 299–333). New York: Brunner/Mazel.

Ross, A. O. (1978). Behavior therapy with children. In S. L. Garfield & A. E. Bergin (Eds.), *Handbook of psychotherapy and behavior change: An empirical analysis* (2nd ed., pp. 591–620). New York: Wiley.

Royer, F. L., & Gantt, W. H. (1966). Effect of movement on cardiac conditional reflex. *Conditional Reflex, 1,* 190–194.

Rozin, P., & Kalat, J. W. (1972). Learning as a situation-specific adaptation. In M. E. P. Seligman & J. L. Hager (Eds.), *Biological boundaries of learning* (pp. 66–97). New York: Appleton-Century-Crofts.

Rugh, J. D., & Schwitzgebel, R. L. (1977). Instrumentation for behavioral assessment. In A. R. Ciminero, K. S. Calhoun, & H. E. Adams (Eds.), *Handbook of behavioral assessment* (pp. 79–116). New York: Wiley.

Rush, A. J., Hollon, S. D., Beck, A. T., & Kovacs, M. (1978). Depression: Must pharmacotherapy fail for cognitive therapy to succeed? *Cognitive therapy and research, 2,* 199–206.

Sallade, J. B. (1980). Group counseling with children who have migraine headaches. *Elementary School Guidance & Counseling, 15,* 87–89.

Salmoni, A. W., Schmidt, R. A., & Walter, C. B. (1984). Knowledge of results and motor learning: A review and critical reappraisal. *Psychological Bulletin, 95,* 355–386.

Sameroff, A. J. (1971). Can conditioned responses be established in the newborn infant: 1971? *Developmental Psychology, 5,* 1–12.

Sanders, S. H. (1980). Toward a practical instrument system for the automatic measurement of "up-time" in chronic pain patients. *Pain, 9,* 103–109.

Sandifer, B. A., & Hollandsworth, J. G. (1981, November). *Investigation of the social validity of an assertion training procedure for graduate nurses in a general hospital setting.* Paper presented at the annual meeting of the Mississippi Psychological Association, Biloxi.

Sarason, S. B. (1981). An asocial psychology and a misdirected clinical psychology. *American Psychologist, 36,* 827–836.

Sartory, G., Rachman, S. J., & Grey, S. (1977). An investigation of the relation between reported fear and heart rate. *Behaviour Research and Therapy, 15,* 425–438.

Sawyer, D. A., Julia, H. L., & Turin, A. C. (1982). Caffeine and human behavior: Arousal, anxiety, and performance effects. *Journal of Behavioral Medicine, 5,* 415–439.

Schachter, S. (1964). The interaction of cognitive and physiological determinants of emotional state. In L. Berkowitz (Ed.), *Advances in experimental social psychology* (Vol. 1, pp. 49–80). New York: Academic Press.

Schachter, S. (1966). The interaction of cognitive and physiological determinants of emotional state. In C. D. Spielberger (Ed.), *Anxiety and behavior* (pp. 193–224). New York: Academic Press.

Schachter, S. (1971). *Emotion, obesity, and crime*. New York: Academic Press.

Schachter, S. (1980). Urinary pH and the psychology of nicotine addiction. In P. O. Davidson & S. M. Davidson (Eds.), *Behavioral medicine: Changing health lifestyles* (pp. 38–69). New York: Brunner/Mazel.

Schachter, S., & Singer, J. E. (1962). Cognitive, social, and physiological determinants of emotional state. *Psychological Review, 69,* 379–399.

Schildkraut, J. J., Keeler, B. A., Papousek, M., & Hartmann, E. (1973). MHPG excretion in depressive disorders: Relation to clinical subtypes and desynchronized sleep. *Science, 181,* 762–764.

Schneider, W., & Shiffrin, R. M. (1977). Controlled and automatic human information processing: I. Detection, search and attention. *Psychological Review, 84,* 1–66.

Schneirla, T. C. (1972). Interrelationships of the "innate" and the "acquired" in instinctive behavior. In L. R. Aronson, E. Robach, J. S. Rosenblatt, & D. S. Lehrman (Eds.), *Selected writings of T. C. Schneirla* (pp. 131–188). San Francisco: W. H. Freeman.

Schoenheimer, R. (1942). *The dynamic steady state of body constituents*. Cambridge: Harvard University Press.

Schrodinger, E. (1945). *What is life? The physical aspect of the living cell*. New York: Macmillan.

Schwartz, B. (1974). On going back to nature: A review of Seligman and Hager's *Biological boundaries of learning*. *Journal of the Experimental Analysis of Behavior, 21,* 183–198.

Schwartz, G. E. (1973). Biofeedback as therapy: Some theoretical and practical issues. *American Psychologist, 28,* 666–673.

Schwartz, G. E. (1978). Psychobiological foundations of psychotherapy and behavior change. In S. L. Garfield & A. E. Bergin (Eds.), *Handbook of psychotherapy and behavior change: An empirical analysis* (2nd ed., pp. 63–100). New York: Wiley.

Schwartz, G. E. (1982). Cardiovascular psychophysiology: A systems perspective. In B. L. Cacioppo & V. L. Petty (Eds.), *Perspectives in cardiovascular psychophysiology* (pp. 347–372). New York: Guilford Press. (a)

Schwartz, G. E. (1982). Cognitive behavior modification: A conceptual review. *Clinical Psychology Review, 2,* 267–293. (b)

Schwartz, G. E. (1982). Testing the biopsychosocial model: The ultimate challenge facing behavioral medicine? *Journal of Consulting and Clinical Psychology, 50,* 1040–1053. (c)

Schwartz, G. E., & Beatty, J. (1977). Introduction. In G. E. Schwartz & J. Beatty (Eds.), *Biofeedback: Theory and research* (pp. 1–6). New York: Academic Press.

Schwartz, G. E., Fair, P. L., Greenberg, P. S., Mandel, M. R., & Klerman, G. L. (1975). Facial expression and depression II: An electromyographic study. *Psychosomatic Medicine, 37,* 81–82.

Schwartz, G. E., Davidson, R. J., & Goleman, D. J. (1978). Patterning of cognitive and somatic processes in the self-regulation of anxiety: Effects of meditation versus exercise. *Psychosomatic Medicine, 40,* 321–328.

Secunda, S. K., Katz, M. M., Friedman, R. J., & Schuyler, D. (1973). *Special report, 1973: The depressive disorders* (DHEW Publication No. HSM 73-9157). Washington, DC: U.S. Government Printing Office.

Seidman, L. J. (1983). Schizophrenia and brain dysfunction: An integration of recent neurodiagnostic findings. *Psychological Bulletin, 94,* 195–238.

Seligman, M. E. P. (1970). On the generality of the laws of learning. *Psychological Review, 77,* 406–418.

Seligman, M. E. P. (1971). Phobias and preparedness. *Behavior Therapy, 2,* 307–320.

Seligman, M. E. P. (1974). Depression and learned helplessness. In R. J. Friedman & M. M. Katz (Eds.), *The psychology of depression: Contemporary theory and research* (pp. 83–113). New York: Wiley.

Seligman, M. E. P. (1975). *Helplessness: On depression, development, and death.* San Francisco: W. H. Freeman.

Seligman, M. E. P. (1981). A learned helplessness point of view. In L. P. Rehm (Ed.), *Behavior therapy for depression: Present status and future directions* (pp. 123–141). New York: Academic Press.

Seligman, M. E. P., & Hager, J. L. (Eds.). (1972). *Biological boundaries of learning.* New York: Appleton-Century-Crofts.

Selye, H. (1956). *The stress of life.* New York: McGraw-Hill.

Selye, H. (1974). *Stress without distress.* Philadelphia: Lippincott.

Shapiro, A. K., & Morris, L. A. (1978). Placebo effects in medical and psychological therapies. In S. L. Garfield & A. E. Bergin (Eds.), *Handbook of psychotherapy and behavior change: An empirical analysis* (2nd ed., pp. 369–410). New York: Wiley.

Shapiro, D., & Goldstein, I. B. (1982). Biobehavioral perspectives on hypertension. *Journal of Consulting and Clinical Psychology, 50,* 841–858.

Shapiro, D., & Surwit, R. S. (1979). Biofeedback. In O. F. Pomerleau & J. P. Brady (Eds.), *Behavioral medicine: Theory and practice* (pp. 45–74). Baltimore: Williams & Wilkins.

Shapiro, D., Tursky, B., Greshon, E., & Stern, M. (1969). Effects of feedback and reinforcement on the control of human systolic blood pressure. *Science, 163,* 588–590.

Shapiro, D., Tursky, B., & Schwartz, G. E. (1970). Control of blood pressure in man by operant conditioning. *Circulation Research, 27*(Supp. 1), 27–41.

Shearn, D. W. (1962). Operant conditioning of heart rate. *Science, 137,* 530–531.

Sherwood, S. (1973). Sociology of food and eating: Implications for action for the elderly. *American Journal of Clinical Nutrition, 26,* 1108–1110.

Shevrin, H., & Dickman, S. (1980). The psychological unconscious: A necessary assumption for all psychological theory? *American Psychologist, 35,* 421–434.

Shevrin, H., & Fritzler, D. E. (1968). Visual evoked response correlates of unconscious mental processes. *Science, 161,* 295–298.

Shevrin, H., Smith, W. H., & Fritzler, D. E. (1971). Average evoked response and verbal correlates of unconscious mental processes. *Psychophysiology, 8,* 149–162.

Sifneos, P. E. (1979). *Short-term dynamic psychotherapy.* New York: Plenum Press.

Skinner, B. F. (1938). *The behavior of organisms: An experimental analysis.* New York: Appleton-Century.

Skinner, B. F. (1950). Are theories of learning necessary? *Psychological Review, 57,* 193–216.

Skinner, B. F. (1953). *Science and human behavior.* New York: Free Press.

Skinner, B. F. (1957). *Verbal behavior.* New York: Appleton-Century-Crofts.

Skinner, B. F. (1959). A case history in scientific method. In S. Koch (Ed.), *Psychology: A study of a science* (Vol. 2, pp. 359–379). New York: McGraw-Hill.

Skinner, B. F. (1966). Some responses to the stimulus "Pavlov." *Conditioned Reflex, 1,* 74–78.

Skinner, B. F. (1974). *About behaviorism.* New York: Alfred A. Knopf.

Smith, D. (1982). Trends in counseling and psychotherapy. *American Psychologist, 37,* 802–809.

Smith, E. R., & Miller, F. D. (1978). Limits on perception of cognitive processes: A reply to Nisbett and Wilson. *Psychological Review, 85,* 355–362.

Smith, M. J. (1975). *When I say no I feel guilty.* New York: Dial Press.

Smythies, J. R. (1970). *Brain mechanisms and behavior: An outline of the mechanisms of emotion, memory, learning and the organization of behavior, with particular regard to the limbic system.* New York: Academic Press.

Snyder, S. H., Banerjee, S. P., Yamamura, H. I., & Greenberg, D. (1974). Drugs, neurotransmitters, and schizophrenia. *Science, 184,* 1243–1253.

Solomon, R. L., & Wynne, L. C. (1954). Traumatic avoidance learning: The principles of anxiety conservation and partial irreversibility. *Psychological Review, 61,* 353–385.

Sontag, S. (1979). *Illness as metaphor.* New York: Vintage Books.

Sperry, R. (1982). Some effects of disconnecting the cerebral hemispheres. *Science, 217,* 1223–1226.

Spielberger, C. D. (1966). Theory and research on anxiety. In C. D. Spielberger (Ed.), *Anxiety and behavior* (pp. 3–22). New York: Academic Press.

Stare, F. (1977). Three score and ten plus more. *Journal of the American Geriatrics Society, 25,* 529–533.

Starling, E. H. (1918). *The Linacre Lecture on the Law of the Heart.* London: Longmans, Green.

Stephen, L., & Lee, S. (1937–1938). *The dictionary of national biography* (Vol. X, pp. 287–293). London: Humphrey Milford. (Original work published 1917)

Stern, R. M., & Higgins, J. D. (1969). Perceived somatic reactions to stress: Sex, age, and familial occurrence. *Journal of Psychosomatic Research, 13,* 77–82.

Stolk, J. M., & Nisula, B. C. (1979). Genetic influences on catecholamine metabolism. In R. S. Depue (Ed.), *The psychobiology of the depressive disorders: Implications for the effects of stress* (pp. 205–220). New York: Academic Press.

Stone, G. C. (Ed.). (1983). Proceedings of the National Working Conference on Education and Training in Health Psychology [Special issue]. *Health Psychology, 2*(5).

Stoyva, J. (1977). Why should muscular relaxation b clinically useful? Some data and 2 1/2 models. In J. Beatty & H. Legewie (Eds.), *Biofeedback and behavior* (pp. 449–472). New York: Plenum Press.

Stoyva, J. M. (1979). Musculoskeletal and stress-related disorders. In O. F. Pomerleau & J. P. Brady (Eds.), *Behavioral medicine: Theory and practice* (pp. 155–175). Baltimore: Williams & Wilkins.

Strupp, H. H. (1968). Discussion. *Voices, 4*(12), 95–97.

Strupp, H. H. (1978). Psychotherapy research and practice: An overview. In S. L. Garfield & A. E. Bergin (Eds.), *Handbook of psychotherapy and behavior change: An empirical analysis* (2nd ed., pp. 3–22). New York: Wiley.

Stuart, R. B., Mitchell, C., & Jensen, J. A. (1981). Therapeutic options in the management of obesity. In C. K. Prokop & L. A. Bradley (Eds.), *Medical psychology: Contributions to behavioral medicine* (pp. 321–353). New York: Academic Press.

Sturgis, E. T., & Scott, R. (1984). Simple phobia. In S. M. Turner (Ed.), *Behavioral theories and treatment of anxiety* (pp. 91–141). New York: Plenum Press.

Suinn, R. M. (1982). Intervention with Type A behaviors. *Journal of Consulting and Clinical Psychology, 50,* 933–949.

Surwit, R. S. (1982). Behavioral treatment of Raynaud's syndrome in peripheral vascular disease. *Journal of Consulting and Clinical Psychology, 50,* 922–932.

Surwit, R. S., Wiliams, R. B., & Shapiro, D. (1982). *Behavioral approaches to cardiovascular disease.* New York: Academic Press.

Sweeney, D. R., & Maas, J. W. (1979). Stress and noradrenergic function in depression. In R. A. Depue (Ed.), *The psychobiology of the depressive disorders: Implications for the effects of stress* (pp. 161–176). New York: Academic Press.

Taylor, C. B. (1980). Behavioral approaches to hypertension. In J. M. Ferguson & C. B. Taylor (Eds.), *The comprehensive handbook of behavioral medicine* (Vol. 1, pp. 55–88). New York: SP Medical & Scientific Books.

Taylor, S. E. (1983). Adjustment to threatening events: A theory of cognitive adaptation. *American Psychologist, 38*, 1161–1173.

Teasdale, J. D., & Bancroft, J. (1977). Manipulation of thought content as a determinant of mood and corrugator electromyographic activity in depressed patients. *Journal of Abnormal Psychology, 86*, 235–241.

Telch, M. J., Agras, W. S., Taylor, C. B., Roth, W. T., & Gallen, C. C. (1985). Combined pharmacological and behavioral treatment for agoraphobia. *Behaviour Research and Therapy, 23*, 325–335.

Testa, T. J., & Ternes, J. W. (1977). Specificity of conditioning mechanisms in the modification of food preferences. In L. M. Barker, M. R. Best, & M. Domjan (Eds.), *Learning mechanisms in food selection* (pp. 229–253). Waco, TX: Baylor University Press.

Thoresen, C. E., & Mahoney, M. J. (1974). *Behavioral self-control.* New York: Holt, Rinehart & Winston.

Thorndike, E. L. (1935). *The psychology of wants, interests and attitudes.* New York: Appleton-Century.

Thorndike, E. L. (1970). *Animal intelligence: Experimental studies.* Darien, CN: Hafner. (Original work published 1911)

Thyer, B. A., Nesse, R. M., Cameron, O. G., & Curtis, G. C. (1985). Agoraphobia: A test of the separation anxiety hypothesis. *Behaviour Research and Therapy, 23*, 75–78.

Tinbergen, N. (1969). *The study of instinct.* Oxford: University Press.

Toffler, A. (1970). *Future shock.* New York: Random House.

Tolman, E. C. (1923). A behavioristic account of the emotions. *Psychological Review, 30*, 217–227.

Trower, P., & Turland, D. (1984). Social phobia. In S. M. Turner (Ed.), *Behavioral theories and treatment of anxiety* (pp. 321–365). New York: Plenum Press.

Tryer, S., & Shopsin, B. (1982). Symptoms and assessment of mania. In E. S. Paykel (Ed.), *Handbook of affective disorders* (pp. 12–23). New York: Guilford Press.

Tryon, W. W. (1984). Principles and methods of mechanically measuring motor activity. *Behavioral Assessment, 6*, 129–139.

Tucker, D. M., Shearer, S. L., & Murray, J. D. (1977). Hemispheric specialization and cognitive behavior therapy. *Cognitive Therapy and Research, 1*, 263–273.

Turk, D. C., Meichenbaum, D. H., & Berman, W. H. (1979). Application of biofeedback for the regulation of pain: A critical review. *Psychological Bulletin, 86*, 1322–1338.

Turner, S. A., Daniels, J. L., & Hollandsworth, J. G. (1985). The effects of a multicomponent smoking cessation program with chronic obstructive pulmonary disease outpatients. *Addictive Behaviors, 10*, 87–90.

Turner, S. M. (Ed.). (1984). *Behavioral theories and treatment of anxiety.* New York: Plenum Press. (a)

Turner, S. M. (1984). Preface. In S. M. Turner (Ed.), *Behavioral theories and treatment of anxiety* (pp. ix–x). New York: Plenum Press. (b)

Turner, S. M., & Michelson, L. (1984). Obsessive-compulsive disorders. In S. M. Turner (Ed.), *Behavioral theories and treatment of anxiety* (pp. 239–277). New York: Plenum Press.

Turner, S. M., Beidel, D. C., & Nathan, R. S. (1985). Biological factors in obsessive-compulsive disorders. *Psychological Bulletin, 97*, 430–450.

Twentyman, C. T., & McFall, R. M. (1975). Behavioral training of social skills in shy males. *Journal of Consulting and Clinical Psychology, 43*, 384–395.

Tyrer, S., & Shopsin, B. (1982). Symptoms and assessment of mania. In E. S. Paykel (Ed.), *Handbook of affective disorders* (pp. 12–23). New York: Guilford Press.

Valenstein, E. S. (1973). *Brain control: A critical examination of brain stimulation and psychosurgery.* New York: Wiley.

van Egeren, L. F. (1971). Psychophysiological aspects of systematic desensitization: Some outstanding issues. *Behaviour Research and Therapy, 9,* 65–77.

van Wulfften Palthe, P. M. (1936). Psychiatry and neurology in the tropics. In C. D. de Langen & A. Lichtenstein (Eds.), *A clinical textbook of tropical medicine.* Amsterdam: G. Kolff.

Venkatesh, A., Pauls, D. L., Crowe, R., Noyes, R., Van Valkenburg, C., Martins, J. B., & Kerber, R. E. (1980). Mitral valve prolapse in anxiety neurosis (panic disorder). *American Heart Journal, 100,* 302–305.

Vermilyea, J. A., Boice, R., & Barlow, D. H. (1984). Rachman and Hodgson (1974) a decade later: How do desynchronous response systems relate to the treatment of agoraphobia? *Behaviour Research and Therapy, 22,* 615–621.

Vinoda, K. S. (1966). Personality characteristics of attempted suicides. *British Journal of Psychiatry, 112,* 1143–1150.

Waid, W. M., Orne, E. C., Cook, M. R., & Orne, M. T. (1978). Effects of attention, as indexed by subsequent memory, on electrodermal detection of information. *Journal of Applied Psychology, 63,* 728–733.

Walk, R. D. (1956). Self ratings of fear in a fear-invoking situation. *Journal of Abnormal and Social Psychology, 52,* 171–178.

Wallace, R. K. (1970). Physiological effects of transcendental meditation. *Science, 167,* 1751–1754.

Wallace, R. K., Benson, H., & Wilson, A. F. (1971). A wakeful hypometabolic physiologic state. *American Journal of Physiology, 221,* 795–799.

Walls, R. T., Werner, T. J., Bacon, A., & Zane, T. (1977). Behavior checklists. In J. D. Cone & R. P. Hawkins (Eds.), *Behavioral assessment: New directions for clinical psychology* (pp. 77–146). New York: Brunner/Mazel.

Warrenburg, S., Pagano, R. R., Woods, M., & Hlastala, M. (1980). A comparison of somatic relaxation and EEG activity in classical progressive relaxation and transcendental meditation. *Journal of Behavioral Medicine, 3,* 73–93.

Waters, W. F., Cohen, R. A., Bernard, B. A., Buco, S. M., & Dreger, R. M. (1984). An autonomic nervous system response inventory (ANSRI): Scaling, reliability, and cross-validation. *Journal of Behavioral Medicine, 7,* 315–341.

Watson, J. B. (1924). *Psychology from the standpoint of a behaviorist* (2nd ed.). Philadelphia: Lippincott.

Watts, F. N. (1983). Affective cognition: A sequel to Zajonc and Rachman. *Behaviour Research and Therapy, 21,* 89–90.

Weinberg, G. M. (1975). *An introduction to general systems thinking.* New York: Wiley.

Weiner, B. (1985). "Spontaneous" causal thinking. *Psychological Bulletin, 97,* 74–84.

Weiss, J. M., Glazer, H. I., Pohorecky, L. A., Bailey, W. H., & Schneider, L. H. (1979). Coping behavior and stress-induced behavioral depression: Studies of the role of brain catecholamines. In R. A. Depue (Ed.), *The psychobiology of the depressive disorders: Implications for the effects of stress* (pp. 125–160). New York: Academic Press.

Weissman, M., Fox, K., & Klerman, G. L. (1973). Hostility and depression associated with suicide attempts. *American Journal of Psychiatry, 130,* 450–455.

Wendt, G. R. (1930). An analytic study of the conditioned knee-jerk. *Archives of Psychology, 19*(123), 5–97.

Wenger, M. A. (1950). Emotion as visceral action: An extension of Lange's theory. In M. L. Reymert (Ed.), *Feelings and emotions: The Moosehart Symposium* (pp. 3–10). New York: McGraw-Hill.

Wenger, M. A., & Bagchi, B. K. (1961). Studies of autonomic functions in practitioners of Yoga in India. *Behavioral Science, 6,* 312–323.

Wenger, N. K., & Hellerstein, H. K. (Eds.). (1978). *Rehabilitation of the coronary patient.* New York: Wiley.

Werder, D. S., & Sargent, J. D. (1984). A study of childhood headache using biofeedback as a treatment alternative. *Headache, 24,* 122–126.

Whitehead, W. E., & Bosmajian, L. S. (1982). Behavioral medicine approaches to gastrointestinal disorders. *Journal of Consulting and Clinical Psychology, 50,* 972–983.

Wigner, E. P. (1964). Events, laws of nature, and invariance principles. *Science, 145,* 995–999.

Wilcoxon, H. C., Dragoin, W. B., & Kral, P. A. (1971). Illness-induced aversions in rat and quail: Relative salience of visual and gustatory cues. *Science, 171,* 826–828.

Wildman, B. G., & Erickson, M. T. (1977). Methodological problems in behavioral observation. In J. D. Cone & R. P. Hawkins (Eds.), *Behavioral assessment: New directions for clinical psychology* (pp. 255–274). New York: Brunner/Mazel.

Williams, D. R., & Williams, H. (1969). Auto-maintenance in the pigeon: Sustained pecking despite contingent non-reinforcement. *Journal of the Experimental Analysis of Behavior, 12,* 511–520.

Wilson, G. T. (1982). Psychotherapy process and procedure: The behavioral mandate. *Behavior Therapy, 13,* 291–312.

Wilson, G. T., & Davison, G. C. (1969). Aversion techniques in behavior therapy: Some theoretical and metatheoretical considerations. *Journal of Consulting and Clinical Psychology, 33,* 327–329.

Wilson, G. T., & O'Leary, K. D. (1980). *Principles of behavior therapy.* Englewood Cliffs, NJ: Prentice-Hall.

Wine, J. (1971). Test anxiety and direction of attention. *Psychological Bulletin, 76,* 92–104.

Winokur, G., Clayton, P. J., & Reich, T. (1969). *Manic depressive illness.* St. Louis: Mosby.

Wolf, M. M. (1978). Social validity: The case for subjective measurement or how applied behavior analysis is finding its heart. *Journal of Applied Behavior Analysis, 11,* 203–214.

Wolfe, B. E. (1984). Forward. In S. M. Turner (Ed.), *Behavioral theories and treatment of anxiety* (pp. vii–viii). New York: Plenum Press.

Wollersheim, J. P. (1974). Bewail the Vail, or love is not enough. *American Psychologist, 29,* 717–718.

Wolpe, J. (1958). *Psychotherapy by reciprocal inhibition.* Stanford: Stanford University Press.

Wolpe, J. (1973). *The practice of behavior therapy* (2nd ed.). New York: Pergamon Press.

Wolpe, J. (1976). Behavior therapy and its malcontents—I: Denial of its bases and psychodynamic fusionism. *Journal of Behavior Therapy and Experimental Psychiatry, 7,* 1–5. (a)

Wolpe, J. (1976). Behavior therapy and its malcontents—II: Multimodal eclecticism, cognitive exclusivism and "exposure" empiricism. *Journal of Behavior Therapy and Experimental Psychiatry, 7,* 109–116. (b)

Woolfolk, R. L., Carr-Kaffashan, L., McNulty, T. F., & Lehrer, P. M. (1976). Meditation training as a treatment for insomnia. *Behavior Therapy, 7,* 359–365.

Woolfolk, R. L., & Dever, S. (1979). Perceptions of assertion: An empirical analysis. *Behavior Therapy, 10,* 404–411.

Woolfolk, R. L., Lehrer, P. M., McCann, B. S., & Rooney, A. J. (1982). Effects of progressive relaxation and meditation on cognitive and somatic manifestations of daily stress. *Behaviour Research and Therapy, 20,* 461–467.

Yager, J., & Young, R. T. (1974). Nonhypoglycemia in an epidemic condition. *New England Journal of Medicine, 291,* 907–908.

Young, H. S. (1974). *A rational counseling primer.* New York: Institute for Rational Living.

Zajonc, R. B. (1980). Feeling and thinking: Preferences need no inferences. *American Psychologist, 35,* 151–175.

\., B. (1984). On the primacy of affect. *American Psychologist, 39*, 117–123.

.M. (1982). Myopic view. *The APA Monitor 13*(4), 4.

.ian, D. (1978). Attribution and misattribution of excitatory reactions. In J. H. Harvey, W. Ickes, & R. F. Kidd (Eds.), *New directions in attribution research* (Vol. 2, pp. 335–368). Hillsdale, NJ: Erlbaum.

Zuckerman, M. Klorman, R., Larrance, D. T., & Spiegel, N. H. (1981). Facial, autonomic, and subjective components of emotion: The facial feedback hypothesis versus the externalizer-internalizer distinction. *Journal of Personality and Social Psychology, 41*, 929–944.

Zung, W. W. K. (1974). The measurement of affects: Depression and anxiety. In P. Pichot (Ed.), *Psychological measurements in psychopharmacology* (pp. 170–188). Basel: Karger.

Zuroff, D. C., & Schwartz, J. C. (1978). Effects of transcendental meditation and muscle relaxation on trait anxiety, maladjustment, locus of control, and drug use. *Journal of Consulting and Clinical Psychology, 46*, 264–271.

Author Index

Subject Index